T0043933

The Woman
All Spies Fear

The Woman
All Spies Fear

*Code Breaker Elizebeth Smith Friedman
and Her Hidden Life*

Amy Butler Greenfield

RANDOM HOUSE STUDIO ▲ NEW YORK

Text copyright © 2021 by Amy Butler Greenfield

All rights reserved. Published in the United States by
Random House Studio, an imprint of Random House Children's Books,
a division of Penguin Random House LLC, New York.

Random House Studio and the colophon are registered trademarks of
Penguin Random House LLC.

Visit us on the Web! rhcbooks.com

Educators and librarians, for a variety of teaching tools,
visit us at RHTeachersLibrarians.com

Library of Congress Cataloging-in-Publication Data
Name: Greenfield, Amy Butler, author.
Title: The woman all spies fear : code breaker Elizebeth Smith Friedman and her
hidden life / Amy Butler Greenfield.
Description: New York : Random House Studio, [2021] | Includes bibliographical
references. | Audience: Ages 12+ | Audience: Grades 7–9 | Summary: "Biography of
Elizebeth Smith Friedman, an American woman who pioneered codebreaking in WWI
and WWII but was only recently recognized for her extraordinary contributions to the
field"—Provided by publisher.
Identifiers: LCCN 2021009061 (print) | LCCN 2021009062 (ebook) |
ISBN 978-0-593-12719-3 (hardcover) | ISBN 978-0-593-12720-9 (lib. bdg.) |
ISBN 978-0-593-12721-6 (ebook)
Subjects: LCSH: Friedman, Elizebeth, 1892–1980—Juvenile literature. |
Cryptographers—United States—Biography—Juvenile literature. | Friedman, William F.
(William Frederick), 1891–1969—Juvenile literature. | Cryptographers—United
States—Biography—Juvenile literature. | Cryptography—United States—History—
20th century—Juvenile literature. | World War, 1939–1945—Participation, Female—
Juvenile literature. | World War, 1914–1918—Participation, Female—Juvenile literature.
| Married people—United States—Biography—Juvenile literature.
Classification: LCC D639.C75 G74 2021 (print) | LCC D639.C75 (ebook) |
DDC 940.54/8673092 [B]—dc23

The text of this book is set in 11.75-point Adobe Caslon Pro.
Interior design by Andrea Lau

Printed in the United States of America
10 9 8 7 6 5 4
First Edition

Random House Children's Books supports the First Amendment and
celebrates the right to read.

Penguin Random House LLC supports copyright. Copyright fuels creativity,
encourages diverse voices, promotes free speech, and creates a vibrant culture.
Thank you for buying an authorized edition of this book and for complying
with copyright laws by not reproducing, scanning, or distributing any part in
any form without permission. You are supporting writers and allowing
Penguin Random House to publish books for every reader.

For Jenny Turner,
a strong woman and a true friend

CONTENTS

CHAPTER ONE

The Doll Shop Spy

I n 1942, in the middle of World War II, some strange letters came to the attention of the Federal Bureau of Investigation. They were all addressed to the same person in Argentina, and they all sounded oddly alike, yet they came from four different American women. The letters were about dolls, and they ran like this:

> *I have been so very busy these days, this is the first time I have been over to Seattle for weeks. I came over today to meet my son who is here from Portland on business and to get my little granddaughters doll repaired. I must tell you this amusing story, the wife of an important business associate gave her an Old German bisque Doll dressed in a Hulu Grass skirt . . .*

When the FBI questioned the women who supposedly had sent the letters, the women knew nothing about them. FBI lab experts confirmed that the women's signatures were excellent forgeries.

Someone knew these women well enough to fake their handwriting. Someone was hiding behind their names. Could it be a spy?

The FBI kept digging for clues. The four women lived in different cities and didn't know each other, but it turned out they had something in common. All of them were long-distance customers of a doll shop at 718 Madison Avenue in New York City.

The FBI checked out the shop. Filled with pricey dolls in fancy costumes, it didn't look like the headquarters of a spy ring. The shop's owner, Velvalee Dickinson, appeared innocent, too. A graduate of Stanford University, she was a fifty-year-old widow who had been in the doll business since 1937. She and her late husband had once been friends with many Japanese officials, but that was before Japan and the United States had gone to war.

The FBI remained leery. They staked out the doll shop, and they examined Dickinson's bank account and safe-deposit box. In January 1944, after they traced some of her money back to Japanese sources, they arrested her as a spy.

Dickinson fought back. Tiny, dark-haired, and delicate, she screamed and kicked, scratching at the FBI agents like a wildcat. When they questioned her, she insisted the money had nothing to do with spies. It came from her doll business and insurance payouts.

The FBI was worried. While they'd been able to connect Dickinson to the letters, they weren't sure how to interpret them. The money trail was also murky, with no clear proof of a link to spymasters. Everything was guesswork, which wouldn't impress anyone when the case went to trial.

One of the lawyers who had to prosecute the case was assistant U.S. attorney Edward Wallace. He had plenty of courtroom experience, and he knew it was time to seek help. He also knew exactly who he wanted to approach—one of America's top code breakers, Elizebeth Smith Friedman.

Like Dickinson, Elizebeth was also small, dark-haired, and college-educated, but the resemblance ended there. As a young woman, she had played a key role in code breaking during World War I. She later cracked the codes of American mobsters, smashing their crime gangs. Now, in 1944, she had a top-secret job at the Navy.

Wallace believed that if anyone could crack the Doll Woman letters, it was Elizebeth. But when he asked the FBI if he could put her onto the case, the FBI balked. It wasn't that they doubted her skill. They had worked with her many times before, so they knew just how good she was. As they saw it, the problem was that Elizebeth was *too* good. They couldn't stand the thought that the credit for catching Dickinson might go to her, and not to the FBI.

When it came down to it, however, the FBI needed a conviction. After an initial protest, they allowed Wallace to share the Doll Woman letters with Elizebeth. Luckily for them, the Navy wanted her skills to remain secret, so her name had to be kept out of the record. In case documents, she would be called "Confidential Informant T4."

Although Elizebeth was busy tracking Nazi spies, she made time to look at the Doll Woman letters. At first, she was given very little background to go on, but even so, she made progress. Soon she was startling everyone with her insights.

As she explained to Wallace, the letters were written in what was called "open code." This meant that ordinary sentences and phrases had been given secret meanings, agreed upon in advance. These phrases were then strung together in ways that made the letter seem more or less natural to a casual reader.

Elizebeth warned Wallace that the precise meaning of this kind of code was hard to prove. There was usually a certain amount of guesswork involved, and that would make the case a challenge to prosecute. Yet her analysis was shrewd and hard-hitting.

Take these sentences, for instance, from a Doll Woman letter dated February 22, 1942:

> *The only new dolls I have are three lovely Irish dolls. One of these three dolls is an old Fisherman with a Net over his back, another is an old woman with wood on her back and the third is a little boy.*

Elizebeth believed that Dickinson was using "doll" to mean "ship." The different dolls stood for different kinds of vessels. The "old Fisherman with a Net" was probably a minesweeper. The "old woman with wood on her back" might be a ship with a high upper deck. The "little boy" could be a small warship, perhaps a destroyer or torpedo boat.

Elizebeth worked out the likely meaning of many other words, too. When the letters mentioned "family," they referred to either the Japanese fleet or other agents, depending on context. The "visit of important gentleman's wife" was probably an "invitation to the Japanese Navy to bomb the harbor." The phrases "Mr. Shaw" and "back to work" were a warning that the USS *Shaw*, a damaged destroyer, would soon be ready for action again.

Elizebeth also pinpointed phrases that identified Dickinson as a secret agent. She could tell that Dickinson was a layperson where ships were concerned, and she made smart guesses about where and how Dickinson had obtained her information. Elizebeth even found clues indicating who else might be involved in the spy ring.

After she traveled to New York to get additional case details, she was able to say still more about the letters. Her findings were sent to the FBI, and the prosecution used them to strengthen their case. In August 1944, Dickinson was sentenced to ten years of jail time.

The FBI and the newspapers were quick to proclaim that "the War's No. 1 Woman Spy" had been put behind bars. Elizebeth was not mentioned.

Elizebeth had mixed feelings about that. For se-

Elizebeth cut out this newspaper article that gave the FBI credit for breaking the "Doll Woman" case. In it, Velvalee Dickinson is pictured before and after her arrest (upper left and center).

curity reasons, she knew she had to stay out of the limelight. If the Nazis ever learned how good she was at code breaking, it would hamper her efforts to bring their spies down. But it annoyed her to see the FBI taking credit for her work.

It wasn't the first time that Elizebeth had been pushed into the shadows, nor was it the last. On the FBI's public website, the account of the Doll Woman case still omits any mention of her, even though the need for secrecy is long past. Married to William Friedman, one of the best code breakers of all time, she is often mentioned merely as his wife. Yet as William himself was quick to point out, Elizebeth was brilliant, too.

Like the open code in Dickinson's letters, Elizebeth could appear ordinary on the surface. Even now, she is easily underestimated. To get her true measure, you must delve deeper, the way a code breaker would, searching for the truth that lies just out of sight.

Elizebeth did not have an easy start in life. Yet she rose to become one of the most formidable code breakers in the world, the scourge of gangsters and spies. How did she do it? Ambition and grit played a part, but she needed opportunity, too.

She found it in a library—and in one of the strangest job offers of the century.

CHAPTER TWO

Starting Out

E lizebeth rarely talked about what her life was like before she became a code breaker. She didn't save much from those early years, either. Look in her files, and you'll find only a few papers, a slim diary, and a handful of old photos from that time. It was a chapter of her life that she kept to herself.

To discover who she was when she started out, you have to comb through all the evidence she left behind, and then go hunt for more. A faded few lines on a census form. A remark made in jest. An old house that still stands square to the road. Like scattered bits of code, none of these snippets gives away much on its own. But piece them together, and the real story starts to emerge.

What you see, early on, is that young Elizebeth Smith was determined to be different. Sensitive to the weight and meaning of letters and words, she wanted even her name to set her apart. There was nothing she could do about her surname—the "odious name of Smith," as she put it in her college diary. Yet she detested that "most meaningless of phrases, 'plain Miss Smith.'" To her mind, it implied that she was "eliminated from any category even approaching anything interesting."

It must have been a comfort that her first name was unusual, if only in its spelling. Her mother, Sopha Strock Smith, had called her Clara Elizebeth. It was the Elizebeth part that stuck, spelled with an "e" in the middle, rather than with the standard "a." Family legend had it that Sopha wanted to avoid the nickname Eliza. Perhaps it was also her way of encouraging Elizebeth to stand out from the crowd.

Sopha was Elizebeth's champion—and Elizebeth certainly needed one. Born on August 26, 1892, she was Sopha's youngest surviving child, with eight older brothers and sisters. They all lived in a brick house that Elizebeth's grandfather had built, on the Smith family farm in Union Township, a few miles east of Huntington, Indiana.

Delicate by nature, with wavy brown hair and hazel eyes, Elizebeth was a tiny presence in that huge family. It was a position that frustrated her. Prone to nausea and stomach problems, she remembered her early years "as one continual period of throwing up."

A portrait of the Smith family, with Elizebeth sitting front and center.

Home was a tense place because Elizebeth and her father did not get along. John Marion Smith had served in the Union Army as a teenager, marching with General Sherman in the Civil War. The experience had soured him, but he was widely respected as a veteran and a good farmer. A staunch Republican, he was also elected to local office. By nature, he was a rigid and controlling man, and he did not think much of females. Sopha tried to shield Elizebeth from his temper.

To Elizebeth, Sopha was her "wonderful little Mother"— a smart and curious woman who was interested in everyone. Like Elizebeth, Sopha was small and dark-haired, and she, too, had been the youngest child in her family. Educated at one of the most advanced schools in rural Indiana, she became a teacher. After she married John Smith when she was twenty-four, she centered her life around family and church, yet she often told fond stories about her student days.

Most likely, it was Sopha who spurred Elizebeth to get a good education. She also gave her daughter backbone. "My mother encouraged me to go my own way," Elizebeth once said. The lesson stayed with her for life.

The Smith family farmhouse.

Elizabeth had a quick mind, and she did well in her studies. At first, she walked to the small Antioch School near the family farm. Later, she and her parents moved into nearby Huntington, where she went to high school. Drawn to words in any language, she took four years of German and five years of Latin. She had a strong voice despite her small frame, and she spoke with "rare force and effectiveness," winning the class orator prize. At a time when nine out of ten students never even graduated from high school, she was aiming at college.

Her father did not approve. Believing that higher education was a waste of time for girls, he refused to pay a penny toward it.

To get around this, Elizebeth applied for a scholarship to Wellesley. She also applied to Swarthmore, and perhaps Earlham, another Quaker college, as well. Some people have taken this as proof that she herself was Quaker, but the real story is more complicated—and it shows that Elizebeth was willing to use every lever to get an education. Her parents were pillars of the local Church of God, and that was the faith she was raised in. But she knew that her father came from Quaker stock, and that he was proud of his forebears. If she could get into a Quaker college, she hoped his pride would prompt him to help pay her costs.

Her well-crafted plans fell apart. She failed to get into Wellesley or Swarthmore. Earlham did not work out, either, perhaps because her father was unwilling to help her. At her graduation in 1910, she had the second-highest GPA in her class, and she stated that she had college plans. Instead, she spent the next year at home, playing piano for church socials.

It was such a dismal year that she tried to erase it from her memory, pretending it had never happened. Later, she would always subtract one year from her age, as if to say that her extra year at home hadn't counted. But if her father thought she would give up on college, he was wrong. She applied again that year.

This time around, she was accepted at the College of Wooster in Ohio. It had no Quaker links whatsoever, but somehow she managed to talk her father into giving her a loan anyway. Still, he drove a hard bargain. She had to pay back every penny, plus six percent extra for interest.

Elizebeth thought it a price worth paying.

At college, she took classes in English, Greek, and philosophy. She studied poetry and the plays of William Shakespeare, and she wrote poems of her own. No longer under her father's thumb, she enjoyed thinking for herself. "I am never quite so gleeful as when I am doing something labeled as an 'ought not'!" she confessed to her diary. She wondered if this rebellious streak was the reason why "so many people remark that I should have been born a man."

Yet even with her father's money, she struggled to get by. To make enough to live on, she sewed clothes and arranged hair for parties. The work wearied her and made her feel "indigo, Prussian, navy, blue." It was hard to keep up with her studies when she had to "make dresses and comb hair for other folks." The sense that she wasn't living up to her potential gnawed at her.

Elizebeth as a teenager.

Other things bothered her, too. She scorned pretense, and she believed in plain speaking. Attempts to beat around the bush made her turn prickly. She had strong opinions, and she wasn't afraid to defend them. But young women who spoke their minds were not always welcome, even at college, and at times she found herself seething with frustration.

In Huntington, where she spent her summers, she felt even worse. "I hate the place," she wrote in 1913. She felt boxed in by the town and by neighbors who didn't approve of her. Most of all, she felt misunderstood by her own family, who scolded her for being touchy and outspoken and having a bad attitude.

Looking for comfort, she went to visit old friends in the country. It soothed her to sleep "out under the stars," to row over flooded farmland, and to paddle a canoe. Music helped, too. One night her "heart was carried completely away by a baritone. . . . It made me want to be able to sing well myself, so badly that—well, I just couldn't sit still with the desire of it."

In the fall of 1913, Elizebeth transferred to Hillsdale College in Michigan. Later in life, she said that this was because her mother was ill. Her family thought it had more to do with a "romance gone wrong," but the truth has been lost to time. Whatever lay behind the move, she soon regretted it. The rebel inside her was hard to satisfy, and she found it difficult to settle. "I wanted, oh so badly, to come here; and disregarded my mother's wishes, and paid a big price to come," she confided to her diary. "Now it all seems so worthless and useless."

Honesty forced her to admit that the move had made her more discontented, not less. But in time, she hit her stride. She became literary editor of the college paper, joined the sorority Pi Beta Phi, and was even elected class president. She also fell hard for a handsome, moody poet named Harold Van Kirk. Known as Van, he had started off as a student minister, but he soon found his true calling in theater. He called her Betty and sent her French sonnets, as well as ardent lines about midnight meetings, written in a bold, dashing hand.

In 1915, Elizebeth finally earned her B.A. degree. And that's when her life took a wrong turn.

———

As soon as Elizebeth finished college, she had to start repaying the loan from her father. It was $600 in all, a hefty sum in 1915—plus the surcharge for interest. She felt the weight of it like a millstone around her neck, dragging her down. She knew it would take her years to pay it all off.

The debt meant that she needed to get a job right away. Her first thought was business. Had she been a man, she probably would have had her pick of positions, but at the time few workplaces welcomed women. Teaching was often the only option for female college graduates, and that's how it played out for Elizebeth. She took one of the few openings she could find: substitute high school principal in a small Indiana town near her home. The job didn't suit her, and in 1916 she quit.

By then, she was in the midst of a full-blown crisis.

It wasn't just the job that had gone wrong. "I had broken my engagement," she later wrote of that time. Her "fiancé–gone astray" was the poet Van. After she earned her degree, Van had visited her in Huntington, spending time with her family as any serious suitor would. But he was younger than she was, so in the fall he had returned to Hillsdale and the fun of college life. That likely put a strain on the relationship, though the exact reasons for the breakup aren't clear.

She didn't know it, but she'd had a lucky escape. Van never lost his way with women, and he later married and divorced at least two heiresses. But he turned out to be liar and a cheat, and he had a vicious streak. Even his children had nothing good to say about him.

At the time, however, the rift with Van made Elizebeth feel desolate. So did the thought of another "run-of-the-mill" teaching job. Yet how else could she pay back the loan?

She found herself facing the future with dread, seeing only "a long stretch of purposeless years with nothing to live for." She feared she would spend her life all alone, chained to jobs she hated, marking papers and marking time. Her feelings were so raw, and her hopes so broken, that she found herself "wish[ing] passionately day after day only to die."

As long as she was alive, however, she needed to pay back her father. So in May 1916, she started to look for work again. Desperate for a fresh start, she boarded a train to Chicago.

There a library visit sent her life spinning in a whole new direction.

CHAPTER THREE

What Do YOU Know?

In 1916, Chicago was a world-famous city, by far the biggest in the Midwest. The poet Carl Sandburg had sung its praises just two years before: "Hog Butcher for the World, / Tool Maker, Stacker of Wheat. . . . / Stormy, husky, brawling, / City of the Big Shoulders." Walking along its windy, bustling streets, you could almost hear the hum of opportunity. Brash skyscrapers, towering high above the city's busy markets and railroads, made almost anything seem possible. Yet even in Chicago, jobs for women were in short supply.

Staying with friends on the South Side, Elizabeth went to an agency, asking for openings. "I thought of myself as sitting down at a desk," she wrote, ". . . and working away at research or something like that." She thought that sort of job would suit her better than teaching.

She was disappointed to hear that nothing of the kind was

available. But it may have been the agency that suggested she head to the Newberry Library.

Decades later, when Elizebeth was asked to talk about her life, she often started with the day she arrived at the Newberry. She felt that the library was where her life truly began. It was a tale that she relished retelling, and her rich accounts shed plenty of light on what happened next. If Elizebeth's life is a code, this is where it becomes easier to read.

Founded in 1887, the Newberry Library was a pink granite treasure trove of rare and remarkable books. A Chicago landmark, the building drew readers from far and wide. When Elizebeth visited, the library had one of its prize possessions on display, a First Folio—that is, a first edition of Shakespeare's plays, printed in 1623. She was awestruck. "I did not even know that a First Folio of Shakespeare was any nearer to me than the moon," she later wrote. Loving Shakespeare as she did, she felt as "an archeologist would have, when he suddenly realized after years of digging that he was inside the tomb of a great pharaoh."

Afterward, she and a librarian bonded over a discussion of Shakespeare. It turned out they had other things in common, too. They both hailed from Indiana, and they both had Quaker ancestors. When Elizebeth explained that she needed a job, the librarian told her about a millionaire who needed help with a mystery about Shakespeare. His name was Colonel George Fabyan—pronounced FAY-bee-an—and he was the owner of an oddball estate called Riverbank.

"It was something so startling," Elizebeth later said, "that I could not grasp it all at once." But she let the librarian call to arrange an interview.

To Elizebeth's astonishment, Fabyan himself came straight to the library. "In came this whirlwind, this storm, this huge man, and his bellowing voice . . . could be heard all over the library floor." He stood 6'4" in his cutaway coat and striped trousers. To Elizebeth, he seemed like a bearded, gray-haired giant. Barely more than five feet tall, she was taken aback when he loomed over her.

"Will you go out to Riverbank and spend the night with me?" he demanded.

Elizebeth was "knocked kind of breathless" by the brazen request. At last she managed to say, "I don't have anything with me to go anywhere and spend the night."

"That's all right," Fabyan said. "We'll furnish you anything you want; anything you need, we have it. Come on!"

Moving like a man who always got what he wanted, Fabyan bundled her out of the library. He "lifted me by one arm, you know, under one elbow and . . . carried me like that, swept me out of there and swept me into this big limousine with a driver." Before she knew what was happening, they were boarding a Union Pacific train.

As Fabyan joked with the conductor, Elizebeth panicked. She felt out of her depth, and she knew she looked that way, too. Her modest gray dress had a "white Puritan collar and cuffs."

When Fabyan loomed over Elizebeth, she felt like a "schoolgirl."

Her thick brown hair was topped with "the simplest kind of hat anyone could wear in those days." None of it made her feel like a match for this enormous millionaire.

"Where am I? Who am I? Where am I going?" she wondered. "I may be on the other side of the world tonight."

Frozen in place, she listened to Fabyan, who was still chatting with the conductor. Then Fabyan slammed down into the seat beside her. With his blue eyes only inches from hers, he shouted, "WHAT DO *YOU* KNOW?"

Elizebeth realized he thought she was "a demure little nobody."

Something in her rebelled. She wasn't a nobody. Recovering her poise, she said firmly to Fabyan, "That remains, Sir, for you to find out."

Fabyan roared with laughter. He liked her spirit.

As his booming guffaws filled the train carriage, Elizebeth turned her head and looked out the window. Fabyan settled down. Then, as the train headed west, he explained what the new job would involve. Was Elizebeth any good at cracking ciphers and codes?

For the rest of their train journey, Elizebeth let Fabyan talk. As far as she could tell, it was what he liked to do best. But their trip was too short for him to explain everything, and soon they were getting off the train. Amazed, she saw another car and chauffeur waiting for them at the station. After a short drive, they reached Riverbank, Fabyan's one-of-a-kind country retreat.

There Elizebeth found herself in a strange new world.

CODE BREAK
CODE OR CIPHER?

Although Elizebeth had heard of codes and ciphers in college, she didn't know much about them. It may have been Fabyan who first explained to her how to tell them apart.

Here's the difference:

With a *code*, you replace entire words and phrases. For example, you could decide in advance on a simple code like this:

$$grass = money$$
$$water = hide$$

If you then send a message that says "Water the grass," it means "Hide the money."

Simple codes like this are easy to remember, but anything complicated will need a code book, which can be hard to lug around. Codes also limit what you can say. For example, if the word "attic" isn't in your code book, you can't say, "Hide the money in the attic."

With a *cipher*, you deal with each letter separately, switching them around or replacing them. A simple cipher might replace every letter with a number, so that A = 1, B = 2, C = 3, and so on. Using this cipher, you could write out "Hide the money" like this:

$$8\text{-}9\text{-}4\text{-}5 \quad 20\text{-}8\text{-}5 \quad 13\text{-}15\text{-}14\text{-}5\text{-}25$$

As long as you remember the method for changing letters, you can say almost anything in a cipher. But beware—a simple cipher is easy for an expert to break!

In everyday life, we often refer to both ciphers and codes

as "codes" and to the people who crack them as "code breakers." Elizabeth's own favorite term for her profession was *cryptanalyst,* a word her husband invented. It was more precise than "code breaker," although she was often called that, too. Under either title, the essence of her job remained the same—to take an encryption (sometimes called a *cryptogram*) and make it reveal the true message, or *plaintext.*

Sometimes Elizebeth also worked as a *cryptographer,* which meant that she was the one coming up with ways of obscuring the plaintext. For the most part, however, she focused on taking cryptograms apart. As she once explained about her work, "we don't make 'em, we break 'em."

CHAPTER FOUR

Riverbank

According to local maps, Riverbank could be found in the small town of Geneva, Illinois. But in Fabyan's view, it was his own personal kingdom—a place where he alone made the rules. Stretching over more than three hundred acres, the private estate was protected by guards and stone walls.

What was going on behind those walls? Fabyan's neighbors weren't sure. They weren't even certain who Colonel George Fabyan really was. Depending on who you talked to, he was an inventor, a scientist, a soldier, or even a lunatic—or maybe all of the above.

The truth? Even now it can be hard to tell. Fabyan liked secrets, and he sometimes lied. Even his name was misleading. Although he adored the title "colonel," it was only an honorary one, granted by the governor of Illinois. He wasn't a military man.

Yet some of Fabyan's unlikely stories turned out to be true. Born to a wealthy family of New England fabric merchants, he had dropped out of school as a teenager. After having adventures in the Wild West, he got back into the family business. Later, he inherited a fortune of $3 million, and he used part of the money to build Riverbank. There he let his eccentric tastes run wild.

Like most visitors, Elizebeth was astounded by the estate. Riverbank had a Roman pool, a Dutch windmill, a Japanese garden, and staff from all over the world. A lighthouse flashed the warning "23 SKIDOO" in Morse code—turn-of-the-century slang for "get lost." The main house had been remodeled by up-and-coming architect Frank Lloyd Wright. Its chairs, sofas, and beds swayed in midair, suspended by chains from the ceilings.

The wildlife at Riverbank was startling, too. Fabyan and his wife, Nelle, kept a private zoo with monkeys, bears, peacocks, alligators, and a gorilla called Hamlet. They also raised cattle, goats, ducks, turkeys, terriers, bees, and English bulldogs. Nelle especially enjoyed going for walks with a touchy chimpanzee named Patsy, who lived on the porch.

All this, however, was a mere sideshow. As Elizebeth soon learned, what was most unusual about Riverbank was its research program. After seeing other tycoons grow bored with their lavish art collections and swanky mansions, Fabyan had invested his own millions in a private brain trust. "You never get sick of too much knowledge," he said.

His own interests were endless, so Riverbank was packed with experts of all kinds. Botanists were breeding new plants. Doctors were improving human posture. Engineers were working on everything from weapons to sound waves to X-rays. Fabyan gave them the funding they needed, then pushed them hard. His chief command? "Be spectacular."

Fabyan's pet project was run by a gracious, silver-haired woman named Elizabeth Wells Gallup. A former high school principal,

Gallup had been educated in Michigan and Paris, and she loved Shakespeare as much as Elizebeth did. She was also fascinated by something called Bacon's cipher.

It was this cipher that Fabyan wanted Elizebeth to work on. Both Fabyan and Gallup believed it was the key to a centuries-old mystery.

—————

The man who invented Bacon's cipher was Sir Francis Bacon, an English scientist and statesman who lived in Shakespeare's day. Bacon was interested in secrets of many kinds, including encryption, but his cipher wasn't a typical cipher. That is, it didn't substitute each letter with another letter. Instead, it used combinations of "A"s and "B"s to spell out a version of the alphabet:

A	*B*	*C*	*D*	*E*	*F*
aaaaa	*aaaab*	*aaaba*	*aaabb*	*aabaa*	*aabab*

G	*H*	*I/J*	*K*	*L*	*M*
aabba	*aabbb*	*abaaa*	*abaab*	*ababa*	*ababb*

N	*O*	*P*	*Q*	*R*	*S*
abbaa	*abbab*	*abbba*	*abbbb*	*baaaa*	*baaab*

T	*U/V*	*W*	*X*	*Y*	*Z*
baaba	*baabb*	*babaa*	*babab*	*babba*	*babbb*

In Bacon's cipher, the word "be," for example, looks like this:

aaaabaabaa

Gallup believed that Shakespeare's First Folio contained secret messages written in this cipher. The messages were from Bacon, she said, and they revealed the true author of Shakespeare's plays. According to Gallup, this was Bacon himself. And that was not the only surprise. Another message from Bacon read, "Queene Elizabeth is my true mother, and I am the lawfull heire to the throne."

Gallup and her supporters, including Fabyan, had accepted these revelations at face value. So had a handful of experts. Yet many scholars denounced Gallup as a crackpot, and she wanted to prove them wrong.

To refute her critics, Gallup had assembled a team at Riverbank, with Fabyan's backing. Their mission was to decrypt the entire First Folio, and they needed another assistant. Would Elizebeth join them?

Elizebeth had mixed feelings. She wasn't sure she liked Fabyan, whose high-handed ways reminded her of her father. Yet the project intrigued her. So did Riverbank. Maybe here she could find a path to a future she wanted.

She took the job.

———

For Elizebeth, it was the start of a wild and wonderful summer. For months she had felt nothing but despair, but at Riverbank she began to revive. "[T]he world began to pop," she later said. "Things began to happen."

Although her pay was only $30 a month, she and the other workers led a glamorous life. "We swam in the Roman swimming pool, we bicycled over country roads, we drove occasionally in the Stutz Bearcat belonging to a young bachelor engineer," she remembered. "We used to go tearing down the Lincoln Highway at

60, 70 miles an hour—Oh!—with that car with no top on it or anything, and you didn't know whether your head was going to blow right off or not!"

Former president Teddy Roosevelt sometimes came to stay at Riverbank. So did actresses, stockbrokers, and daredevil pilots. And even when there weren't famous guests to meet, Elizebeth and the other workers were served fine meals, and they dressed up for dinner. At night they "always had pitchers of ice water and fresh fruit with fruit knives" placed at their bedsides. It was a far cry from life back on the Smith family farm.

Elizebeth (left) with Elizabeth Wells Gallup (right) and her sister Kate Wells (center).

Just as she had feared, however, Fabyan was a difficult boss. "He gave orders on every phase of life, even dictating what sort of clothes I should wear and where I should buy them," she recalled. He insisted she shop at an expensive department store in Chicago, where everything cost more than she wanted to spend, but when she complained, she got nowhere. Fabyan hated to be challenged, and he had a terrible temper.

Everyone at Riverbank dreaded the evenings when Fabyan sat in his "hell chair." This was a wicker chair suspended by chains near an outdoor fire. Behind it was a web of rope stretching sixty feet high, making Fabyan look like an oversized spider hulking beneath it. "[W]henever he wanted to bawl anybody out, which he did frequently, he would have them brought there," Elizebeth said.

Fabyan in his "hell chair."

Swaying back and forth in the hell chair, Fabyan would smoke and shout at his victims. He would "give them hell," Elizebeth said. "Thus the name."

She counted herself lucky that Gallup was a gentler soul who treated her kindly. But the work itself was not easy. At first, it took Elizebeth eight hours or more to decrypt a simple text. Determined to prove herself, she set her mind on mastering Gallup's method.

———

The gist of the job was simple enough. Elizebeth and the rest of the team had to search for two distinct typefaces, or fonts, on pages from the First Folio. According to Gallup, those typefaces were how Bacon had slipped his messages into Shakespeare.

To understand what Gallup had in mind, imagine a line of Shakespeare, printed in a mix of two fonts:

TO BE, OR NOT TO BE:
THAT IS THE QUESTION

Look closely, and you'll see that one font has fancy "serifs," that is, finishing strokes on the letters. The other font is very plain.

If you call the serif letters Type "a" and the others Type "b," you can decode the words as:

ba aa ba aba aa aa
baba aa aaa baabaaba

Put these letters into groups of five, and you get **baaab / aabaa / aaaba / baaaa / aabaa / baaba**. In Bacon's cipher, that stands for **S—E—C—R—E—T**.

In this example, the differences in the letters are easy enough to spot, but Elizebeth had to detect something much subtler.

A little twist in the tail of a "y."

A slightly thinner "i."

A tiny loop on the crossbar of a letter "t."

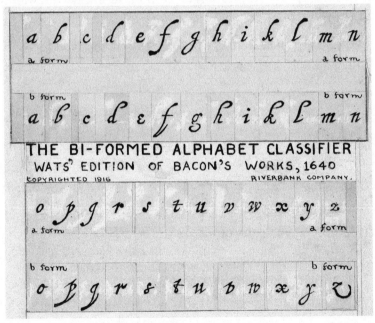

This was one of many alphabet "classifiers" that Gallup's team used, showing possible "a" and "b" forms of various letters. Few letters in the First Folio matched these exactly, so the work involved many judgment calls.

Gallup could identify the two types without trouble, but the rest of the workers struggled. Even with a magnifying glass, it was easy to slip up and miss things. Still, Gallup thought Elizebeth showed promise. Soon she became a valued member of the team, often chosen to explain the work to Riverbank's eminent guests.

Yet no matter how hard Elizebeth worked, she continued to have trouble decoding the secret messages. Most of the time, she ended up with nonsense.

At first, she admired how Gallup was able to spot her errors and correct her work. Yet as the weeks passed, Elizebeth became troubled. She noticed that Gallup wasn't always consistent about how she identified typefaces. It also seemed strange that not even the best workers could reproduce her results. Elizebeth began to have qualms. "[M]y admiration . . . turned to uneasy questioning, and then to agonizing doubt."

Was Gallup mistaken? Was she seeing messages that weren't really there?

———

Elizebeth was right to have doubts.

According to Gallup, the First Folio had two—and only two— distinct typefaces: Type "a" and Type "b." Every single letter belonged to one type or the other. But this simply wasn't true.

In 1623, when the First Folio was printed, every page had to be set up for the press by hand, using tiny metal letters called *movable type*. The casting process meant that no two metal letters were ever precisely the same, even before wear and tear. The exact mark the type made on the page also depended on the amount of ink and pressure used. All of these factors determined how a given letter looked on the page, and many of them were out of the printer's control.

Nowadays, experts agree: There are many typeface variations in the First Folio, and they appear at random. When Gallup tried to divide these variations into only two groups, she was seeing patterns that didn't exist.

That summer, however, no one dared question Gallup about her methods—at least not at Riverbank. Even Elizebeth hesitated to challenge her mentor. Gallup was kind and sincere, and she'd had an education that Elizebeth could only envy. It seemed likely she knew what she was doing. Besides, if Elizebeth asked questions, it might send Fabyan into a rage. What if he fired her?

Before the summer was over, however, she shared her doubts with another Riverbank worker, a young scientist named William Frederick Friedman. Could she trust him? She hoped so.

Neither of them knew it yet, but it was the start of a partnership that would transform their lives—and the future of American code breaking.

CODE BREAK
FROM BACON TO BINARY

In Bacon's original cipher, something odd happens to the letters J and U. Bacon wrote in Latin, which didn't need them, so they were later crammed in as I/J and U/V. But Bacon's idea still works even if you add J and U separately:

A	aaaaa	H	aabbb	O	abbba	V	babab
B	aaaab	I	abaaa	P	abbbb	W	babba
C	aaaba	J	abaab	Q	baaaa	X	babbb
D	aaabb	K	ababa	R	baaab	Y	bbaaa
E	aabaa	L	ababb	S	baaba	Z	bbaab
F	aabab	M	abbaa	T	baabb		
G	aabba	N	abbab	U	babaa		

Below, you can see one of Bacon's mottoes written in the modern version of his cipher. It became one of Elizebeth's favorite mottoes, too. To read it, try breaking the letters into groups of five.

ababaabbababbbababbaabababbaabaaaaabbaabba
aabaaabaaabaabaabbbbbabbbababbaaabaabaaab

Bacon's cipher is also called the *biliteral cipher*, meaning that it uses two letters. But as Gallup's method showed, you don't actually need letters to make it work. All you need are two different elements. A dot and a dash will do. Or a red line and a blue line. Or two different fonts or emojis.

You can also take Bacon's cipher and express it using 0 for a and 1 for b. Put that way, Bacon's cipher becomes an example of binary code, the language of computers:

A	00000	H	00111	O	01110	V	10101
B	00001	I	01000	P	01111	W	10110
C	00010	J	01001	Q	10000	X	10111
D	00011	K	01010	R	10001	Y	11000
E	00100	L	01011	S	10010	Z	11001
F	00101	M	01100	T	10011		
G	00110	N	01101	U	10100		

CHAPTER FIVE

A Dear Good Friend

Elizebeth never forgot the moment she met William Fried-man. On her first evening at Riverbank, she was waiting for dinner when William arrived. "I was sitting there on a bannister or something. And I saw him come up the steps," she said over half a century later. "He was so beautifully dressed . . . there was no country informality about his attire at all." Dark-haired and quick-witted, William had charming manners, hazel eyes, and a "strongly intellectual face." He made an indelible impression on Elizebeth.

At twenty-four, William was only a little older than she was, but he had grown up in a very different world. Born in Russia on September 24, 1891, he was the first son and second child of Frederick and Rosa Friedman, who named him Wolfe.

That same autumn, Russia was wracked by famine. Millions of people were going hungry, and hundreds of thousands of them would starve to death. As a Jewish family, the Friedmans faced other dangers as well. Antisemitism was rising in Russia, making it harder for Jews to get education, jobs, and housing. Even worse, Christian mobs were killing and maiming Jews in brutal pogroms and riots.

In search of a better life, the Friedmans moved to the United States when Wolfe was still a baby. Frederick came first, quickly followed by Rosa and the children, who traveled in steerage. They ended up in Pittsburgh, where Wolfe became William—and an American citizen.

The move was hard on the whole family. Frederick was a gifted translator who spoke eight or nine languages, but in America he had to take whatever job he could get. He found work selling Singer sewing machines door-to-door. The daughter of a well-to-do wine merchant, Rosa toiled in Pittsburgh as a peddler for a clothing firm.

Frederick and Rosa had three more sons in Pittsburgh. When Rosa's parents joined them, the family had even more mouths to feed. With their scant budget pushed to the breaking point, the Friedmans were always in debt. Growing up, William feared "the wolf always at the door," a fear that haunted him for life. As a small, worried child, he hid pennies under a floorboard—a "hoard" to protect his family if "evil times" came.

Evil was something young William could imagine all too vividly. Although his family had escaped Russia, they knew that terrible things were happening to the friends they had left behind. When William was eleven, rioters in his hometown of Kishinev attacked their Jewish neighbors, killing forty-nine and injuring over four hundred more. They also destroyed some seven hundred Jewish homes. It was one of the worst such pogroms on record. Had the Friedmans still lived there, they might not have survived it. No wonder, then, that William's childhood was marked by fear.

Despite all these worries, William did his best to make his parents proud. He was good at chess, and he was a natural scholar and athlete. He also had a way with words, winning a prize in a speech contest. His speech, which defended a jailed socialist, did not please his high school principal, but he graduated near the top of his class.

That summer, William took a job as a clerk at the Erie City Iron Works. Fascinated by science, he dreamed of being an electrical engineer, but he couldn't see how he could pay for the training. Instead, he enrolled at Michigan Agricultural College, mostly because he could get free tuition there.

William (left) at Michigan Agricultural College in 1910.

It didn't take long for William to realize—as he put it to a friend—that he wasn't suited to "scratching a living out of the soil." Borrowing money for a train ticket, he headed instead for Cornell. There he got a scholarship to study genetics. It was a field so new that the word had only just been coined, and it was a good match for William's talents. He liked complex problems, and he liked breaking new ground. After he finished his degree in 1914, he stayed at Cornell doing advanced research in the Department of Plant Breeding.

As he was well aware, however, the study of genes had a dark side. This was the pseudoscience of eugenics, whose many followers believed they could improve the human species through careful breeding. Convinced that some people were inferior, they tried to stop them from having children.

Teasing classmates nicknamed William "Eugenics Bill," but the record shows that he was interested in improving plants, not people. Not everyone he met felt the same way. For two summers, he worked on corn hybrids at the famous Cold Spring Harbor Laboratory on Long Island, New York. The eminent director of the lab, Charles Davenport, recently had started a Eugenics Record Office there. Its goal? To study human bloodlines, and to eliminate what Davenport saw as "unfit" persons—such as Jews—from the American gene pool.

Davenport promoted eugenics not only in America, but across the world. He later cultivated ties with Nazis who shared his beliefs. Yet if he was among the worst eugenicists in America, he was far from the only one. Back at Cornell, William worked with another advisor who promoted eugenics, too.

William must have felt uneasy in such company. As a graduate student from a poor family, he also had money worries. So in 1915, when the head of his department told him about a strange letter he had received from a man named Colonel Fabyan, William paid attention. Fabyan was about to expand into gene research at Riverbank, and he wanted a bright young man to lead the way.

Odd as the setup was, William was interested. It sounded like Riverbank was a place where he could be his own master, do the work he loved, and earn good money. In June, he agreed to move there as the head of Fabyan's new Genetics Department.

Although William's job title was impressive, his working conditions were anything but. At Riverbank, he lived in a damp windmill, where he did experiments with fruit flies and African violets. He was an excellent photographer, so Fabyan also ordered him to take photos of Shakespeare's First Folio for Gallup's team.

William didn't mind the extra duty. As a child, he had loved Edgar Allan Poe's "The Gold-Bug," a tale about a cipher that leads to buried treasure. Ciphers and codes interested him—and so did Elizebeth. The two of them began spending more and more time together.

———

When Elizebeth finally shared her doubts about Gallup's project, William admitted he was uneasy, too. In his enlarged photographs of the First Folio, he couldn't see the patterns that Gallup saw. He and Elizebeth discussed the problem. They both liked Gallup, and they were sure she would never knowingly lie. But that didn't mean that what she said was true.

They became convinced that the secret messages were an illusion. To say so, however, might mean losing their jobs. Loath to take that risk, they spoke only to each other about their concerns, and the secret brought them closer. Before long, they had given each other nicknames—Billy Boy and Elsbeth. Soon they were sharing bike rides, jokes, struggles, and dreams.

Both Elizebeth and William had fallen in love before, but neither had ever known anything like this. It was as if each were a cipher to which the other had the key. By the end of 1916, William had fallen head over heels.

Elizebeth was slower to commit herself. As she confided in her diary, the breakup of her previous engagement had left her "mangled and torn and castigated and macerated in soul." Although she was slowly healing, she despaired that she would "never *feel* again." Yet she treasured William's friendship. At some point, she introduced him to her mother, who liked him. He also met her favorite sister, Edna, who came to visit Riverbank.

Elizebeth and William at Riverbank.

Only two years older than Elizebeth, Edna was a widow already. She saw herself as a woman of the world, and she encouraged William to keep pursuing her sister. "I think that E cares a very great deal more for you than she lets herself or anyone else believe," she wrote to him.

Shortly before Christmas 1916, while at Riverbank, Elizebeth came down with appendicitis. She had to be rushed to the hospital for an operation. Perhaps that was what made William declare himself. At any rate, something forced his hand, and his feelings came out into the open. Elizebeth was still wary of entanglement, but sparks began to fly between them—a "Flame which we kindled together."

In January, the flame nearly flickered out. Elizebeth was back in Indiana by then, taking a leave of absence from Riverbank so that she could look after her mother, who was dying of cancer. William wrote to her and pressed her to think about their future, but Elizebeth put him off. "It seems so hard to be thinking of anything personal, when Mother's life hangs in the balance," she wrote.

Her mind was so full of her mother's distress that she couldn't focus on anything else. The doctor had few treatments for Sopha's tumors, but he tried piercing her skin to drain off fluid. To Elizebeth, this seemed barbaric. Shocked by the pain her "Mother-kins" had to endure, she spent "hours pacing back and forth," trying and failing to ease her mother's agony. The depression that had lifted at Riverbank now claimed her again.

William became her "Comforter" as she confessed her despair. "It is so awful—Billy Boy—to look on the face of death like that— the beckoning face. I've been pretty close myself at times—but it's so different when it's one's Mother." She was also ground down by a "battle of wills" with her father, who saw no need for a new doctor.

Haunted by the need to pay back the money he had loaned her, she agonized about how to meet her expenses. "I cannot afford not to be making at least a little money," she wrote to William. She had hoped to work from home, but that was impossible when her mother was so ill. "I try to make myself work, but I cannot."

For the most part, she was careful to keep her letters platonic, calling him a "dear good friend," a "Dear boy," and "one of the truest friends I've ever had." But he meant more to her than that, and she sometimes admitted it. She told him that she missed his "rocking"—which apparently involved them sitting close together, perhaps in one of Riverbank's swinging chairs. By early February, she was writing, "To be your North Star—Billy Boy—I'd *like* to be!" In another note that same day, she said, "I think of you infinitely, tho' I can't say it."

———

Those last days with her mother changed Elizebeth. Above all, they sharpened her desire to make something of her own life. "I want, oh, so much, for us both to 'achieve,'" she wrote to William.

At the end of February, Sopha died. Soon afterward, Elizebeth returned to Riverbank. By then, she was no longer willing to waste time on Gallup's false theory. William backed her up. He, too, had lost patience with the Shakespeare project.

Neither of them relished the idea of telling elderly, kindhearted Gallup that her decades of effort were pointless. Instead, they approached Fabyan with their doubts.

As they had feared, Fabyan lost his temper. Ignoring their concerns, he shouted that he didn't pay them to ask questions, but to follow his orders.

Under Gallup's patient direction, the Shakespeare project continued exactly as it had for years. Elizebeth was still expected to search for two kinds of typefaces in the First Folio. William was still expected to take photographs of the letters.

Later that month, however, Fabyan issued new orders. Gallup would continue with the Shakespeare project, but Elizebeth and William were told to set up a separate Department of Ciphers. Elizebeth didn't know what to think, but the timing couldn't have been better. Within a few weeks, she and William would become the most important code-breaking team in the country—just as the United States went to war.

CHAPTER SIX

The Skeletons of Words

In March 1917, when Elizebeth and William started River-bank's Department of Ciphers, World War I had been raging in Europe for over two years, and the conflict had spread across the globe. The United States was trying to keep out of it, but it was hard to stay neutral. German submarines had killed Americans, and relations with Germany were fraying.

That spring, the papers were full of war news. The conflict struck many people as horribly modern, fought as it was with recent inventions like tanks, airplanes, and poison gas. All were lethal. One of the biggest game changers, however, was a new technology that seemed relatively harmless: radio.

Unlike telegraphs, which needed wires and cables, radio messages traveled through the air. That meant they could be sent across any terrain, including enemy lines, and still arrive almost instantly. Both sides made the most of this high-tech leap. Soon they were sending hundreds of radio messages every day, tapping them out in the dots and dashes of Morse code.

Only if you were a fool, however, did you send messages disguised by Morse alone. Anyone with a receiver and an antenna could detect radio signals, and Morse was widely known by both sides. To keep your messages secure, you encrypted them first, then sent the encryption in Morse.

With all these veiled messages flying through the air, World War I soon became the war of the code breakers. By cracking your enemy's codes and ciphers, you could learn their military secrets. Everything was up for grabs, from battle plans to spy reports to the locations of supply depots. If you learned enough secrets, you could win the war.

Code breaking even helped drag the United States into the war. In January 1917, a German diplomat named Arthur Zimmermann sent a telegram in cipher to the German ambassador in Mexico City. The telegram said that if the United States declared war, Germany wanted Mexico on its side. To sweeten the deal, Zimmermann promised that Mexico would get Texas, Arizona, and New Mexico as a reward.

The British intercepted the telegram and cracked it. In February, they shared the message with the United States. When the message was revealed to the public, Americans were outraged. Soon afterward, when German submarines attacked more American ships, the United States entered the war.

America now needed top-notch code breakers of its own. Unfortunately, it had very few military men with the right skills—"possibly three or at most four persons," Elizebeth later wrote. The War Department, which oversaw the United States Army, realized it had a problem.

Elizebeth and William were about to become the solution.

———

Never one to miss an opportunity, Fabyan had already offered the services of Riverbank's Department of Ciphers to the U.S. Army. As soon as war was declared, the Army sent Captain Joseph Mauborgne to inspect Fabyan's operation.

Like Fabyan, Mauborgne was a giant of a man, but in all other ways, he was a quite different person. A gifted artist and violin player, he was a radio expert and one of the Army's best code breakers. In 1911, he had cracked Playfair, Britain's prized military cipher, just for the fun of it. Impressed by Elizebeth and William, he filed a favorable report. Fabyan's estate was about to become the nation's main code-breaking center.

Soon Riverbank was awash in secret messages. They came not only from the War Department, but also from the Navy, the State Department, the Justice Department, and even the post office. Urgent material was sent by telegram. The rest arrived in heavy mail sacks.

Elizebeth and William were expected to break everything.

The work was daunting, especially at first. Only a year before, Elizebeth had been an assistant high school principal and William had been studying fruit flies. But they knew they were fast learners—and with their country depending on them, they refused to give up.

As they pored over the secret messages, they noticed certain patterns. For example, a cryptogram that looked like a random string of letters might turn out to have more "V"s in it than anything else. Elizebeth and William knew enough about cryptography to guess that "V" might stand for "E," the most common letter in the English language. They made tables of how often other letters appeared in the message, then compared this with the distribution of letters in normal English. This was called *frequency analysis,* and it could crack simple messages wide open.

Of course, sometimes the plaintext wasn't in English. Some messages were in German, others were in Spanish, and a smattering of them were in other languages. Often the context told them what to expect. Messages sent by the Mexican Army were likely to be in Spanish, for example.

Fabyan hired translators to help. But Elizebeth and William found that the work went much faster if they mastered the basics of the languages themselves. William had inherited his father's gift for this, and Elizebeth was already well trained in German and Latin. Soon they were cracking messages in many languages.

For guidance, they read whatever cryptography manuals they could find. Chief among these was a handbook by an Army officer named Parker Hitt, an expert who had gone to France to serve with American forces. They even had a chance to meet Hitt's wife, Genevieve Young Hitt, who was also a code breaker.

While handbooks were helpful, the messages themselves were the best teachers. Studying them by the hundreds, and then by the thousands, Elizebeth and William devised new tests and tables and shortcuts that helped them to find patterns and solutions. They then taught these methods to their small team. As Elizebeth put it, she and William "became the learners, the students, the teachers, and even the workers all at once." Soon they were surpassing what the Hitts had achieved.

She and William also came up with basic working practices that they would use for the rest of their lives. They worked on grid paper, using capital letters. They numbered and saved every worksheet. They always used pencil, not pen. (It was necessary, they found, "to use the eraser quite as much as the pencil.")

Above all, they worked together—not alone, as most code breakers did. They found it was easier to spot errors and get results when you had "different minds, centered on the same problem."

A team of two could make more progress than four people working separately.

No other team, however, could match Elizebeth and William. Soon they were breaking even the toughest codes and ciphers. Amazingly, they could crack almost any message within two hours. Elizebeth loved the moment when a solution emerged. "The thrill of your life," she later called it. "The skeletons of words shine out and make you jump."

*William and Elizebeth
at Riverbank in 1917.*

Working as a team meant that Elizebeth and William were spending hours together each day. Often they sat at the same table, tossing ideas back and forth. With every hour that passed, they saw more deeply into the secret messages in front of them. They also saw more deeply into each other.

William had already lost his heart to Elizebeth, and by now he was desperate to marry her. He told her that she was beautiful and brilliant, and that he wanted them to build a life together. The "magic" of Elizebeth's "beautiful loosened hair" made him long to put his arms around her "in a passionate embrace."

Elizebeth hesitated. She had strong feelings for William, and she could see that he was a very different man from her father and from Fabyan. All the same, she remained wary. Experience had taught her that engagements could end in pain. Besides, she had seen too many women lose their rights after marriage, including her mother. Exhausted by her own battles with her father, she knew she could not face a lifetime of such arguments. Perhaps it was better to stay single, to be sure of avoiding them.

It didn't help that their backgrounds were so different. At the time, marriages between Jews and Christians were uncommon and usually frowned upon by both sides. Knowing this, even William, wildly in love, had spent a long time "wrestling with myself, and with my upbringing, and with my past and with the future" before he proposed.

Elizebeth herself was open-minded about religion. "I believe in an all-wise and all-good God," she wrote in 1915, "who is not bound by human limitations" and "is both in and of nature." Although she had been raised on Bible verses, she now spoke of God mostly in metaphor: "Spring spells God, and God is Love." To her, God was "the Painter" of the sky.

She could not see herself converting to Judaism, but neither did she intend to convert William. Could an arrangement like that work? She knew her family would not like it. Although her sister Edna approved of a "Smith-Friedman Alliance," the rest of her conservative Christian family was unlikely to be so accepting. She knew William's family wouldn't welcome her with open arms, either.

Then, too, there was the problem of money. Neither of them had very much.

In the face of so many doubts and obstacles, the logical decision was not to marry. During a car trip to nearby Aurora, they "talked over the impossibility of our union. . . . The reasons we both enumerated very calmly—and they seemed weighty indeed."

Yet Elizebeth could not walk away from William. The bond they shared was unlike anything she'd known before. And as they worked together, hour by hour, it was deepening. In early May, less than a month into their wartime service, she told William she would marry him.

Now they just had to tell their families.

CHAPTER SEVEN

Will We Win?

The reaction to their engagement was even worse than Elizebeth and William had feared. Her father responded coldly to the "sudden" match, and when he later announced it in the local paper, he did not mention in print that William was Jewish. When William went to Pittsburgh to tell his parents, they were horrified. His mother collapsed.

"You would have thought that Bill had committed murder," his brother Max said. "If he had still been living in Pittsburgh, he would have been ostracized." Elizebeth was frantic. "Oh, Billy, Billy, what have we done?" she wrote. "What if your mother should die?" The idea was too terrible to contemplate. "Oh, dear Heart, it must come right!" she told him. Then she wrote, "I love you," for the very first time.

To their relief, Rosa Friedman soon recovered. But she continued to oppose the match, and there seemed to be little hope of a family blessing on either side. Yet that didn't deter Elizebeth and

William for long. On May 21, 1917, they made a secret trip to Chicago, where a rabbi married them. In their wedding photos, they both look subdued, as if stunned by their own daring.

With no time for a honey-moon trip, they went straight back to code breaking.

For Elizebeth, it was a tense time, and not only because of the workload. Ever since her engagement with Van had fallen apart, she had felt too numb to love anyone. Now she was not sure she could ever love William the way he loved her. Even after the wedding, she held herself back. At first, she returned his kisses only out of "compassion."

"I . . . believed that there could be no happy marriage in this world of *pitifully human*

William and Elizebeth on their wedding day.

beings," she later wrote. Deep down, part of her believed that marriage—even to a "good" man like William—was a trap. She braced herself for misery.

What she got instead was "the Miracle." That was how she put it in her diary, and how she thought of it ever afterward. "[T]o fall in love with One's Husband" seemed the stuff of fairy tales. And yet it happened to Elizebeth that summer.

A month after her wedding, she wrote in wonder, "Is it possible I am to have them, after all—Youth, and Love, and Life?" In a few short weeks, everything had changed, and she felt transformed. No longer holding back, she fell for William, body and soul. "He became my all in all."

She was constantly astonished by his devotion. Once, when they were in a meeting, he sent a note fluttering down to her: "My dearest—I sit here studying your features. You are perfectly beautiful!!" Elizebeth saved the note in her diary, writing, "Dear Boy!"

One clear August evening, they pledged a new vow. "Tonight my Lover-Husband and I made a tryst with the future," Elizebeth wrote. "The goal is set; will we win? We planned it all—cheek to cheek—facing the swelling power of the new moon."

They were committed to being partners in everything, in work as well as love. Together, they were determined to go far.

———

Love and ambition were powerful fuel.

That summer, Elizebeth and William made breakthrough after breakthrough. Their job was secret, and few people knew who they were or what they were doing. But among intelligence circles, Riverbank was becoming famous, not only in the United States, but also farther afield.

That fall, a mysterious British visitor turned up at the estate, lugging a briefcase. Fabyan told Elizebeth and William that the brawny stranger was from Scotland Yard, but it's likely he came from another branch of British agents. When he opened his briefcase, it was stuffed full of intercepted letters. Instead of words, many of these letters had numbers listed in groups of three, such as 26-2-3 and 4-1-7.

Elizebeth and William set out to break them. Swiftly, they

worked out that the letters were written in two different book ciphers. This meant that each cipher was based on an ordinary book—one that the sender and receiver both owned.

Book ciphers are easy to read if you know the book and the system of encryption. When you see a number like 26-2-3, you go to page 26 of your book, find the second line, and look for the third letter. (In some systems, you might instead search for the second column or the third word.) You write that down, then move on to the next set of numbers, until you have the whole message.

The trick, of course, is to break the cipher *without the book*. Using both statistics and intuition, Elizebeth and William did exactly that. They worked backward from the messages, looking at repeated patterns and making logical guesses about what each letter could be. In a remarkably short time, they broke the messages. By then, they knew enough about the books that they could guess what they were. Eventually, they even found copies of them. Both books confirmed every single guess they had made.

Decoded, the letters revealed a German plot that centered on India. As part of the British Empire, India was contributing both men and supplies to Britain's war effort. Germany wanted to stoke unrest there to weaken Britain and distract it from the war in Europe. So German agents funneled money to Indian immigrants in the United States, who used it to fund a revolt in their home country.

By the time Elizebeth and William first saw the letters, British and American officials already knew the broad outline of the plot, and many Indians who had worked with the Germans had been arrested. The decrypts, however, made the case against them much stronger. Emotions ran high at one of the trials, and in the courtroom one defendant shot another dead. Most were given short sentences in prison. Across the country, the case hit the headlines.

The only Friedman who testified at the trials was William. Elizebeth had hoped to serve as cowitness, but instead she continued the daily grind of code breaking. As she put it, "someone had to stay behind and oil the machinery at Riverbank." But they both knew it was a joint code-breaking coup, one they had achieved together.

Those who knew the Friedmans sometimes wondered who was the better code breaker. Was it Elizebeth or William? It was hard to say. "I was never able to decide which was the superior," a World War I colleague once wrote. "They were both brilliant and modest about it all."

Both relied on a complex blend of statistics and instinct to crack puzzles. Both worked hard to develop their skills. Both were also competitive, even in their time off.

Elizebeth enjoyed telling how William once tackled a fun cipher challenge that was said to be unsolvable. He cracked it in fifteen minutes. "Of course when I learned that," she wrote, "I too had to try my hand." The result? "I unlocked the forever-to-be-hidden secret in 17 minutes."

Yet if the two of them shared many skills, they also had different natural gifts. William's greatest strength was analysis. He could take apart a cipher, piece by piece, as if it were a machine. Elizebeth, by contrast, had exceptional intuition. At times, it seemed almost as if she could see into a code maker's mind. Her sudden insights often floored William. Time and again, she amazed him with a "shrewd 'guess'" that was worth more than "a whole day's painstaking labor."

Working alone, each was a top-notch code breaker. But when

they worked together, something magic happened. Attuned to each other to an almost spooky degree, they achieved things that others considered impossible.

One of the best examples of this involved a new British coding device called a Pletts Cryptograph. The British believed the device was unbreakable, and they wanted to use it on the front lines. The French and Americans were interested in it, too. As a final test, the U.S. Army sent five Pletts messages to Riverbank. To William, the task looked hopeless at first:

> *I took one look and saw there were five messages, just five, and they were all very short—each had about 35 letters. I said, "Oh! It's silly to try this. I have other fish to fry."*

But Fabyan—whom William called the Colonel—wouldn't let the matter drop:

> *The Colonel said, looking hard at me, "Young man, on the last day of each month, you get a little green piece of paper with my name in the lower right-hand corner of it. If you would like to continue receiving those bits of paper, you'll start working on these messages right away."*

Not wanting to forgo his paychecks, William said: "Yes, Sir!"

Over the next two hours, William worked out that the messages must be based on two keyword ciphers. He was convinced that the first keyword was "cipher." For the life of him, however, he could not work out what the second one was.

He consulted Elizebeth. She was "sitting across from him very busily engaged on something else." As she recalled,

*He asked me to lean back in my chair, close my eyes and make
my mind blank. . . . Then he would propound to me a question
to which I was not to consider the reply to any degree, not
even for one second, but instantly to come forth with the word
which his question aroused in my mind. . . . He spoke the word
"cipher," and I instantaneously replied, "machine."*

It was the right word.

After that, it took only minutes to break the messages. The first one said, "This cipher is absolutely indecipherable."

Mere hours after the secret messages had been delivered to them, Elizebeth and William sent back the plaintext. Confident in the devices, the British army had already distributed eleven thousand of them. Now the machines had to be abandoned.

For the British, the episode was an embarrassment. For Elizebeth and William, it was a triumph. Working together, they were solving problems that no one else could. As partners, they seemed almost invincible.

Secretly, however, someone was undermining them. It was the very same person who had brought them together—their boss, George Fabyan.

CODE BREAK
THE KEY TO THE CIPHER

The "unbreakable" Pletts Cryptograph relied in part on *key-word ciphers,* a type of *substitution cipher.* In a substitution cipher, each letter of the message you want to send is swapped out for a different letter. Both messages will have the same number of letters, but the second one will be unreadable.

To create a simple keyword cipher, you first write out the alphabet. Beneath it, you write your keyword, followed by the remaining letters of the alphabet in order. Each letter of the alphabet should only appear once. Here's what it looks like when the keyword is "cipher":

A	B	C	D	E	F	G	H	I	J	K	L	M	N	O	P	Q	R	S	T	U	V	W	X	Y	Z
C	I	P	H	E	R	A	B	D	F	G	J	K	L	M	N	O	Q	S	T	U	V	W	X	Y	Z

Imagine you then wanted to write a message saying, "I know the keyword." Encrypted, it would look like this:

D G L M W T B E G E Y W M Q H

Without the keyword, it's hard to work out what the original plaintext could be.

The Pletts Cryptograph raised the bar because it combined *two* keyword ciphers. These were set on rotating rings that could be spun independently. In addition, one of the cipher rings had twenty-seven spaces, instead of the usual twenty-six. By turning the rings, you could encrypt each plaintext letter with a different scrambled alphabet. That made the message much harder to crack.

CHAPTER EIGHT

Underlings

E lizebeth and William were a sensational code-breaking team. But Riverbank had room for only one star—and that was George Fabyan. He never let either of them forget it.

Despite their many triumphs, Fabyan still treated Elizebeth and William badly. He kept on paying them poorly, issuing absurd orders, and shouting them down if they argued with him. As Elizebeth wryly noted, Fabyan acted as if he were "the supreme commander of our personal lives." To him, they remained "underlings."

By the fall of 1917, Elizebeth and William were both intent on breaking free. Determined to get as close to the front lines as possible, William asked the United States Army for a commission to serve as a code breaker overseas. Elizebeth, meanwhile, applied to work for the Navy. To their dismay, they received no replies.

The reason for the silence? Fabyan had betrayed them.

Desperate to recruit both Elizebeth and William, the Army

had approached Fabyan. It wanted to take over Riverbank's entire Department of Ciphers and move it to Washington, DC. Fabyan refused to cooperate, and he didn't tell Elizebeth and William about the offer. When Army officials wrote directly to the Friedmans, the letters never reached them. Fabyan was reading their mail before they did, and he destroyed any letters he didn't want them to see.

Possibly Fabyan went even further than that. One Army officer who later visited Riverbank thought the place was bugged—particularly the rooms where Elizebeth and William were working. That kind of technology was still in its infancy, but Riverbank was known for its acoustic engineers and inventions. It's not out of the question that Fabyan was eavesdropping on his star employees to make sure they made no attempt to leave Riverbank.

After a while, the Army stopped writing to the Friedmans, and it made other plans to wrest control of code breaking from Fabyan. Sending secret messages from Washington to Riverbank was a logistical hassle and a security headache. Besides, Army officials had become wary of Fabyan himself. They believed his hunger for publicity made him a security risk.

The Army pinned its hopes on its own new code-breaking bureau, known as MI-8. Founded in the summer of 1917, MI-8 got off to a slow start, but as it grew, it took over much of Riverbank's work.

By the fall of 1917, Elizebeth and William were anxious about the slowdown. Fabyan was worried, too. He offered to set up a school to train code breakers for the Army, all expenses paid. Desperate for skilled officers, the Army accepted.

In October 1917, the first officers showed up. Over seventy more arrived in January and February 1918, with the last few coming in March and April. Elizebeth and William trained them all. They also trained some of the officers' wives.

Wanting to share their techniques even more widely, Elizebeth and William also started writing pamphlets about code breaking. Known as the Riverbank Publications, these were cutting-edge studies. But when Fabyan printed the pamphlets, he claimed the copyrights for himself. The true names of the authors did not appear on the title pages.

It was yet another betrayal, and it created plenty of confusion. For years, it wasn't clear who had written the groundbreaking pamphlets. Even now, it's hard to tell exactly who wrote what.

Eventually, William was credited as their sole creator. Later, Elizebeth was named as coauthor on one of them. Yet drafts and further records indicate that Elizebeth helped with at least two other pamphlets. Given that she tended to keep quiet about her achievements, she may have worked on others, too. On government forms, she noted at least twice that she was "co-author with William F. Friedman of numerous cipher books," by which she meant the pamphlets.

Why, then, did William end up with almost all the credit?

The answer may lie in the long struggle to get the copyrights back from Fabyan. William fought hard for this, but for years the outcome was uncertain. Perhaps Elizebeth thought that if she insisted on joint credit, she would muddy the waters. After all, most people had a hard time believing that a woman could break codes, let alone write papers about them. And if people started doubting her claims, they might doubt William's, too. Then she and William would end up with nothing.

She also may have felt that William was entitled to the lion's share of the credit. Consider, for example, Riverbank Publication

No. 17, the first paper that set out their basic working methods. A draft copy indicates that Elizebeth wrote only one section, leaving the bulk of the pamphlet to William. Nevertheless, Elizebeth deserves more credit than she got. In Publication No. 16, *Methods for the Solution of Running-Key Ciphers,* her work may have amounted to joint authorship. "Even in those days I was admitted to have been one of the authors," Elizebeth later said of it. In writing to her, William called it "our R-K pamphlet."

As far as Fabyan was concerned, however, the pamphlets were his. It was not the first time that he had undercut Elizebeth and William. And it wouldn't be the last.

———

In the spring of 1918, when the training courses came to an end, Elizebeth and William still did not know that Fabyan was undercutting them behind their backs. Yet they were growing restless and uneasy. All the officers had reported for active duty, leaving the two of them behind at Riverbank, with less and less military code breaking coming their way.

For months, William had been trying to find a way to join the code breakers in France. "He felt like a draft evader," Elizebeth later said. "[H]e was embarrassed." Fabyan had offered to help but kept secretly blocking him. Desperate to get overseas, William at last raised such a ruckus that Fabyan agreed to let him go. First, however, he

William in uniform with Elizebeth at his side, 1917.

made William promise to return to Riverbank when the war was over.

By June, William was a first lieutenant with the Army's military intelligence unit. Before he left for France, he and Elizebeth posed for pictures. Solemn and thin, he stands tall in his high-collared uniform. Elizebeth nestles by his side with a wan smile. There are circles under her eyes.

After barely a year of marriage, the war that had brought them together was driving them apart.

CODE BREAK
HIDING IN PLAIN SIGHT

In February 1918, Elizebeth and William's code-breaking class took time out for a photo. At first glance, it looks like an ordinary wartime portrait. Officers in uniform stand stiffly at attention in two long rows. In front of them sit Elizebeth, William, and Fabyan, along with two other women, both assistants in the Cipher Department. Everyone looks solemn, waiting for the photographer to capture the shot.

George C. Marshall Foundation

It's hard to believe that this photo carries a secret message. Yet it does—and the message is encrypted in Bacon's cipher.

Close up, it's possible to see that some people in the photo are facing straight forward. They are the "a" form. Others face sideways—either slightly or sharply. They are the "b" form. Observe them carefully, and you will find that they are spelling out words.

The class didn't have enough people to complete the final letter of the message. But it's still possible to work out what it says:

KNOWLEDGE IS POWE(R)

It was one of William's favorite quotations, adapted from a saying by Sir Francis Bacon himself: *Knowledge itself has power.*

Elizebeth (sitting, center) is an "a." William (sitting, right) is a "b."

The technical name for this type of hidden communication is *steganography*—the practice of concealing a message within another message, image, or file. Invisible ink is another example. Harmless-looking digital images that contain malware are yet another.

In later life, William kept a copy of this photo under glass on his desk. It was a great example of a message hiding in plain sight.

CHAPTER NINE

Don't Be Afraid to Take a Step

For Elizebeth, the separation was not only an emotional blow, but a professional one, too. She wanted to go to France with William, but the Army did not allow female code breakers to serve so close to the front lines. The policy riled Elizebeth. "I, a mere woman, could not follow to pursue my 'trade,'" she wrote years later. The unfairness of it still rankled her.

Looking for another way to serve, she again applied for jobs in the Navy. This did not lead anywhere, either—probably because Fabyan was still stealing her mail. Instead, Elizebeth remained at Riverbank. Since the Army now had its own trainers, all she could do was work on the few messages that continued to come in.

Bored and unhappy, she lived for William's letters. He started writing to her on the first train that took him out of Riverbank, and he wrote still more as he crossed the ocean. When he reached the American headquarters in Chaumont, France, where he would be based for the rest of the war, he told her all about that, too. On every page, his love for her shone out.

She was his "Darling," his "Dear One," his "Dearest-in-All-the-World," his "Love-girl," his "Beloved Mine," his "Inspiration Gold," his "Divine Fire." When he sent her a telegram for their "Sixteenth Monthiversary," he joked that each letter and punctuation mark was a code standing for "I love you!" In countless ways, he cheered her on, telling her that "I adore, adore, adore You!"

Only rarely did he ask anything of her. "Honey Mine, please, I think it would be lovely if you lit the candles on Friday night and just thought a silent prayer for your Lover," he wrote soon after his departure. "And I am sure it would cheer the old folks if you told them." By then, his parents had made their peace with his marriage. "They think the world of you," he told her. He had yet to learn that Elizebeth and his parents would never be close.

Stuck in war-torn France, four thousand miles from home, he missed Elizebeth terribly. After long hours of code breaking, he went back to his room in a private French home, among streets so dark that he sometimes needed the light from his cigarette to find his way. On his mantel, he had arranged not one photograph of Elizebeth, but seven.

He dreamed about her all the time. In his nightmares, she left him, but other dreams were better. In one, he wrote, "I was a Hero, I saved you from a lion that escaped from somewhere." In another, he told her, "We were together again and I held you in my arms once more—so tight. I thought I should burst with happiness and joy at being with you once again."

Elizebeth's own letters to William have not survived. Perhaps they were lost in France, or perhaps she later destroyed them. But William sometimes quoted her, and his responses often hint at what she wrote. So, in a sense, some of her words are encrypted in his.

Aware that wartime censors could open her mail, she was discreet and even stilted at first. "Adored One, why worry about the Censor?" William protested. "I want you to write me as if you were talking to me. . . . Your words of love are the living breath to me—and meat and drink. I want to hear you whisper your passion, your hopes, your fears—all—all—to me."

To his delight, Elizebeth soon set her shyness aside. Writing freely about her hopes and fears and longings, she told him that her love for him was "shameless." "I thought, last year, that I loved you—but that was as a zephyr to a gale, compared to this engulfing, enveloping worship of now," she wrote. He was thrilled.

When she confessed, with a poem, that she had not truly fallen in love with him until after the wedding, it shook him. "Dear Heart—I didn't know," he wrote. But he thought it was "far better to have had you marry me on faith and hope—then to have you fall desperately in love with me, than the other way around." In the same poem, she told him that she was "wishing and waiting and counting the months till you come back to me." It meant everything to him that he was now everything to her.

In letters that were passionate and practical by turns, they did whatever they could to elide the miles between them. At times, they even took comfort in baby talk, where "Billy" became "Biwy." But mail service was erratic, which tested them. "Just imagine, almost a month since even a letter from you," William wrote. "Oh, Honey, Honey, how will I ever learn to stand it!" When Elizebeth, in turn, went for eight weeks without hearing from him, she felt "infinite pain and loneliness."

It couldn't have helped matters that William had mentioned, early on, that a French waitress had complimented him on his "'belle noir cheveux'"—his "good-looking black hair." William, who had no interest in anyone but his wife, thought this was "funny," but Elizebeth worried. When his letters failed to arrive, nightmares dogged her. Nevertheless, she kept writing. She tried to believe that William still loved her, and that in time he would come home. She told him she prayed for a future when "I may keep you as wholly mine."

At night in his lonely French billet, William lighted his oil lamp and gazed at her photographs. He was working sixteen-hour days, but security meant that he could only tell her the barest details about what he was doing. "The work is so hard, and the results so very, very meagre," he wrote soon after his arrival. "Sometimes I fear that I haven't got it in me at all. I cannot explain to you—but just imagine yourself at work absolutely in the dark, up against the most baffling problem . . . oh, I tell you, Honey, it's going to be an awfully hard task to make good."

After working in tandem with Elizebeth, it felt strange to go back to breaking codes by himself, but that was Army policy. "You know how much 'group work' counts in our business," he wrote to her. "What can one person alone accomplish? Well there's not enough of 'round-table work' here. Independent work mostly. I'll fix that if possible."

It wasn't long before he made his mark. "I had one of those idea days yesterday—you know what I mean, Honey," he wrote in August. After a sleepless night, he had solved a tough problem "out of the clear blue." That fall, his commander introduced him to a visiting colonel as "our wizard on Code."

For Elizebeth, the outlook was bleaker. The government rarely needed Riverbank anymore, so Fabyan pressured her to return to the Shakespeare project. The situation grew unbearable. To her horror, she discovered that Fabyan had been going through her mail, making sure she didn't receive any job offers. She could not be certain that anything was private anymore, not even her love letters from William. She felt increasingly trapped. A male coworker was harassing her, and she later told close friends that she had to fend off Fabyan, too.

She did not tell William everything she was facing, but he knew she was unhappy. He thought she should look for another boss. "Honey, don't be afraid to take a step," he wrote that summer. "You have ability and more brains than any other woman I've known. You can fill any job a woman can and many jobs that men fill." Later, her letters alarmed him so much that he cabled her to say she should leave Riverbank right away.

By then, Elizebeth had already flown, heading home to Indiana in early September. Moving back in with her father was no treat, but it was better than being cornered by Fabyan. To earn money, she took a job as an assistant librarian in Huntington. She returned to the "prison"—her term for Riverbank—only to collect her belongings.

Furious, Fabyan insisted it was her duty to remain at Riverbank until William returned. Elizebeth refused. When William heard, he cheered her on. He was more than ready to be done with Fabyan himself, he told her. "I know we shall never return to Riverbank," he wrote. "I am afraid we were getting chained to the job . . . and I am glad that we are free." They were both relieved to be out of Fabyan's reach.

They did not yet understand how long that reach truly was— or how dangerous an enemy Fabyan could be.

CHAPTER TEN

Escape

When the war ended in November 1918, Elizebeth and William rejoiced. On the night that peace was being brokered, his first thought was for her. "Dearest Woman in the Universe," he wrote. "This is surely a fateful day." In Indiana, Elizebeth confessed that she was "consumed by thoughts of dear, intimate things that burn one up with a fire of longing and ache of wanting you." They were both impatient to be together again.

Fabyan was impatient, too—for different reasons. A mere two days after peace was declared, he insisted that William return to Riverbank at once. "You have had a long enough vacation," he wrote. Fabyan demanded to know when Elizebeth's "vacation" would be over, too.

Stuck in Huntington, Elizebeth was—as she later put it— "beginning to realize what it meant to be a champion swimmer stranded in the Sahara." Yet she couldn't imagine going back to Riverbank.

William agreed that they should stay away from Fabyan. He was appalled that the man had stolen their mail—and their job offers. "I should be a grade higher now," William wrote angrily to Fabyan in December 1918. "Elizebeth should have been richer by much valuable experience, and our financial affairs should have been in a far better condition."

Nothing they said changed Fabyan's mind. He was set on their returning to Riverbank. Not only that, but he also wanted them to return to the Shakespeare project. Elizebeth and William were outraged. They refused to waste their time on a bankrupt theory that would destroy their reputation as code breakers.

Yet if they weren't going back to Riverbank, what would they do instead? How would they live? Where would they go? It was hard to make concrete plans when they were so far apart. But they could dream.

William hoped the government would offer him a code-breaking job, but he knew that was unlikely in peacetime. Instead, he thought he might return to genetics—an ambition Elizebeth encouraged. "Elsbeth, my Dearest, when you say that you want me to go on with my research work—blaze the trail and all that—do you realize that those chaps . . . are usually not bank presidents?" he wrote. He felt lucky that she didn't expect him to make wads of money, but he was concerned about their finances all the same.

To improve their prospects, Elizebeth was saving every penny she could. William was impressed with the results. "Well, Honey, so we have $500 and no debts in the world. Well, isn't that nice! You capable personage, you. I love you, Elsbeth Friedman. You're a worthy partner to a financial success if we ever make a *howling* one."

At a time when most American women still could not vote, William was determined to treat Elizebeth as his equal. When she wrote that she was worn out from cleaning and cooking for her father, William said he wanted their marriage to run on different lines. She should be free to use her talents, just as he did. If that meant he needed to help with the sweeping or washing, he was willing. He added that he didn't care about having a "spick and span" house: "*Home* does not entail a spotless kitchen and a fault-less parlor," he wrote. "Home does entail the presence of hearts that beat in unison. . . ."

Theirs would be a very modern marriage. "I don't want a 'rubber stamp' type of wife," he told her a few weeks later. "What makes you so wonderful is your individuality, and I want you to develop it." She had talked about being a writer, and he was prepared to back her all the way—even if it meant that "[s]omeday I may be known as Mrs. Friedman's husband!"

Just as he worried about her, she worried about him. A flu pandemic was sweeping the world that winter, with people dying by the millions. To prevent the virus from spreading, the library where Elizebeth worked had shut down for four weeks, and people were required to wear masks in public places. She feared the situation might be worse where he was. She was concerned about the Bolshevik revolution in Russia, too. William told her not to worry about "the damfool Bolshevists." He had every intention of coming home soon.

To their frustration, however, his discharge was delayed. The Army saddled him with writing an official account of their war-time code and cipher operations—"all the histories and data and things—the final say." It was an honor to be given the job, but he had to stay in France until it was done. The work dragged on and on.

Finally, in February 1919, William was told he was free to go.

"Won't our reunion be better than any honeymoon you can think of?" he wrote to Elizebeth. "I love you! I love you! I love you, love you love you!!" It would take time to arrange passage across the Atlantic, but he told her he would be home soon.

Elizebeth headed east to meet him. Staying with friends in Rochester, New York, she received the telegram he sent from New York City on March 6:

```
CAN YOU LEAVE TONIGHT WIRE TRAIN

MEET YOU MUCH LOVE

     BILLY
```

In the bustle of New York, they had their reunion at last.

———

Overjoyed to be together again, Elizebeth and William traveled from New York to Pittsburgh so he could see his parents. Then they started to map out their future.

They focused on William's job search first. Although they traveled as far as New York for interviews, they kept well away from Riverbank. To their shock, however, that wasn't enough to protect them. Angry and

"Hero to war and home again," *wrote Elizebeth on the back of this photo.*

unwilling to be crossed, Fabyan used his wealth and his business connections to stalk them. "He was having us watched," Elizebeth said. "He knew every move that we made."

Wherever they went, Fabyan sent insistent telegrams, often to the very office where William was interviewing. Each one made the same demand: "Return to Riverbank at once." The telegrams also said that William was still on Riverbank's salary roll, implying that he was not a free agent. Employers backed away, and no one offered William a job. Elizebeth believed that Fabyan had scared them off.

He was scaring Elizebeth and William, too. How had he known where they were? How had he learned which companies William was visiting? They never found out, but it was now clear to them both that Fabyan's power extended far beyond Riverbank, and that they had never really escaped him.

With their options running out and their savings dwindling, they felt they had no choice but to return to Riverbank. First, however, they made demands. They wanted better pay, and they wanted Fabyan to stop interfering with their personal lives. They told him they would not live at Riverbank, but in the nearby town of Geneva. They also insisted he name them as authors on any papers they wrote. Finally, they demanded that they be allowed to challenge Mrs. Gallup's theory about Shakespeare.

After Fabyan agreed to all the conditions, they returned to Riverbank. True to form, Fabyan then went back on his word. Elizebeth and William managed to set up a separate household in Geneva, but not a single other demand was met.

Betrayed yet again, Elizebeth and William felt trapped and desperate. William's health began to buckle under the strain. Never robust, he became depressed and lost weight.

They knew they had to get out of Riverbank, but it was hard to see how they could ever escape Fabyan. He was rich and ruthless, and he felt he owned them. He also had a violent streak that made a friend warn them to be careful. To have any chance of leaving Riverbank, they would need powerful allies—and they would have to work in absolute secrecy.

On the quiet, they got in touch with some of their wartime contacts. In April 1920, they were offered jobs with a secret code-breaking outfit run by the former director of MI-8, Herbert Yardley. They both had reservations about Yardley, but almost anything seemed better than staying at Riverbank. Ready to make their move, they told Fabyan about the job offers.

Outraged, Fabyan showered them with his usual mix of threats and false promises. They had to finish their work in progress before they left Riverbank, he told them. Anything else was "a breach of loyalty." To sweeten the deal, he agreed to double whatever salary Yardley had offered them.

Perhaps because of their concerns about Yardley, Elizebeth and William made the mistake of trusting Fabyan. But months passed, and nothing changed. Fabyan presented them with endless work that had to be finished up, but he paid them not a penny more than usual. He had betrayed them yet again—but what could they do? At first, they could see no way out.

Then, in October 1920, Joseph Mauborgne got in touch with them.

———

Mauborgne was the man who had inspected Riverbank for the Army in 1917. He held both Friedmans in high regard, and they trusted him. By 1920, he was heading up research into codes and ciphers for the Signal Corps, the Army unit in charge of communications. When he asked William to reenlist and join his team, William eagerly signed up for the required tests.

Held at the Army's Camp Grant, not far from Riverbank, the test day was a disaster. Ready to prove himself as a code breaker, William was also quizzed about subjects he hadn't studied since high school. What really did him in, however, were the results of his physical the next morning. He was told he had a heart defect, and it was serious enough for the Army Board to turn him down.

Alarmed, William went to two local doctors, who found no sign of any problem. William then learned that the chief doctor at Camp Grant was Fabyan's brother-in-law. Yet again, Fabyan had found a devious way to trap William and Elizebeth at Riverbank.

William and Mauborgne tried to get the Army Board to overturn the decision, but it was too late. Then Mauborgne came up with another proposal. Would William take a civilian job with the War Department instead? William was quick to say yes—and to ask for a job for Elizebeth, too. He warned Mauborgne to say nothing to Fabyan.

By then, Mauborgne needed no warning. Having seen Fabyan's dark side, he was urging caution on William. "I expect violence," he wrote.

It took some time to work out the details, but in December 1920, both William and Elizebeth secretly accepted positions with the War Department. The jobs would start in Washington, DC, on January 1, 1921.

They just had to escape Riverbank first.

It was Elizebeth who engineered their final breakout. She called it "our secret plot to be able to get away without getting our throats cut." Always a model of courtesy, William hated to do anything underhanded, but Elizebeth made him promise he would say nothing to Fabyan until the very last moment. "We've got to be just as tricky as he is," she said.

Without telling anyone, they packed up their house in Geneva. Only once the rooms were bare did they make their move. Dressed for train travel, they made one last visit to Fabyan. They told him they were leaving that afternoon—for good.

For once, there was nothing Fabyan could do to stop them. They left that same day, on the three o'clock train, bound for a new life in Washington.

CODE BREAK

RAIL FENCE LOVE LETTER

Did William and Elizebeth write their wartime love letters in code? As far as we can tell, they didn't—at least not during the war itself. They must have known that censors would flag any such letters as suspicious. At best, the letters would be delayed. At worst, the two of them might get into trouble.

After peace was declared, however, William dared to put a short, simple cipher at the end of one of his letters.

This was called a *rail fence cipher*. Elizebeth would have known exactly how to handle it, without thinking twice.

Starting in the upper left corner, she would have read *down* the first line of letters, then *up* the next line of letters. If you keep snaking down, then up, then down, you get the letters in the right order:

I-L-O-V-E-Y-O-U-V-E-R-Y-M-U-C-H-
I-S-H-O-U-L-D-S-A-Y-S-O-!-!

To make a rail fence cipher work, you need to fill in the whole grid. Here, William used two exclamation points to make the grid come out right. Some messages use random letters instead, such as an "XX."

A rail fence cipher is a type of *transposition cipher*. Unlike a substitution cipher, it doesn't replace any of the letters in the original message. All the letters stay the same, but they are moved around—*transposed*—into the wrong places.

While William's rail fence cipher is easy to read, transposition ciphers can get much more complex. Simply by writing his message out in a line, William could have made it more challenging (although he might have gotten into trouble with the censor):

IEROU !LVYH L!OUM SDOVO UISSE YCHAY

By performing many transpositions on the same plaintext, and shuffling the columns, you can create a baffling message.

If you want to get really complicated, you can apply both transposition and substitution to the same message. Modern data encryption uses a mix of the two techniques, allowing us to send messages and do business safely on our phones and computers.

CHAPTER ELEVEN

At Home

In late December 1920, Elizebeth and William arrived in Washington, DC. Their first perch was the swanky Raleigh Hotel, famous for its roof garden, tenth-floor ballroom, and Beaux Arts glamour. Amid its gold-embossed columns and potted ferns, Elizebeth and William scanned the apartment sections in the local newspapers, looking for a place of their own.

During the war, Washington's population had soared. By 1920, over 400,000 people lived in the city, and there wasn't enough housing to go around. Elizebeth and William grabbed the first furnished apartment available—a piano teacher's studio. It was "furnished" only with a table, benches, and two pianos, and they had to stay out during the day, when the teacher gave lessons. At night, however, the apartment was theirs, and it was a place where Fabyan couldn't interfere in their lives. They bought two beds, fitted out the bare kitchen, and settled in.

Washington was exciting, but also strange. The Friedmans were especially taken aback by the traffic. "[E]verybody shoots past blind corners, taking long chances," William told a friend. "Naturally there are a few smashups every day. The speed limit is eighteen miles in the city, but everybody goes thirty to thirty five, or forty, even in the down-town section."

If the capital had its dangers, it had plenty of pleasures, too. The winter was the mildest they had ever known, the "days very sunny . . . nights not too cold." Used to the bitter winters at Riverbank, they marveled that there was "no ice whatsoever, and no bad wind, and very little snow."

Elizebeth was "starved for theater," so she was thrilled to live in a city where they could attend performances "at least three times a week." On evenings when she and William stayed at home, the apartment pianos came in handy. They played music: Elizebeth on the ivories, William on the violin. Soon Joseph Mauborgne and other friends joined in. "We used to have crowds below, on the street, when the windows were open," Elizebeth remembered.

In Washington, Elizebeth and William found it easy to reconnect with old friends like Mauborgne and to make new ones. Not only were the Friedmans lively company, they were also loyal in times of trouble. One old friend—an officer they'd trained at Riverbank—came to them one evening on the verge of a breakdown. They stayed up late with him, and William helped him get treatment at the Army's mental hospital. After a few weeks, the officer felt like a "new man." Sixty years later, he still believed that the Friedmans had saved his life.

In Washington, William's own low spirits lifted. No longer painfully thin, he was eating well. That summer he played tennis, swam, fished, and canoed on the Potomac River. He was in such good spirits that he was even willing to respond to letters from Fabyan. Now that the man was no longer their boss, he was easier to handle.

"Everything is fine!" William wrote to a Riverbank friend that June. "Like the work and the people very much. A great deal more to live for, and many more friends, and things to do. And freedom—oh! Boy."

Elizebeth was also pleased to be free, but she was not so happy about the job. She and William had been in-structed to build new secure code sys-tems for the Army. The big problem? She had been hired not as William's equal but essentially as his assistant, at roughly half the pay.

Elizebeth and William canoeing on the Potomac in the early 1920s.

Elizebeth had grown up in a world where women earned less than men. Nevertheless, working for half pay must have disheartened her. What bothered her even more, however, was that William had leapfrogged her when it came to ability, too.

In 1917, she and William had been a perfectly balanced pair. His technical insights were matched by her intuitive leaps. In France, however, William had wrestled with even more difficult codes. The struggle—and his eventual triumph—made him formidable.

During that same period, Elizebeth had stagnated. Barred by her gender from joining William in France, she instead had spent her time dealing with Fabyan and then her father. None of it taught her anything new about code breaking. When William returned from France, she felt the difference between them keenly. Through no fault of her own, she was no longer his equal with codes and ciphers.

"By the end of the war, I was more or less known as a military cipher expert," she wrote, "but I was better known as the wife of my husband." William "had made a reputation so startling that I regarded the task of catching up to him as being altogether hopeless."

No one else could keep up with William, either. After returning to Riverbank in 1919, he had been tasked with cracking America's most advanced coding machine, invented by AT&T. At first, Elizebeth had worked with him, but after putting in twelve-hour days for six weeks, she and the rest of the team gave up. It was William who stuck with the problem—and stunned everyone by finding the solution.

Soon afterward, he wrote his landmark article, *The Index of Coincidence*. One of the most important papers in the history of code breaking, it introduced powerful new ways of using statistics to break codes. As usual, Fabyan tried to lay claim to his work, calling it Riverbank Publication No. 22, but its insights were William's alone. In a single stroke, he had set the field on its modern foundations.

Elizebeth was proud of her husband's brilliant mind, but she also yearned to be brilliant in her own right. The growing gap between them depressed her. Maybe she'd hoped that the move to Washington would change things, but it didn't. Yet again, it was William who was the leader and she who followed.

It may have been around this time that Elizebeth started to take another look at feminism. As a young college graduate, she had regarded suffragists with a skeptical eye. Women could be oppressors, too, she thought, and she took a dim view of "inane woman's rights, man-rebellious twaddle." Since then, however, she had gotten a hard education in all the ways that women received second-class treatment.

Soon she would join the League of Women Voters, where in time she would become a local leader in the fight for women's rights. In the 1930s, she chaired a panel on the future of feminism. She also took other progressive stances, like making a point of using her own full name—Elizebeth Smith Friedman—instead of the more common and acceptable form, Mrs. William F. Friedman. She came to see the suffragists as heroes. To her, they were "those courageous souls who made the fight that we might all be free."

In 1921, however, all that was still on the distant horizon. For Elizebeth, the pressing reality was that she was stuck in a job where she felt like second best, with her time worth half that of her husband's.

At the end of the year, in recognition of his remarkable gifts, William was promoted. He became the chief cryptanalyst of the Army Signal Corps. Soon afterward he was appointed an officer in the Army Reserve.

Elizebeth took a different path. After a year on the job, she quit.

———

Later in life, Elizebeth said that she left her job because she wanted to write. On the face of it, that was excuse enough. For years, she had composed poems, scribbled down short story ideas, and dreamed of publication. She had detailed outlines for books, including one on the history of the alphabet.

She also had William's support. "You can write, sweetheart—wonderfully," he had told her in 1918. Understanding that it would "take a long time and much pains if you're ever going to write for publication," he wanted her to pursue what she loved.

But if writing was a draw, it was not the only one. Another hidden desire motivated her, too. The evidence for it lies tucked away in her files, on a yellow scrap from a legal pad. There, in a loose scrawl, Elizebeth admitted that she "resigned in our hopes to have a child." Overlooked for almost fifty years, that scrawl is like the key to a cipher, unlocking a hidden layer of Elizebeth's inner life.

Children were not something she talked about much, but she and William had been quietly dreaming of them for years. In their wartime letters, it was Elizebeth who first broached the subject, saying she sometimes wished that they'd had a child before he left for France. At night, she dreamed of a little girl—and once of triplets. The triplet dream made William laugh, but otherwise he responded with enthusiasm: "I want them so—more than I can tell. *Ours, ours*—won't that be wonderful!"

After the war was over, they decided to wait until they were "safe." Most likely, that was a code that meant "when we are beyond Fabyan's reach." Yet once they were settled into their new life in Washington, far away from Fabyan, there was no longer any reason to delay. Elizebeth soon would turn thirty, well beyond the age when most women in the 1920s started their families, and they were both eager to be parents.

Did she hope that staying at home would improve her chances of bearing a healthy baby? It was a common belief at the time, and one that William probably shared. After she quit, William even told a friend that he had persuaded her to take time off. If that was true, Elizebeth may not have needed much persuasion.

She seems to have been glad to leave a job that had not made her happy.

Nothing, however, could stop her from keeping busy. Tired of living in a piano studio, she scouted out a much better apartment, with five rooms, a fireplace, and a sheltered porch where William could tinker and experiment with radios. Elizebeth reported that they "went head over heels in debt" furnishing the place. They even purchased a secondhand piano so they could keep making music together. At the new place, their circle of friends continued to expand.

That summer, as she turned thirty, Elizebeth went to the Midwest for a long visit with old friends and family. William missed her profoundly, at work and at home. With the war over, neither Congress nor the Army was inclined to spend much money on code breakers, so it was hard to hire another assistant. The one he finally got was a cross-eyed ex-boxer with cauliflower ears, who could only type, not break codes.

"I am all alone," William grumbled to an old colleague. "Help is scarce and the poor War Department is getting poorer every day. Consequently I have my hands full." To Elizebeth, traveling around the Midwest, he wrote, "Honey, the house has been like a tomb." He signed it, "Your lonely old bear of a husband."

In her letters, Elizebeth sounded vibrant but restless. "Blessed Love! Am I wicked to be glad you are missing me? But if I hadn't come away, I couldn't have known you'd write me such darling letters, could I?" She blithely sent William "60 trillion kisses" but told him "you mustn't love me *too* much." She also refused to route her travels through Pittsburgh to see his family. "This is my five weeks and I shall live them to the end as my whims dictate. I may come home, not by Buffalo, but by Timbuctoo! Who knows?"

Unlike William, she was having fun. Spending time with friends and her beloved sister Edna, she went swimming and picnicking by Lake Erie. Her letters must have made William more acutely aware of all he was missing. "After it got dark, we told stories and sang around the fire—it was a glorious night with the moon making fairyland of the lake."

By the fall, Elizebeth was back in Washington. Still restless and hoping for a child, she poured her energy into writing. In addition to her history of the alphabet, she started another book—a manual on code breaking for teens. Rigorous but playful, she approached the subject with humor, starting off with the word "SYMPA-THIZERS":

> *Now, there are only two things I can do to that word to change it from a well-known friend to a perfect stranger. I can seize the word by the scruff of the neck, give it a good shaking, and make it look like a respectable town in the land of the Never-Never: PRZYMIHATSES. That's what is called* transposition, *because we have merely rearranged or* transposed *the letters from their original arrangement or order. . . .*
>
> *Now the only other thing I can do . . . is to replace them by other letters, or by symbols, figures, dancing men, or what not. For example, I can take this sentence "Sympathizers being rounded up here." and replace each letter by the one that follows it in the ordinary alphabet, and my, but doesn't it look like gibberish?*
>
> *TZNQBUIJAFST CFJOH SPVOEF VQ IFSF*
> *That's what is called* substitution. . . .

Elizebeth rooted for her readers even as she pushed them to excel. "Eureka!" she exclaimed at the end of one exercise. "We have it!"

She worked hard at her writing, and she wanted to see her books published. But she still hadn't finished them when the Navy came knocking on her door in the autumn of 1922. They needed an expert on codes and ciphers right away—and they wanted to hire Elizebeth.

CHAPTER TWELVE

On the Doorstep

"I didn't want to work for the Navy," Elizebeth later said, "but I found they were just sitting on my doorstep all the time." Week after week, the Navy kept at her. After four months, Elizebeth decided that "the only way to get rid of them was to go there for a little while until they found someone else."

The Navy was persistent because it was desperate. Expert code breakers were scarce, and recently they had lost one of their best: Agnes Meyer. A woman with great gifts in math, music, and languages, Meyer had worked as a Navy code breaker since 1918, and in the early 1920s she was creating new codes for them. But in 1922, she left the Navy for a job where the pay and prospects were better.

At first, the Navy hoped to get William to fill the vacancy. When he wouldn't budge from the Army, the Navy approached Elizebeth instead. She did not take this as a compliment. "This was a case of, 'If we can't have William Friedman, we will make use of his brains through his wife,'" she later said. "That's the story of my life. Somebody asks for my husband, and they can't get him, so they take me."

The Navy may have wanted a back door to William, but what they got in February 1923 was a gifted expert in her own right. Moreover, they got her for the bargain salary of $1,900 a year. That was $300 more than Meyer had earned, but well below William's salary at the War Department. The Navy didn't get Elizebeth for long, however, because she soon discovered that she was expecting a baby.

It was a wretched pregnancy. The terrible nausea she had known as a child came galloping back, and it was relentless. According to family stories, she "could keep nothing on her stomach" for a full nine months. In June, she resigned from the Navy job that she had never really wanted. But she didn't improve. The nausea only ended when she gave birth to her daughter, Barbara, on October 14, 1923.

Barbara was a beloved child in every way, but it was not an easy time. Although the nausea was gone, Elizebeth was in agony after the birth. For months, she could barely walk.

William unwisely mentioned her condition in a letter to Fabyan. Never a man short of advice, Fabyan recommended a cure of "warm barley gruel" and back exercises, including scrubbing floors. "I have no desire to make a scrub woman out of Elizabeth [sic]," he declaimed, "but I know of nothing to take its place, providing it is conscientiously done."

Elizebeth had X-rays instead.

William and Elizebeth with Barbara.

They revealed latent back issues made worse by pregnancy and childbirth. She was put in a plaster cast, then a brace. After that, she wore a special girdle until her back healed.

By then, she and William were living in rural Maryland, in a big house called Green Mansions. Set far back from the road, it had a wraparound porch, an apple orchard, and a garden with prizewinning irises. The Friedmans shared the place with friends who had a daughter of their own.

Despite William's long commute to Washington, he and Elizebeth were happy. On a shady knoll by the house, they relaxed in hammocks and swinging chairs like the ones they'd known at Riverbank. Toddler Barbara wandered around freely with Crypto, their Airedale watchdog. Crypto was "a kind of private bodyguard," Elizebeth wrote—"the first of many dogs and cats we supplied for our children."

During Elizebeth's long months of nausea, the Friedmans had hired a housekeeper named Cassie. A single, Black woman in her early thirties, she came from Washington, DC, where she helped support her widowed brother and his children. Elizebeth considered her "an extraordinarily fine person," and young Barbara adored her. She stayed with the Friedmans for seven years, until her early death from cancer. Later on, the Friedmans also hired a woman named Carlotta as a day nurse to help out.

Unfairly, both Cassie's and Carlotta's last names have been lost to history. Yet it was their presence that made it possible for both Elizebeth and William to pursue paid work. And even with help, the Friedmans had a lot to juggle.

At the War Department, William's star was rising. In addition to his code-building duties, he was becoming Washington's on-call code breaker. At one point, he was even asked to decipher radio signals thought to come from Mars. He also decoded telegrams that exposed corruption in President Warren G. Harding's cabinet in 1924. The scandal, known as Teapot Dome, landed the secretary of the interior in prison. It also put William in the papers.

William was news not only because he was a code breaker, but because he was Jewish. At the time, Congress was about to pass a new immigration act that made it easy for so-called Nordic people to immigrate to the United States. The entry of others, including Jews, was sharply curtailed. The new policy was shaped by the kind of eugenicists that William had met in his college days, and Cold Spring Harbor's Charles Davenport led the charge.

Some newspapers pointed to William as proof that Jewish immigrants were far from "undesirable." Here was a man who had "rendered a great service to his country," in both war and peace. "We'll take our chances of becoming 'contaminated' with a hundred thousand 'aliens,'" one reporter wrote, "if they produce only one William Frederick Friedman in a generation!"

The Friedmans clipped the article and saved it.

While William commuted into Washington every day, Elizebeth remained at home. A doting mother, she kept records of her baby's every accomplishment, as well as her cryptic babblings. Yet Elizebeth continued to work, too. At a time when middle-class women were expected to retire after they started a family, this was a daring decision.

At first, her work involved writing the books she hoped to publish one day. But soon she and William jointly took on another job—creating a secret code for millionaire Edward Beale McLean.

The lavish, loose-living owner of the *Washington Post*, McLean was a buddy of both President Harding and the secretary of the interior. When William broke the Teapot Dome telegrams, McLean worried that his own secrets could be easily read, too. Summoning William, he asked if he could buy a secure code for private use.

William and Elizebeth talked over the idea. McLean was willing to pay a good price, and Elizebeth could do the bulk of the work from home, with William helping in the evenings. After checking with a lawyer, they agreed to build the code. Six months later, when the job was done, McLean dragged his feet on payment. Despite his immense wealth, he failed to settle the full bill for years.

McLean's conduct enraged Elizebeth. She wanted to take action, but William held back. All his life, William found it hard to demand payments that were owed to him. Having grown up in a world of widespread antisemitism, he feared that "any demand for his rights" would lead to ugly comments about money and Jews.

To be cheated, and to have no recourse, was painful. It reminded the Friedmans of their ordeals with Fabyan, and they resolved never to get into such a situation again. "We were becoming weary," Elizebeth wrote, "of very wealthy men and their dealings in money matters." They had learned a "life time lesson" that "rich men never pay their bills."

In August 1925, Elizebeth and William moved on—quite literally. Taking their savings and what money they could get from McLean, they bought a home of their own. Brand-new, it was located at 3932 Military Road in northwest Washington, making William's commute much easier. The modest two-story house would be their family home for more than twenty years.

They had barely settled in when the government came looking for Elizebeth again. This time, the man who wanted to recruit her was mournful-eyed Captain Charles Root of the Coast Guard. He wanted to know if Elizebeth was willing to serve in a new kind of war—a war against smugglers and gangsters.

CHAPTER THIRTEEN

The Rum War

In late 1925, when Captain Root sought out Elizebeth, the Coast Guard was in trouble. It was fighting what later became known as the Rum War—and the Coast Guard was losing.

What kicked off the Rum War was Prohibition, America's ban on alcohol, which cut off the nation's supply of wine, beer, and spirits. When the ban went into effect in 1920, reformers who had campaigned for it were pleased, but plenty of Americans refused to comply with the new rules. Downing homemade hooch and bathtub gin, they also turned to smugglers who sold them rum, brandy, and other drinks. By 1924, illegal liquor worth a staggering $500 million (equal to over $7.7 billion today) was coming into the United States each year.

It was the Coast Guard's duty to stop that liquor before it reached the shoreline. From the start, they were fighting an uneven battle, and the conflict got uglier as new players came on the scene.

Within a few years, rumrunning was dominated by the killers and thugs of organized crime.

Before Prohibition, criminal gangs were small-timers. Often in the pay of local political bosses, they had no national reach. But liquor smuggling was so lucrative that it encouraged powerful new gang alliances—and alcohol profits made those gangs almost untouchable. The mobster Al Capone was said to make upwards of $50 million a year from illegal booze. Money like that made it easy to run rings around law enforcement.

To the dismay of reformers, Prohibition was turning out to be crime's best friend. In fact, the trade had helped *create* modern organized crime. By the mid-1920s, gangsters were ruling the roost in big cities like New York and Chicago. Some gangs bought off anyone who opposed them. Others simply gunned them down.

The gangsters tried both tactics on the Coast Guard. Some officers could be bribed into leaving them alone. But when that didn't work, the rumrunners didn't hesitate to shoot at Coast Guard vessels and crews. The Rum War was the result—an ongoing battle at sea and along the shores.

When Root approached her, Elizebeth already knew that the Rum War was no joke. If she got involved, she would be squaring off against dangerous men—men who wouldn't hesitate to target the mother of a small child. She had every reason to send Captain Root away. But she didn't. She saw him as a "conscientious officer" who was in desperate need of help, and she listened to what he had to say.

———

Few people knew more about the Rum War than Charles Root. At fifty-one, he had served in the Coast Guard for most of his working life, and he had been tracking the gangsters for years. He knew, for instance, who their suppliers were. The Bahamas, Belize, and the islands of Saint Pierre and Miquelon sold them millions of gallons of liquor. Canada, Cuba, and Mexico were also reliable sources of drink.

A rumrunner with cases and barrels of illegal liquor on deck.

Root had also seen how the gangsters spared no expense on their rumrunning fleets. Some gangs bought aircraft engines for their boats, to make sure they could outrun the Coast Guard. The top gangs went even further, buying vast "mother ships" that could be loaded with up to sixty thousand cases of drink. These "floating warehouses" were then anchored in international waters for six months or even a year, beyond the reach of the Coast Guard. The gangsters used middle-sized boats called "intermediates" to ferry the cargo to speedboats near the coast. These zippy "contact" boats then ran the liquor into shore.

How could the Coast Guard compete? At the start of the Rum War, they had only seventy-five vessels, not all of them fit for pursuit. Even when they bought more, it wasn't enough. As Elizebeth later explained, the Atlantic coast alone, "with its coves and inlets, its chopped waterline, with its many secluded spots where boats might secretly dock and unload, created a problem which defied description." For the Coast Guard, the Rum War was less a game of cat and mouse and more a case of a needle in a haystack.

Outmanned and outgunned, the Coast Guard had to outsmart the rumrunners. That, at least, was Root's take. Head of the Coast Guard's Intelligence Section—and, for a time, its only member—he tracked every detail he could discover about the rumrunners' vessels. On charts and lists, he recorded their names, their owners, their bearings, and their radio signals.

In 1925, a few rumrunners still sent their messages the old-fashioned way, via carrier pigeon and floating bottle. But most gangs were using radio. They broadcast from so-called wildcat stations, which were secret and unlicensed and kept odd hours. When the gangs realized that Root was eavesdropping, they hired the best cryptographers money could buy, for up to $10,000 a year. That was more than four times what the Coast Guard could offer. Soon the rumrunners were transmitting their messages in codes and ciphers that Root could not break.

Stumped, Root turned to the Navy and to William at the Army. At first, they helped Root out, but then they had to stop. Both the Army and the Navy were forbidden to engage in law enforcement. Besides, they had more than enough to do already, creating codes and breaking messages for their own services.

Root realized the Coast Guard needed its own code breaker—and it needed one fast. His first choice was William, who turned him down. So Root approached Elizebeth instead.

From the get-go, Elizebeth understood that Root was another one of those people looking for a back door to her husband, taking her on so "they'd get the use of his brains." But she didn't dismiss the offer out of hand. She was not one of the reformers who had campaigned for Prohibition, but she believed in the rule of law, and the rise of the gangsters appalled her. At a time when organized crime was taking over American cities, Root was offering her a way to fight back.

Her official employer, she learned, would be the Treasury Department, which oversaw both the Bureau of Prohibition and the Coast Guard. She would then be loaned long-term to Root's Intelligence Section. And Root himself was willing to do whatever it took to hire her. "I made the condition that I wouldn't work in an office," Elizebeth wrote. "If I could take the stuff home and work on it, all right." Root agreed.

That December, Elizebeth became the newest recruit in the Rum War—and the Coast Guard's secret weapon.

CHAPTER FOURTEEN

The Making of Her

Elizebeth's start at the Coast Guard was low-key. "I didn't even have an office downtown," she later wrote. "I went to Captain Root's office, collected papers and information and the like." She then took everything home. When she had solved her packets of encrypted messages, she returned them to the office and got new ones.

At the office, she also "got together the present situation: how many rumrunners were involved, where they were going, what they were doing . . . and made sure that I had all of the dates." Her war work had taught her that these details were crucial. If you knew what the messages might contain—a boat's name, say, or a port—it was easier to crack them.

Sometimes all she had was the messages themselves. Yet even then, she could often produce results, due to her gift at spotting patterns. Take this message, intercepted by the Coast Guard on Sunday, January 30, 1926, at 6:30 a.m.:

EBQKPI QYHGC CSQCJ SMSFSQ PCESFSQ CGWSS
CRSMFS UIVJWCI PQK VJWCIJQS LYMSE
TJQVYWL.

The Coast Guard had no idea what to make of this, but Elizebeth did.

She would have noticed right away that the message was broken into irregular groups. These might be words—and they were a sign that she was dealing with amateurs. Smart gangs usually sent their messages in four- or five-letter groups to make them harder to crack.

Even better, one of the groups was only three letters long: "PQK." Odds were that it was a common three-letter word, possibly "the" or "and."

Elizebeth would have noticed other patterns, too. For instance, "Q" is a rare letter in ordinary messages, but it makes up a whopping ten percent or so of this one. And the letter that appears most often in the message is "S," at seventeen percent. Perhaps it stood for "E," the most frequent letter in the English language. If so, that would mean that "PQK" couldn't be "the," but it might still be "and."

"It pays to go very slowly at the start, using your best judgement for every letter," she advised other code breakers. "Above all, don't jump at conclusions too quickly, or you'll surely stub your toes." If a guess didn't lead to good results, she backtracked and tried another one.

After playing around with letter counts and making more guesses, Elizebeth might then have worked out that not only did "S" = "E," but "E" = "S." Another pattern? *Yes!*

It turns out that pairs are the key to the cipher. Elizebeth wrote the solution out in neat penciled letters:

SUNDAY NIGHT TEN TO ELEVEN
AT SEVEN THREE TWELVE BY
FORTY FORTY ONE MILES CONFIRM

The sender was naming a time (Sunday night) and a spot in the ocean (N 40°41' by W 73°12'). That spot happened to be near Long Island, a favorite landing place for rumrunners. Most likely, the sender was setting up a meeting point. Thanks to Elizebeth, the Coast Guard now knew that the spot was worth watching.

By breaking messages like these, Elizebeth swiftly proved her value to the Coast Guard. But after only two months on the job, she had to leave. She was facing another rough pregnancy.

Born prematurely on July 28, 1926, her son John Ramsay thrived. This time Elizebeth had better medical care and recovered quickly, too. Soon she was solving ciphers for the Coast Guard "in emergencies." In April 1927, she went back to working full-time. Just as before, she was based at home, as a "Special Investigator."

Root was clearly delighted to have her back. In a memo, he praised her "shrewdness in the breaking down of enemy ciphers." Yet even with all her skill and experience, it was hard for Elizebeth to get the respect she deserved. Root gave much of the credit for her success to William, noting that she had both "the services of her distinguished husband" and his "secret methods of solving ciphers." Later on, William's own colleagues made similar assumptions. As one of them said, "Our impression, and I think it was a mistaken one, was that much of her success was a result of Mr. Friedman's effort."

At first, William did help Elizebeth now and then. He liked to rummage through the messages on her desk, and he sometimes contributed to solutions. "We got fun out of that," Elizebeth recalled. At times, the messages they solved made them chuckle.

WILLIAM FREDERICK FRIEDMAN   ELIZEBETH SMITH FRIEDMAN
BARBARA   FRIEDMAN
JULY 28 ÷ ANNOUNCE THE ARRIVAL OF ÷ 1926
JOHN RAMSAY FRIEDMAN.

The birth announcement for John Ramsay Friedman in 1926.

Once they broke a message going out to a rumrunner that said, "Inform Andrew his wife has just had twins." They also broke the reply: "Sorry, Andrew has no wife."

Although they enjoyed these joint efforts, these were the exception, not the rule. Even if William had wanted to do Elizebeth's job, it simply wasn't possible. As the chief code breaker at the Signal Corps, he was already snowed under at work. Not only was he compiling new codes for Army use, he was also teaching cryptography to Army officers, as well as breaking ciphers and codes on demand. From time to time, he also had to represent U.S. interests at high-level meetings. All this meant that he put in long hours already, with little time to spare for outside work.

Elizebeth mostly handled the messages on her own. No one at Root's office had the skills to help her. A secretary typed and filed messages, but the code breaking was up to Elizebeth. "I was . . .

'a loner' as far as any assistance in the solution of secret messages was concerned," she later said. Undaunted, she tackled the job with gusto.

From the moment Elizabeth started work again in the spring of 1927, she was in high demand. Hundreds of messages had piled up, and the Coast Guard needed them solved. "This traffic covered a period of more than a year, was from many different sources both on the Atlantic and Pacific Coasts, and the volume was increasing daily," Elizabeth reported. Within two months, she had solved almost everything.

Caught up, she began cracking messages in real time, many of them from the West Coast. Although some of the encryption systems were already familiar to her, others were not. To break them, she used every trick she knew. The work required not only insight, but also great patience and focus. A single miscopied letter could waste hours. Everything had to be checked and rechecked.

Following the routines she and William had developed at Riverbank in 1917, she worked in pencil, sometimes on graph paper. She saved every worksheet and every attempt at a solution. Again and again, she made the garble of letters yield the true message.

After that, there was still more work to be done. "As rapidly as the systems were broken, each day's traffic was translated by me into plain text." Anything that looked urgent "was telegraphed in cipher to the Pacific Coast. If not of immediate importance it was forwarded by air mail."

The deadlines were never-ending, and there were times when she wondered if she had chosen the right line of work. Sometimes she wished she could use her code-breaking skills in a less pressured job, perhaps in the pursuit of lost ancient languages like Hittite and Mayan:

> *[W]hen I am summoned by telegram to a city two or three thousand miles away, to read several thousand messages to be used in a court case the following Monday, or some equally impossible demand, I think with a sigh of the sheltered life of the man who sits in a museum and spends thirty years deciphering one page of Hittite.*

But her work was getting results, and that buoyed her up. Thanks in no small part to her decryptions, the Coast Guard was

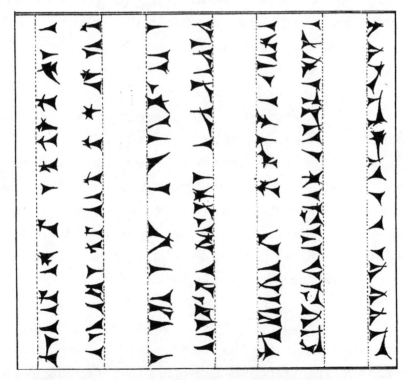

The Friedmans loved to design their own cryptic cards, and they made this one look as if it were written in ancient Hittite. Folded in just the right way, it reveals a holiday greeting in English.

intercepting many more rumrunners, depriving the crime bosses of their profits. Between 1927 and 1928, illegal liquor imports fell by an estimated sixty percent—from 11 million gallons a year to 5 million.

The Coast Guard hoped that the tide of the Rum War was turning. But the gangsters soon fought back with a blizzard of new codes and ciphers. It was a code-breaking battle, and Elizebeth was in the thick of it.

By late 1930, Elizebeth reported that she had now cracked "nearly 50 distinct and separate systems of secret communication." Many were extremely complex, using as many as "three to five methods . . . each of which must be solved as an entity in itself."

The rumrunning gangsters were paying for some of the best cryptography on earth, she realized. Even World War I had seen nothing to equal it. Whenever she cracked one system, more challenging ones rose to take its place—and day after day, she was forced to grapple with them alone.

It was demanding work. At times, it seemed almost impossible. But it was also the making of her.

Just as William's skills had grown by leaps and bounds while he was overseas in France, Elizebeth's talents were now undergoing a similar transformation. In just over three years, she solved a staggering twelve thousand secret messages for the Coast Guard and its allies in the Rum War. She also kept an eye on less vital communications, examining up to twenty-five thousand messages a year overall.

The ability to spot patterns is key to code breaking, and Elizebeth already had an eye for them. Yet the ever-increasing demands of her work raised her gift to a whole new level. If practice makes perfect, Elizebeth was approaching perfection. And over time she chalked up more and more victories.

Portrait of Elizebeth, 1930.

She was upping her game in other ways, too—especially when it came to gathering intelligence. The more data she had, the easier it was to decrypt the messages. To get what she needed, she made the most of her contacts in every division, working not only with the Coast Guard, but also with other agencies involved in the Rum War. In doing so, she helped weave those agencies into a more effective fighting force.

To break a new code system, for example, she might ask a Coast Guard officer about the position of vessels, check with a customs official about cargo reports, and confer with a Bureau of Prohibition agent about possible suspects. Often this meant making a trip into downtown Washington, but sometimes she had to travel much farther to get the information she needed. In the spring of 1928, she made her first coast-to-coast trip, which allowed her to work directly with Prohibition and Coast Guard agents in California. By being on the spot, and by pulling together information from different agencies and locations, she often saw links that no one else could see. These links helped her break more messages, which she then shared with the agencies best poised to act on them.

Today, this kind of multisource, multiagency intelligence work is common in law enforcement, but back then it was new, and Elizebeth was a pioneer. The results spoke for themselves. As she became better and better at the job, she became an intelligence powerhouse, able to advise the Coast Guard and other agencies on everything from potential dangers to easy targets.

———

Elizebeth's own favorite rumrunner case started in October 1929. As the stock market crashed and the United States tumbled into the Great Depression, she was sent to Houston to help with a court case. Over several weeks, she sat in the steamy city, poring over a trunkful of suspicious messages that no one else could crack. When she broke them, she wasn't surprised to discover that they were from rumrunners. What did surprise her was that the 650 messages used twenty-four different code and cipher systems.

From the start, she spotted that twenty-three of the messages belonged in a separate group. Even when decrypted, they left out a lot of details, so at first she couldn't place them, but it was clear that they had nothing to do with the court case. They turned out to be related to the *I'm Alone*—a rumrunning boat that was already in the news.

Earlier that year, the Coast Guard had spotted the *I'm Alone* in the Gulf of Mexico, sailing in coastal lanes that rumrunners often used. When the Coast Guard demanded the right to board, the *I'm Alone* fled. After the Coast Guard caught up, the captain of the *I'm Alone* admitted that he had a cargo of liquor on board. After a long chase, the Coast Guard shot and sank the vessel.

The sinking was widely condemned. Not only had it taken place in international waters, but it turned out that the *I'm Alone* had been manned by Canadians sailing under a Canadian flag. That made the American attack illegal, with some Canadians calling it piracy. The British ambassador registered a protest, the American Embassy in Paris was stoned, and Canada sued the United States for over $386,000. For a nation grappling with the Depression, that was an eye-watering sum.

Elizebeth's twenty-three messages saved the situation for the United States. They helped prove that the real owners and managers of the *I'm Alone* were American smugglers. One was a racketeer who controlled a crime syndicate worth $15 million a year.

After these facts were established, a joint commission cut Canada's claim by over eighty-five percent. Elizebeth and her twenty-three messages had helped save the United States more than $336,000.

Like most of her work, the *I'm Alone* job was done on the quiet. Most people knew her merely as William Friedman's wife, who worked from home on the side. The Coast Guard and its close partners, however, knew the truth. In their circles, Elizebeth was finally getting noticed for her solo achievements.

And she was not done yet. As messages continued to pour in, she honed her powers still further. Soon she would fully come into her own, accomplishing the seemingly impossible—and astonishing the world.

CODE BREAK

BARBARA'S CIPHER

Elizebeth had to travel alone for work, but she rarely traveled for pleasure without her family. One exception came in late 1932, when William urged her to join him in Spain, where he was attending a conference. Elizebeth finished up some tricky code-breaking work and arranged for Barbara and John to stay with her sister in Detroit. Then she crossed the Atlantic on the liner *Île de France* and met William.

Their time together in Spain was one of the great adventures of their life. But they missed the children a lot, and they were delighted when nine-year-old Barbara sent them letters in cipher.

Barbara used a *Caesar cipher*, which replaces each letter with one farther along in the alphabet. A shift of +1 means that each A becomes B, each B becomes C, and so on, until Z becomes A. With a shift of +2, every letter moves along *two* places, so that A becomes C and B becomes D. You can shift all the way to +25, if you like.

Here's a line taken from a Caesar cipher letter that William wrote to Barbara:

XF XFSF NVDI QMFBTFE XJUI ZPVS MFUUFST
JO UIJT DJQIFS.

If you simply shift all the letters back by one place, it's easy to read. Barbara put this trick to good use at summer camp, when she wrote her letters in cipher so that the camp director couldn't read them.

A Caesar cipher is easy to break, but not everyone is trained to spot one. Elizebeth was thrilled to see Barbara using it at the "tender age of nine." Several years later, when Elizebeth was asked about her "greatest thrill," she answered, "Cipher letter in Spain from Barbara."

CHAPTER FIFTEEN

Firepower

By 1930, Elizebeth was one of the world's top cryptanalysts, but most Americans had never heard of her. Some people even misspelled her job title as "Crypt Analyst," which led to mix-ups. "I am . . . not a new sort of high-class mortician," Elizebeth found herself explaining, with exasperated humor. She added that she wasn't "concerned with burying things," but with "digging up" undercover messages.

In July 1931, she acquired a new title: "Cryptanalyst in Charge." After years of working solo, she had convinced the Treasury Department to fund a larger unit. Under her command, they would support the Coast Guard and six other Treasury branches. The price tag was $14,600 a year, but Elizebeth was sure that the expanded unit would improve the Treasury's bottom line. With better intelligence, the Coast Guard would have fewer wild-goose chases. As Elizebeth pointed out, that would mean "*saving* many thousands annually in fuel."

Along with her new title, Elizebeth received a raise of over fifty percent. That boosted her pay to $3,800—nearly three times the average U.S. salary. But instead of working from home, she now had to commute to an office in the Treasury Annex, a block away from the White House. The hours were long. The standard government work week was Monday through Friday, plus a half day on Saturday, but she requested a special security pass to stay in the building after hours. Sometimes that was the only way to get all the work done.

The new team was supposed to help with the workload. First, however, Elizebeth had to recruit them. Knowing she had little hope of finding trained code breakers, she intended instead to search for novices with the potential to go far.

She wanted to hire women, but by law she had to choose from lists of people who had taken civil service exams in math or science. Since only men were encouraged to pursue careers in these subjects, the lists she was given had no women on them. She ended up with four young men instead. The only women in the unit were the secretaries—and Elizebeth herself.

In the 1930s, not everyone could wrap their minds around the idea of a female boss. For the most part, however, Elizebeth had no trouble. "Many times I've been asked as to how my authority . . . was accepted by these men," she wrote, "but I must declare with all truth that with one exception, all of the men young or older who had worked for me and under me and with me, have been true colleagues."

Some men later admitted they'd had "great misgivings" about working under a woman. These faded away after they actually met Elizebeth. She was a good teacher and a pleasant boss, and they were awed by her code-breaking skills.

Elizebeth gave her new recruits a "crash course" in code

breaking, all while carrying on with her usual workload. She also had them index the messages she had broken so far, so that known patterns would be easier to spot. After six months, she could trust her team with simple decrypts. After a year, they could crack most of the complex ones.

Elizebeth appreciated the extra firepower. Still, the hardest code-breaking work remained hers, due to what she modestly termed her "greater experience."

———

Outside the office, Elizebeth threw herself into family life. In good weather, she and William ate on the porch with Barbara and John, sheltered by a huge elm tree. In winter, they had dinners by candlelight. All four of them had a great sense of humor, and they laughed themselves silly over family jokes and the antics of their much-loved cats and dogs.

As Elizebeth saw it, her daughter was an easy child—sweet-natured, gracious, and "reasonable." She had to work harder to understand her son. Although "very loveable and affectionate," John was stubborn and had a temper. Elizebeth adored them both and tried to encourage them in every way she could. She saved their drawings, helped with homework, offered advice, and shared funny poems. A family favorite was "The Fate of the Flimflam" by Eugene Field:

> *"Oh, woe to the swap of the sweeping swipe*
> *That booms on the hobbling bay!"*
> *Snickered the snark to the snoozing snipe*
> *That lurked where the lamprey lay. . . .*

Elizebeth recited this "a thousand times" when the kids were small.

In the backyard, Elizebeth planted a garden, and William built a swimming pool, brick by brick. He also took photos of everyone: Elizebeth reading to the children, Barbara swinging, the kids on their bikes. Barbara remembered her father hanging up the damp prints "between the

Elizebeth reading to Barbara and John.

shower curtain & the wall on a clothesline."

Elizebeth and William also made time for their friends. They enjoyed playing music with them, and they threw parties that people talked about for months afterward. Both of them also liked sports. A keen swimmer, Elizebeth considered herself an "ardent bicyclist," too. William was a doubles tennis champion and later took up golf.

Because they worked long hours, they almost always had a housekeeper of some kind. After Cassie died in 1929, the Friedmans found it hard to find anyone who was her equal, especially as Carlotta had already left by then. But plenty of women applied for the job. One woman kept house for them while living with her husband in the Friedmans' furnished attic. Later in the Depression, an Italian American woman who had lost all her money came to work for them. Although Elizebeth never felt as close to these women as she had to Cassie, their help was crucial, especially when she had to be away for weeks on a case.

Many people questioned a married woman's right to work—let alone to take a job that involved travel. But William cheered her on. During her first West Coast work trip in 1928, one of the children had whooping cough, but even so, William was good at holding the fort. Whooping cough could be "just a little bit bothersome," he admitted. Yet he didn't think it was a reason for Elizebeth to cancel her trip.

Although Barbara and John often missed their mother, they loved spending time with their dad. Full of fun, William was a hands-on father. Barbara later remembered him often "hugging me warmly. He laughed a lot." He also made sure that she got to her skating lessons on time. Now and then, he and John went out on the ice with her.

Once a week, William took the kids to the movies—even though he was so tired he often fell asleep in the theater and had to be poked awake. At night, he read Sherlock Holmes stories to them. He even made up his own tales about "Henry the Whale."

Elizebeth knew that the kids were in good hands with William. Yet when she had to travel, it was

William with Barbara and John.

still hard for her to "pack my bag and hug my children a good-by which is to last a week or month or longer." But what else could she do? Some messages had to be broken on location because of legal restrictions. Others required her to consult with local agents. At times, too, she was needed as an expert witness for trials. Entire court cases could hang on her testimony.

This was especially true of the cases against Conexco—a shadowy behemoth that controlled the rumrunning traffic on the West and Gulf Coasts. It was officially registered in Canada as the Consolidated Exporters Corporation, a bland name that made it sound like a law-abiding company. In reality, Conexco worked with Al Capone's gang and other mobsters to supply liquor to the underworld.

Elizebeth had started tracking Conexco as early as 1925, when she began working for the Coast Guard. Over the next few years, her decrypts revealed the enormous scope of Conexco activities. By 1930, she knew enough to start mapping out one of its biggest networks. In this chart, she laid bare part of its secret structure.

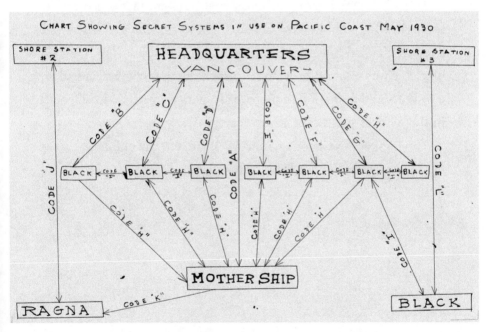

Elizebeth's map of Conexco's West Coast network.

Based on the West Coast, the gang was headquartered in Vancouver, with two additional shore stations. It owned a mother ship far out to sea, packed with tens of thousands of bottles, plus other vessels that were usually called "blacks." (They got that name because they kept their lights off to avoid detection.)

The entire network kept in touch by radio, using not one code, but *twelve*—each for a different part of the system. That made the operation hard to crack. Barely anyone would detect all twelve codes. Even fewer would guess that they were being used by the same secret group.

Elizabeth broke each code and read every message. Then she created her chart, showing how the parts of the network were connected to each other. She also identified some of the key operators involved. In doing so, she turned a spotlight on a shadowy criminal outfit.

Thanks in part to her efforts, a trial of twenty Conexco agents began in May 1933 in New Orleans. They were charged with what a reporter called "the greatest rum-running conspiracy" of them all. The case was so important that the government's lawyers had taken two years and $500,000 to prepare. To win, they needed Elizebeth in the witness stand.

Saying goodbye once again to William and the children, Elizebeth traveled to New Orleans to testify.

CODE BREAK
CRACKING A CONEXCO CODE

With millions in profits, the gangsters who ran Conexco could afford the best cryptography in the business. Elizebeth heard a rumor that a former British Navy officer was their chief code maker. "Whoever he was," she said, "he was a good producer for Conexco."

For the most part, Conexco used *enciphered codes*. These mixes of codes and ciphers were a headache to crack. But how exactly did they work?

Here's an example, taken from Elizebeth's records:

(1) As a Conexco employee, you wrote out your plaintext message:

ANCHORED IN HARBOR

(2) Using a book that Conexco provided, you looked up the code numbers for those words or phrases. Since ANCHORED was 07033 and IN HARBOR was 52725, that gave you:

07033 52725

(3) You added 1000 to each of those numbers:

08033 53725

(4) Using another book, you looked up each number and found what its letter code was:

BARHY CIJYS

(5) You enciphered the letters with a substitution cipher:

MJFAX ZYWKH

(6) You then broadcast these final letters via radio, using Morse code:

```
- -    . - - -    . . - .    . -    - . . -
- - . .    - . - -    . - -    - . -    . . . .
```

For someone who knew the system and had the right code books, it wasn't too hard to work backward and decode the radio message. But for an outsider who had no idea how the system operated, it was next to impossible. Only a code breaker of Elizebeth's caliber had a chance. And for a while, she was stumped, too.

"When this was first encountered, and I had puzzled over it for all the time I could spare," Elizebeth wrote, "I decided to make the assumption that it was enciphered code." It was an inspired hunch—what she and William sometimes called a "Golden Guess." But what ciphers and codes had been used? And how were they layered?

Luckily, some Conexco messages included words that weren't in the code books. These words could only be put through the cipher step (step 5) before they were sent out in Morse. It was a weakness in the system, and it helped Elizebeth break the cipher layer. The code layers were much harder to crack, but with patience, analysis, and a flair for guesswork, she got there.

Once Elizebeth knew what all the steps were, the rest of the messages were easy to read. But every few months, Conexco's code maker would switch to a new system. Then Elizebeth had to start all over again.

CHAPTER SIXTEEN

Fame

The Conexco trial put Elizebeth in the spotlight. From the moment she took her place in the witness box, she caused a stir.

In 1933, court experts were usually men in suits. Yet here stood a woman in a pink dress and a flowered hat, calling herself a "crypt-analyst." The term was so new that the New Orleans court reporter wasn't sure how to write it out. But Elizebeth was all business as she explained that it meant she was an expert in breaking secret code and cipher systems. When prompted, she read out a series of Conexco messages that she had decrypted. Taken together, they laid bare the workings of Conexco's day-to-day operations.

Shaken, Conexco's defense team accused her of faking the decryptions. They suggested she was making things up to help the government's legal team. Still on the witness stand, Elizebeth rebutted that idea. Her readings were "not a matter of opinion."

Instead, she relied on the science of cryptology. "Any other experts would find, after proper study, the exact readings I have given here."

Her clear, calm testimony helped the government win its case. The chief conspirators—including the leader, Bert Morrison—went to prison. The prosecutor, noting that Elizebeth had "made an unusual impression on the jury," wrote that they couldn't have won the case without her.

Elizebeth also made an impression on reporters, who discovered that a female code breaker made good copy. That year, a number of papers ran articles about her, billing her as "Clever Mrs. Elizabeth Friedman . . . Govt. Cipher Expert." She didn't mind the misspelling of her name that much, but it bothered her when reporters had a lot to say about her appearance. Many remarked on how small and good-looking she was, calling her "a pretty government scryptanalyst," "a pretty middle-aged woman," "a smiling lady in a frilly pink dress."

Elizebeth didn't see why newspapers should comment on frills. She also hated the "middle-aged" comment, perhaps because it hit on a sore point. Usually a stickler for accuracy, she was still being cagey about her true age, almost always making herself exactly one year younger. On everything from official census forms to sworn statements, she put her birth date down as 1893 instead of 1892, and she went on doing this for years. Even William did not know the truth.

No reporter ever cottoned on to her fib, but the newspaper coverage rattled her. She didn't mind reporters covering the facts of the case, but she saw no reason for them to write about her age and her clothes. She was going to have to get used to it, though. Like it or not, she was news—and she was about to become bigger news still.

In the spring of 1934, Elizebeth was called back to New Orleans for another Conexco case. This time she made an even more striking impression.

To the relief of many Americans, including the Coast Guard, Prohibition had been repealed a few months before. Unpopular with the majority of Americans, it had proved too expensive to enforce. Liquor became legal again. But judges were still catching up with the backlog of rumrunning cases, so the trials against the likes of Conexco continued.

At the trial, Elizebeth had to face off against defense lawyer Edwin Grace, who worked for the Capone family. Trying to get her testimony discounted, he questioned her expertise again and again. Elizebeth finally turned to the judge.

"Your Honor, is there a blackboard available to the court?" she asked.

When a blackboard was brought forward, Elizebeth gave the whole court a lesson in the basics of cryptology. Her off-the-cuff talk was lucid and convincing. Soon Grace and his team "were nervously indicating that they had had enough."

To Elizebeth's surprise, the blackboard story "set the press on fire." One story, headed "Class in Cryptology," stated that Elizebeth "had conducted a class in solving code messages," showing "how experts translate into plain language the most complex of code and cipher."

"Complex? Code?" Elizebeth later jotted down when summing up the article. On the contrary, she had demonstrated "the *simplest* of all *ciphers*." But that didn't stop the story. "While I pursued my business quietly in New Orleans, short and long articles were appearing all over the country."

The stories kept coming even after the trial was over. "She Breaks Up Smugglers' Plots by Decoding Their Notes for Uncle

Elizebeth clipped and saved this 1934 article about the I'm Alone *case.*

Sam," in the Washington *Sunday Star.* "Millions Are Saved to Nation by Decoder of Smugglers' Notes," in the *Christian Science Monitor.* "Solves Ciphers for Uncle Sam," in the *United States News.* Some articles included her photograph.

Elizebeth had mixed feelings about the coverage. Many of the reporters were careless about the facts, to the point that she could barely recognize herself in their articles. In her own line of work, attention to detail mattered. Why didn't it to the newspapers?

She also hated it when reporters showed no regard for the secret nature of her job. Often they asked her to explain exactly how she broke each code. "No, I can't tell you how I do it," she told them once. "In the first place, it'd take a week or two to explain it. And in the second place we have to keep our ideas secret so that we don't give other smugglers any new ideas."

Still, all this interest in her work was proof that she was doing something right. Back when she was plain "Miss Smith," she had yearned to make her mark on the world. Now she was getting noticed. And when the circumstances were right, she sometimes savored her newfound fame.

One of her favorite days came right after the blackboard trial was over, when she was invited to appear on NBC radio. Elizebeth agreed to the interview, as long as her children could come to the studio as well. Barbara and John were then ten and seven years old, and Elizebeth was always looking for chances to expand their world. Holed up with the technicians, the children got an inside view of radio.

As Barbara and John stood "bursting with excitement in the control room," Elizebeth sat in the studio with Margaret Santry, a popular radio host. Santry gave her a gushing welcome. "I'll confess, Mrs. Friedman, I was thunderstruck the other day when I met you for the first time. I simply wasn't prepared to find a petite, vivacious young matron bearing the formidable title of Cryptanalyst for the United States Coast Guard."

Since Elizebeth was tired of people talking about her looks, this wasn't a promising start, but the interview got better from there. Santry encouraged her to talk at length about her work and the science of code breaking. She covered the personal angle, too. Given that both Elizebeth and her husband were code breakers, Santry wondered, "[D]oes the habit of thinking in code ever creep into your family life?"

"I guess it's bound to—it's so much a part of our life," Elizebeth admitted.

"And are your children experts in code, too?" Santry asked.

Barbara was "quite an expert for her age," Elizebeth responded. She told Santry that when she and William had traveled to Spain, Barbara "sent us messages in cipher all the time."

The day at NBC made Elizebeth feel like a star. A local artist even sketched her while she was in the studio. The flattering portrait later appeared in the *Washington Post*, with an account of the interview.

Best of all, the radio format gave her a chance to speak for herself. Compared with the careless reporting of the newspapers, it made a nice change. And it may have gotten Elizebeth thinking about other ways she could tell her own story.

Five months later, when asked to complete a short profile for a Who's Who of notable American women, Elizebeth sent back a long letter. Normally modest to a fault, she covered her triumphs in detail, adding that "my own experience has been unique." She then added that she was "preparing to write a chronicle" of her career thus far.

If she hoped that the editor would express an interest in her "chronicle," she was disappointed. All the man wanted was the short profile. Still, the notion of a memoir kept coming back to her. She knew she would have to keep some case details secret, but she was sure there was scope for a book—if only she could find the spare hours to write it.

———

One of the stranger effects of fame, Elizebeth discovered, was that the public started writing to you. People sent her heaps of letters. Many demanded that she solve messages and mysteries. Others offered her "unbreakable" coding and cipher systems—usually for a high price. No offer, however, was quite like the one Elizebeth received from a "Mr. W. Andresen" of Moyobamba, Peru.

A big-game hunter, Andresen had read about Elizebeth in a magazine. Like many other amateur code breakers, he challenged her to break some messages in a new system that he himself had devised. He hoped to interest the government in his methods.

```
W.Andresen.Moyobamba.

Repetition of my message to Reader's Digest 15.11.37.

025191410142403258010230208216599210060101602030111252511811102333138094261625
016021030830267005032011243812525076010581101921142114250125602014022260166501o3
342031021242408203207200141614422428022570902207084356710204323182031490513440o7
3040162114505427172480302502210346941004609026090900813534089020171013913430o725
430016012270968405044071562912021170352380601508140404311324701024062171566401o4
506130061842904103113030184314316433112551402001216176661113607183321893606909ll
21002021146324343525114026062112365501094101100416901097082390602101152094323824
61102701187116860209907238101620107723175240224915821435192591301501186118
```

A small part of one of Andresen's messages.

Unlike Elizebeth's other fans, Andresen offered her an unusual prize: a tiger skin. The offer, Andresen explained, depended "partly on my wife," who was looking after the tiger skin. It seemed this was no easy task in Peru's jungle climate. If there was no solution from Elizebeth before Christmas, Andresen felt "bound" to give the tiger skin to his wife instead.

The letter amused Elizebeth. In her reply, she thanked Andresen for thinking of her but told him she had no time to spare for his puzzle. She also told him what the problem with his system was.

Most people thought it was hard to come up with an unbreakable cipher or code, she explained, but the reality was that a "twelve year old boy" could do it, "so long as only two or three examples of the method are available for study." The challenge was coming up with a system that was secure, practical, and speedy enough to be used for thousands of messages a day. Andresen's system featured elaborate lines that had to be hand-checked for accuracy. It was simply not up to the task.

Elizebeth sent her "best wishes to Mrs. Andresen and the hope that she will enjoy absolute possession of the tiger skin." After that, she heard nothing more from Andresen. But plenty of other letters kept pouring in, proof that Elizebeth was becoming a celebrity.

———

If there were times when Elizebeth enjoyed her growing fame, she also knew it had its downsides. The worst aspect was one that she did not like to discuss but that she could not completely ignore.

It put her in danger.

Thanks to all the newspaper coverage, gangsters and mobsters across the country now knew exactly who was decoding their secret messages—and whose evidence was sending them to jail. "After those smugglers got out of prison, some of them were in very, very mean moods," Elizebeth later recalled. During at least one trial, she was given bodyguards. But there was rarely any ongoing protection while she was on the road or once she returned home to 3932 Military Road.

She and William did their best to make light of the risks, especially in front of their young children. They did not always succeed. "Daddy joked about her being taken for a

Elizebeth on her way to a trial in 1934.

ride because that's what those mobsters did in those days," Barbara Friedman remembered. "And it scared me to death."

Maybe William joked about it because the threat felt too close to home. As he and Elizebeth had every reason to know, the agents who enforced Prohibition were suffering heavy losses. Between 1920 and 1933, a shocking ninety-seven agents died in the line of duty.

These record losses took place during Prohibition itself, so perhaps Elizebeth drew a breath of relief when the policy was repealed in 1933. Two years later, she and her unit were assigned at least one task that was utterly safe—creating new code systems for the Treasury Department.

But other aspects of her job continued to be dangerous, and sometimes the peril came from an unexpected direction. Certainly, that was true in 1937, when Elizebeth took on the job that came closest to killing her.

CHAPTER SEVENTEEN

The Trip of a Lifetime

The case that nearly killed Elizebeth started in a small Chinese herb shop in Vancouver, Canada. It was owned by wealthy Gordon Lim, a graduate of Oxford and Beijing University. By all accounts, he was a "very elegant gentleman."

The Royal Canadian Mounted Police, better known as the Mounties, had arrested Lim for drug smuggling in 1925 and 1926. Both times the courts had dismissed the case. Then, in March 1937, the Mounties caught Lim selling a small amount of opium. Suspecting that Lim was actually running a vast smuggling ring, they raided his shop. Inside his safe, they found a cache of seventeen short, encrypted messages on slips of yellow telegram paper.

For weeks, the Mounties puzzled over the messages, but they had no idea how to read them. At last, they asked the United States Customs Bureau for help. The Bureau turned to Elizebeth.

Working across international lines was not always easy, but a case involving drugs was nothing new for Elizebeth. Starting in the mid-1930s, drug smuggling had become a big part of her workload. She knew that drug lords could be just as dangerous as the rumrunning gangsters had been—and just as ingenious with their ciphers and codes.

When the Mounties' messages reached Elizebeth in June 1937, she was given very little to go on. All she knew was that the case involved Gordon Lim and opium. The messages were short and written in five-letter combinations—very much like most rumrunning messages. The letters all came from the English alphabet, but the Mounties suspected the plaintext was in Chinese, probably in Cantonese dialect.

Neither Elizebeth nor her team was fluent in Chinese, but Elizebeth had learned some basic characters while breaking another drug case earlier that year. That, too, had involved a Chinese message—a very long one. After consulting with Chinese speakers, she and her team were able to crack key portions of that message within a week. They pinpointed the ship that was carrying the drugs, and customs agents raided it as soon as it docked.

The Gordon Lim messages were a much tougher problem. They were very short, which limited Elizebeth's chance to spot patterns. ("[T]he shorter a message is," she once wrote, "the longer does it keep you working.") Even worse, the messages weren't all encoded with the same method. When added to the language barrier, that made the problem almost impossible to crack.

Nevertheless, Elizebeth and her team gave it a try. Using statistics, they detected four different encryption systems, each with multiple layers. They even worked out that the first layer of the encryption, the one that used English letters, was based on digraphs—that is, pairs of letters.

This was bad news. While there are only 26 letters in the English alphabet, there are 676 possible pairings, and the meaning of each letter in a digraph depends on how it is paired. For instance, the letter "A" will have a different meaning if it appears in "AE" rather than "AF."

With digraphs, your best hope is to chart the frequency of the pairings and use that to guess what each might represent. With messages in English, for example, the pairing that turns up most often may well represent "TH," the most common digraph in ordinary English.

Of course, English frequencies were no help in breaking Lim's messages, which were thought to be in Chinese. But Elizebeth and her team slowly worked out a possible way of converting the digraphs into numbers. They believed that these numbers could be related to a Chinese code book.

Code books were common in China because they were used for sending telegrams. "Chinese characters can't be sent over wire or cable or radioed or anything like that," Elizebeth noted. Instead, you had to consult the official telegraph books. These contained thousands of Chinese characters, with a unique four-digit number assigned to each one. (In a way, it was like an early version of modern Unicode, which assigns numbers to letters and to symbols such as emojis so that all computers can read them.) To draft a telegram, you wrote down the numbers for each character you wanted, and then you sent the string of numbers.

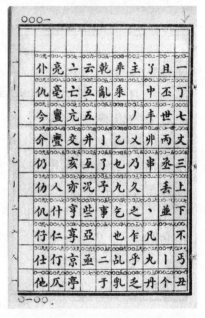

One of William's Chinese code books.

In the United States, it was hard to get hold of these telegraph code books, but William had a few. Elizebeth and her team studied them, hoping to convert the numbers they'd decrypted into a readable message. All they got was nonsense. Did that mean they needed to crack another layer of encryption? Or did it mean that every guess they'd made so far was wrong?

Nobody could tell.

They were stuck.

After a while, Elizebeth's team told her it was time to give up. "They considered it hopeless to do anything more because there wasn't enough material," Elizebeth said. "There are something like fifty-two thousand characters in the Chinese language so you can imagine seventeen messages which were nine or ten groups long each one, what a gigantic hunt would have to go on." Given the odds, "my staff refused to do anything more with it. They said it isn't worth working on; there isn't enough material. We can't do anything with it."

Elizebeth knew they had a point. Reluctantly, she took the messages and stowed them in her desk drawer. Then she moved on to other jobs.

But the Gordon Lim case continued to weigh on her mind. "[T]here was something so intriguing about it that I could not let it go," she wrote. In her spare moments, she found herself thinking about it. "[O]nce in a while I'd get out these papers and try something else, some little idea that had come to my mind."

After many weeks, she had an idea that worked.

———

Elizebeth's first breakthrough came when she decided "to attack *from the ends* of messages." She did this because she had noticed a certain formality in Chinese communications. "I had a feeling that they would end messages in a conventional and habitual manner with phrases like 'reply immediately,' 'send money,' 'send goods at once.'"

Set phrases like this are a gift to a code breaker. In this case, they would cut fifty-two thousand possible characters down to only a handful of likely candidates. If one of those fit, Elizebeth could use it to chip away at the rest of the puzzle.

Hoping her idea would prove right, Elizebeth lined all the messages up starting from their ends. Then she "selected three messages which for some intuitive reason I believed might end with the character for reply."

Elizebeth's intuition had always been remarkable. Now that she was breaking thousands of messages every year, and examining tens of thousands more, it was now second to none. Her brain was fine-tuned for spotting patterns that others missed.

In the three messages Elizebeth selected from the Gordon Lim case file, the pattern she spotted was this: the digits "6010" appeared at the end. Thinking this might correspond to "reply," she then spotted the combination "7193 6010." She thought that might mean "cable reply."

By then, it was September 1937, and she'd had the messages for three months. She now asked the Mounties to send more details about the case, hoping that these might help confirm her insights. What she really wanted, though, was a Chinese expert who could speak the Cantonese dialect.

The U.S. government struggled to find one. For decades, Chinese immigrants and people of Chinese descent had faced severe discrimination, so few worked in federal jobs or moved in government circles. But the Library of Congress sent Dr. Julia Chen, a scholar who spoke Mandarin, to Elizebeth. Luckily, Chen had a rough knowledge of Cantonese, enough to help with the problem.

Chen impressed Elizebeth as "charming and tireless . . . superbly educated and very brilliant." When Elizebeth shared her guess about "cable reply," Chen thought it was plausible. But Chen questioned some of her other results, saying they made no sense in Cantonese.

Elizebeth had an idea. "I asked her to speak the Chinese words aloud together so that I could hear if the *sound* made sense to me."

The syllables Chen spoke were "IX" and "CHEN." To Elizebeth, they sounded like "*Ixion*"—a vessel owned by a company that had trafficked drugs before. Now she was sure she was on the right track.

She kept going. It was like filling in a very tricky crossword. Each character she cracked revealed more patterns and clues about the encryption, but if she made a single wrong guess, it could throw off the rest of the puzzle. Sometimes she had to backtrack to correct a mistake, throwing out hours or days of work. Yet, bit by bit, she was unlocking the messages.

In October, with the messages nearly solved, she got in touch with the Mounties again. "I sent word to Vancouver that I felt that I had the thing really cracked but that I needed a Cantonese interpreter."

Her message reached the Mounties at a critical moment. Gordon Lim's trial was scheduled to begin in Vancouver the following Monday, October 18, but the Mounties still hadn't found a way to break his messages. They decided they needed to bring Elizebeth out to Vancouver right away. She could work closely with their own Cantonese expert and then testify at the trial.

Elizebeth was in the office when the call came. It was Saturday the sixteenth, just past noon. The Mounties wanted her "to be without fail in Vancouver the following Monday morning." That meant Elizebeth had fewer than forty-eight hours to get there. Going by train would take four days. The only solution was to fly.

————

Like most Americans, Elizebeth had never traveled by plane before, not even for a short hop. She was excited to have the chance to fly, especially if it helped crack a case. "I had one of the young men in my office call the airport," she recalled, "and there were a possible two planes for me to get that day." One would depart at 3:40 p.m., the other at 10:00 p.m.

Getting the 10:00 p.m. flight would give her more time to prepare. But "something told me I had to make" the 3:40 plane, Elizebeth later remembered. "I don't know what it was. Why I . . . felt so impelled to do that, but I did."

The timing was tight, though, and she had a lot to do to prepare. First of all, she needed cash, and the banks were all closed. A downtown department store came to her rescue. "[B]less their darling hearts, [they] finally cashed a check, a personal check for five hundred dollars for me."

After that, William drove her home, where she talked with the housekeeper, packed her bags, and kissed her children goodbye. Still ahead of her was the drive to the airport, through heavy traffic. How on earth could she make that 3:40 p.m. flight?

With William at the wheel, they headed for downtown Washington again so that Elizebeth could pick up a briefcase from her assistant. After a quick street-corner handoff, she and William drove like mad for the airport.

Somewhere along the way, or perhaps a little earlier that day,

Elizebeth admitted to William that she had misgivings. Perhaps her hunches were wrong. Perhaps she wouldn't be able to crack the messages in full. Had she promised the Mounties too much? Should she even be making this trip?

William told her "not to hesitate." It wasn't just loyalty that prompted his answer. He knew that Elizebeth's instincts were the finest in the business. He was sure that once she was in Vancouver, the full solution would come to her.

They pulled into the airport just in time. Against all odds, Elizebeth made the 3:40 flight.

————

Aloft, Elizebeth's spirits rose. She started a letter to her children, describing the trip. The only woman on the plane, she marveled at the view of "the country so stunning, with its rivers and streams, green wooded mountains, and even flat farm country laid out in such patterns that it seemed as if a directing mind from above had planned it."

The next leg saw her flying in a "beautiful *United Mainliner.*" When they landed at Chicago, it was dark, and she saw "Lake Shore Drive in myriad of lights . . . as thrilling as the New York skyline when coming in from sea in a ship."

Her next plane was a Skysleeper, where the "hostess gave me hot chocolate and cookies and tucked me in with two blankets and two pillows." At 3:00 a.m., she was woken for a change of planes at Cheyenne, Wyoming. "It was a strange feeling to be there for an hour . . . there in the middle of the great prairies. I felt as if the stretches on all sides were limitless."

On the early-morning leg to Boise, she experienced "*rough* flying," where she was "tossed up in the air at least six inches." Yet

2. TRANSCONTINENTAL & WESTERN AIR SKYSLEEPER, SEATS 25 PASSENGERS.

In Chicago, Elizebeth sent her son John this postcard of a Skysleeper,
"a plane exactly like the one I fly to Salt Lake City."

when she arrived at Vancouver, she wrote to her children, "I'm afraid I'm spoiled for other kinds of travel hereafter!" Headed for bed, she added, "Happy landings, as the hostesses say! Certainly wish you all had been with me."

It had been a remarkable trip, one Elizebeth would remember all her life. But that night, as she stretched out in her Vancouver hotel room, she had no idea exactly how lucky a trip it was.

The next morning, after she reported for duty with the Mounties, she heard the news. Another United Mainliner had crashed as it crossed the Rockies. Bad weather had confused its pilots, who flew into a snowy Utah mountain at cruising speed. It was the plane Elizebeth would have been on if she had taken the 10:00 p.m. flight out of Washington.

Everyone on board was killed.

CHAPTER EIGHTEEN

Turbulence

The plane crash became a touchstone in Elizebeth's life, a marker she came back to again and again. In later years, she told the story of the flight many times—always with a shiver in the telling and a sense of wonder at her own survival. She never forgot how close she had come to disaster.

On that October Monday in 1937, as search crews struggled to reach the plane wreck, Elizebeth could hardly take in what had happened. "The story came as a considerable shock to me," she wrote, and she had an uncanny "feeling of being resurrected."

Back home in Washington, news of the terrible crash was spreading. William was eating breakfast when the report came through on the radio. From what he could gather about the flight times, he thought Elizebeth was probably safe, but he wasn't sure. There was always the chance she had been delayed en route. "I phoned the airport . . . but they could tell me little, and what they did say was wrong," he wrote to Elizebeth. Even worse, the local newspapers "carried big headlines" stating "Prominent D.C. Woman on Lost Plane."

Elizebeth saved this newspaper headline about the plane crash.

It was only when William received a cable from Elizebeth that he knew for certain that she was alive. She had sent it the evening before, when she had first arrived in Vancouver. "Darling: I was awfully glad to get your telegram," he wrote. "I'm greatly relieved."

Elizebeth's sister Edna was also hit hard. "Well did I have a scare last Monday!" she wrote to Elizebeth. "Shortly after receiving your card which I had looked at only hurriedly, someone brought in a paper with the headline about the plane crash." Stunned, Edna took another look at the card. On it, Elizebeth had noted the time her flight was leaving Chicago—hours earlier than the plane that had crashed. Edna was reassured.

The next morning, more news about the crash came in. "Well, my darling, I see that *all* the 19 people on that Mainliner of the United were killed," William wrote to Elizebeth. "You had what appears to be a narrow escape."

In Vancouver, Elizebeth had to focus on her work. The Lim trial was beginning, and the Mounties needed results. They gave Elizebeth a few more messages in what turned out to be yet another system. She also met the Mounties' Chinese interpreter, Dr. Henry Leong, who knew a "staggering number" of Chinese dialects.

Working closely with Leong, Elizebeth was able to make fast, accurate guesses about the messages. By the end of Monday, the work was going so well that she had "both A + B series of messages reading perfectly." William cheered her on by mail. "Swell! I told you . . . it would all come out. And it did. See?"

Three systems still had to be broken, but by Tuesday morning Elizebeth was ready with "a big idea or two." The messages "bloomed like flowers." And they were "very, very damning. They would have convicted anybody because they named the narcotics, the amounts, and when it was to be shipped from Shanghai and all sorts of details." Elizebeth had clinched the case against Gordon Lim and his partners.

Lim did his best to delay the proceedings—something he was expert at. At one point, he even checked into a hospital with emergency appendicitis. A "good old criminal trick, of course," Elizebeth commented, "but it worked."

The Mounties asked Elizebeth to return when the Lim trial resumed. In the meantime, she was free to go back home.

Elizebeth returned to Washington not by plane, but by train. It took her half a week to cross the country. Swaying in sleeping berths and dining cars, she had plenty of time for thought.

She was proud of the work she had done, and she had warm memories of the Vancouver Mounties. Working with them, she later said, was "one of the pleasantest experiences of my career." But she was still sorting out what she thought about the plane crash.

The Mounties believed her escape was a "good omen." As one

of them told her, "To use an old war-time expression, your number is not up yet." On the face of it, she seemed to agree with their stoic response. In the future, she would say that the reason she had not flown on that 10:00 p.m. flight was "fate," because it was "not her time to go." Her children came to regard her as "an extreme fatalist," who calmly looked peril in the eye.

Such fatalism, however, was only one layer of the cipher that was Elizebeth. Below that, there were other layers, where her reaction to the plane crash was far more complicated.

Deep down, she was unsettled by her narrow escape. Page through her papers, and you can see signs of the episode's impact on her. All her life, she would preserve her luggage tag from "United's Mainliner" as if it were a lucky charm. She also kept postcards and letters from the trip, as well as newspaper clippings about the plane crash. In her decisive script, she wrote on them "important" and "save."

The headline that shook her the most—then, and long afterward—was the one William had forwarded to her. "DC WOMAN ABOARD LOST PLANE" was how she remembered it. The woman turned out to be a Washington socialite, but it could

The Mainliner tag, still in Elizebeth's files.

so easily have been Elizebeth instead. And what if it had been? For years, Elizebeth had taken danger in stride, but now she was finding it harder to dodge questions of mortality.

Other questions dogged her, too. While she didn't develop a fear of flying, a more profound uneasiness seized her, and she began to ponder the direction of her life and work. Was chasing after smugglers what she really wanted to do with her time?

That winter, she came to a decision. She told William she wanted to quit her job.

––––––––

The only reason we know that Elizebeth wanted to quit is that William wrote a letter to her about it. Elizebeth herself left no such letters behind. Perhaps she never set her thoughts down in writing, or perhaps it was a time she wished to forget. Maybe it simply didn't fit the story she wanted to tell about herself.

Whatever the truth of the matter, William's brief letter makes us look again at what we know about her life. Like a keyword, it unlocks part of her cipher. The record shows that she was a dauntless code breaker. A pioneer feminist. A strong and powerful woman. But the letter—which clearly states that she wanted to quit—reminds us that even dauntless women can have their moments of doubt.

Over the years, Elizebeth had often dreamed of other careers. Writing still called to her, and she also longed to study ancient languages. Possibly these dreams were in the back of her mind when she spoke to William that winter about quitting her job. But according to the letter William wrote, she said something else, something unexpected. She told him that she wanted to stay at home.

In Elizebeth's social circles, most married women *did* stay at home. But for Elizebeth it was a break in the pattern—a sign that she was struggling. And there were other signs of strain, too.

Regarded by her friends as a person of "irresistible energy and unbelievable persistence," Elizebeth had been living at full throttle for years. She rarely took vacation days. Indeed, she often stayed on task through lunch and late into the evenings. When traveling, she worked even harder. But the Gordon Lim case meant that she was required to travel far more than usual. The trial, appeals, and delays would force her to make three open-ended, coast-to-coast trips in under six months. This came at a time when William's work travel was starting to step up, too. Meanwhile, Barbara and John, at fourteen and eleven, needed everything from skating-lesson drop-offs to late-night homework advice. It was a lot to juggle.

That winter Elizebeth's health took a nose dive, and she had to take time off. In the spring, she got so sick that she landed in the hospital, missing more than a month of work, as well as another coast-to-coast trip. William had to answer her letters and cancel her commitments.

In short, Elizebeth had plenty of reasons to think about giving up work in 1938. A near miss of a plane crash. A crushing workload. Shaky health.

But if you continue to burrow into the coded layers of her life, you will find another, more secret reason, too. It was so hush-hush that she and William could barely discuss it.

It had to do with security leaks.

———

From 1917, when Elizebeth and William first started working for the government, they were always tight-lipped about security matters. Much as they loved to talk about codes and ciphers, they watched their words with care. They knew better than to reveal government secrets. "Just never, never say anything" was the rule they lived by.

Yet no matter how careful they were, the military still saw them as a security risk. The problem was not so much what they did as who they were—a married pair of cryptanalysts, one of whom was getting coast-to-coast press coverage.

The fact that Elizebeth and William worked for different services only made matters worse. In this period, the Army and the Navy were fierce rivals, often acting more like enemies than allies. "[W]e were two separate nations," said one Navy officer who served in this era, and "the distrust and . . . ill feeling went right to the top." Army and Navy intelligence officers were deeply suspicious of each other—and also of the Coast Guard.

As long as Elizebeth and William both worked for the Army, everything was fine. But as soon as she left and took a job with first the Navy and then the Coast Guard, military officials suspected her and her husband of leaking secrets to each other.

In 1924, when William cracked an "unbreakable" Navy code machine, he was accused of garnering inside information from Elizebeth. "Of course there was no truth in that at all," Elizebeth later said.

After looking into the matter, William's superiors finally accepted that he had done the work himself. Still, Elizebeth and William continued to find themselves under scrutiny. And as time went on, the clouds of suspicion were harder to disperse.

In 1937, shortly before Elizebeth's narrow-escape plane flight, she and William got into trouble again. This time the cause of the ructions was—of all things—an issue of *Reader's Digest*. But in many ways, the true problem had begun years earlier, with a scandalous secret agency that once had been at the heart of American code breaking.

It was called the Black Chamber. And it had a past as cryptic as its name.

CHAPTER NINETEEN

The Black Chamber

On a steamy morning in June 1930, William strode through a dull-green hallway in the concrete maze of the Munitions Building in Washington, DC. Behind him trailed three young men, his new assistants. Reaching a deserted corridor in the seventh wing, William stopped in front of room 2742. He took a small card out of his pocket and consulted it. Then he twisted the combination lock and heaved open the steel door.

There was another steel door behind it.

Taking out a key, William opened that door, too. The space behind it was so dark that he had to strike a match to find the light cord. In the flare of the flame, his assistants saw a windowless room, roughly twenty-five feet square. It was jammed full of filing cabinets, covered with dust. There was barely enough space to open them.

Once everyone was in, William pulled the doors almost shut. Neat as a pin in his dapper suit, he stood in the grimy, tomblike room and turned solemnly to the young men. "Welcome, gentlemen, to the secret archives of the American Black Chamber!"

Working out what the Black Chamber was, and what it meant to Elizebeth and William, is like rummaging through the filing cabinets in that tomblike room. If you keep searching, you'll find connections spanning many years, each offering a small piece of the story. And as you search, you may come across a few surprises.

One surprise is that Elizebeth and William nearly ended up working for the Black Chamber themselves. In 1920, while they were still at Riverbank, they were both offered jobs there. At the time, the Black Chamber had been running less than a year, and it still hadn't found a permanent home. Funded by both the War Department and the State Department, the outfit was based in New York City, at a town house on East Thirty-Eighth Street. Almost no one had any idea what went on there. It's likely that Elizebeth and William only knew that it did some kind of code breaking for the government.

They were desperate to escape Riverbank, so the job offer was tempting. But if they didn't know much about the Black Chamber, they knew Herbert Yardley, its founder and director, all too well. They mistrusted his taste for the high life, with Elizebeth calling him downright "unsavory." As director of MI-8 in World War I, he also had claimed credit for some of their code-breaking work.

Yardley, for his part, was uncomfortable with Elizebeth's sharp intelligence. She has an "*edge* on her," he once told William. Perhaps it's no wonder that the Friedmans ended up turning Yardley's offer down.

Did they judge Yardley too harshly? Probably not. He was a slippery man, and his Black Chamber was a shady operation. Its specialty was reading the coded cables of foreign diplomats who were based in the United States. Time-honored agreements said those cables were strictly off-limits in peacetime, but Yardley went ahead anyway. Soon he was in possession of all kinds of secrets, which he passed along to America's own diplomats.

For a while, the Black Chamber prospered. So did Yardley. But then a new secretary of state came to Washington, the upright Henry L. Stimson. Told of the Black Chamber's existence, Stimson was horrified. "Gentlemen do not read each other's mail," he famously said. He shut the Black Chamber within months, at the end of October 1929.

Top brass at the Army didn't care if the Black Chamber's work was fit for gentlemen. To them, what mattered was that it gave the United States an advantage over potential enemies. So without telling Stimson, the Army quietly created the Signal Intelligence Service (SIS). William was named its chief. In essence, he was stepping into Yardley's shoes. He also inherited the Black Chamber's archives.

For years, William had been charged with protecting Army communications. That mission continued, but now he had a new one: breaking into the secret messages of foreign powers whenever American security required it. For William, who liked to be aboveboard in everything, this posed ethical dilemmas. But he wanted to keep his country safe, so he did the work he was asked to do.

Meanwhile, Yardley was out of a job. It was the start of the Great Depression, and he could not find another one. Desperate for money, he wrote *The American Black Chamber*, a sensational account of his exploits there. Published in 1931, it caused a worldwide uproar. Even Americans were startled to hear that their country had broken the codes of nineteen different nations in peacetime. Alarmed, many of those countries began creating new systems that were much harder to crack. Yardley had singlehandedly thrown America's code-breaking advantage away.

William and Elizebeth were shocked by Yardley's book. Not only had it betrayed American interests, it was full of fake facts as well. On a top-secret copy, shared with his colleagues, William jotted comments in the margins. At one point, he recorded in disgust, "This is the purest bunk."

Bunk it may have been, but it had consequences, especially for William. After Yardley's sellout, the American military brass worried a great deal about the loyalty of their code breakers. They also started to panic about the press. As head of the SIS and Yardley's effective successor, William was closely watched. And when Elizebeth started appearing in the papers, the top brass got agitated.

———

Soon after Elizebeth did her first radio interview, the Navy started complaining to the Coast Guard about "undesirable publicity." It didn't matter that Elizebeth had steered the conversation away from anything remotely secret. The Navy didn't want government code breaking anywhere near the spotlight.

The Coast Guard had a different take. So did the Treasury Department, Elizebeth's ultimate boss. As they saw it, Elizebeth was helping to improve their public profile. It was not easy to gain Americans' sympathy when you'd spent years cutting off their liquor supply, but articles about a tiny woman bringing gangsters to justice made their departments look like the good guys. If anything, the Coast Guard and the Treasury were in favor of *more* publicity about Elizebeth. By winning taxpayers over, they hoped to protect themselves from funding cuts. Ignoring the Navy, they happily fanned the flames of her growing fame.

Elizebeth continued to have mixed feelings about all this publicity. She was appalled by lurid stories like "How the G-2 Woman

Trapped the Dope Ring," which portrayed her as a femme fatale. Yet she was delighted by accurate profiles, and she remained open to interviews with trustworthy reporters, especially women. She even hoped to find a writer to work with her on a memoir. For the most part, publicity of the right kind appealed to her, just as it did to the Treasury and the Coast Guard.

She did not yet realize that almost any kind of publicity could be risky. That understanding only came in August 1937, when a story blew up in her face.

William, Elizebeth, and their son, John, in the mid-1930s.

The story that caused all the problems was called "Key Woman of the T-Men." (The "T" was short for "Treasury.") In sprightly fashion, it covered Elizebeth's many triumphs, including her victory over the Conexco smugglers. It also highlighted her key role in the *I'm Alone* case, which had saved the United States a small fortune. Because it was written by one of her friends, Leah Stock

Helmick, the piece had Elizebeth's full cooperation. Both women were thrilled when the article won a *Reader's Digest* contest.

After the article appeared in print, however, top Army and Navy officials were livid. Helmick had identified William as the head of the SIS, and she had coyly suggested that the agency was breaking foreign codes. All true, but the military, which was still recovering from Yardley's bombshell, did not want to see such things in print. Although Elizebeth's Treasury bosses were pleased with the article, William got chewed out by his superiors. They didn't care that other Army officers had approved the story—or that William knew next to nothing about it. They let him know they were furious.

The article "caused me no end of embarrassment," William wrote later. "[H]igh up officials in both the Army and the Navy were displeased." Not long afterward, he told a colleague that "my superiors have bluntly told me that my name must not appear in the public press" for any reason whatsoever. "From this," William added, "you will gather that they are pretty jittery and want to keep quiet even the fact that there is such a thing as cryptography going on."

Was the response overkill? Perhaps. But there was more at stake than it seemed. Aside from mentioning William, the article also noted that Elizebeth had broken Chinese codes. By itself, this was a harmless enough statement. But William's bosses knew something that Elizebeth and Helmick did not—which was that William and his team had broken some of Japan's top-grade ciphers.

In code-breaking terms, Elizebeth's Chinese codes and William's Japanese ciphers were in no way alike. But William's bosses were alarmed to see him publicly linked in any way with the breaking of Asian-language codes. They knew that many people would—wrongly—assume that William was helping his wife to break Chinese codes. Some might then guess that he had broken Japanese ones, too.

The top brass also remembered all too well how Yardley's boastful book had made Japan dump its old codes and ciphers, then create much harder ones. With Japan posing a growing threat in the Pacific, the United States couldn't afford to have that happen again. And yet here was a *Reader's Digest* story providing a tip-off for any Japanese official who happened to see it.

William believed these fears were overblown. His bosses, however, were adamant that the article amounted to a security breach.

At some point, someone told Elizebeth to stop talking about Chinese codes. Whoever approached her, she got the message. In a memo she wrote just after the *Reader's Digest* story appeared, she warned the head of the Coast Guard that her work with Asian-language messages had to stay quiet:

> *In view of the present situation in the Far East, I know definitely that to mention that we have ever solved a message in Japanese or Chinese will bring down upon the Coast Guard, the certain anathema of the Navy Department, and possibly of the State and War Departments.*

Discreetly, she added, "I have definite reasons for making these statements and shall be glad to make a full explanation verbally, if you so desire."

———

That fall, when Elizebeth flew out to the Gordon Lim trial, she must have been hoping to stay out of the public eye. As she saw it, her work, though crucial, was only a small part of a much larger trial. Soon, however, she saw that the case was attracting attention—and so was she. Her name was going to end up in the papers again, linked to Chinese codes. That, she now knew, would have all kinds of consequences.

If she kept working with Chinese codes, she would have this problem over and over again. But that was what her job required her to do. There was no way out—unless she gave up the job.

To quit would be a big step. She had worked hard to get where she was, and she might never again find a job where she enjoyed so much respect. She also still loved the essence of code breaking— that thrilling moment when a hidden message yielded its secrets.

Yet, more and more, she was seeing that the job had serious downsides. It was running her ragged. It also exposed her to dangers, as the near-miss plane crash reminded her. And it was certainly stirring up trouble for William.

Was that why she told William she wanted to quit? Did she think that was what William wanted her to do?

If so, she was wrong. William had other ideas.

CHAPTER TWENTY

Ad Absurdum!

For years, William had upheld Elizebeth's right to work, even when that meant long weeks away from their family. He had also supported her when she chose to stay home and have children. This time around, though, he had reservations.

They talked over what to do. William's bosses might be pleased to see his wife quit her job and park herself at home, but William couldn't see that suiting Elizebeth herself. In January 1938, when the Gordon Lim trial resumed and she went back to Vancouver, he set his thoughts down in a letter—the same letter that serves as the only clue that she wanted to quit.

He began by mentioning something else she had told him, about seeing a friend on the West Coast who had welcomed her warmly but who seemed to be living a rather empty life. William was worried that the same thing could happen to Elizebeth if she decided to retire:

What if you had only bridge and bridge luncheons to look forward to? That, my dear, is one of the principal reasons why I have been reluctant to agree to your quitting office. We could get along on my own salary—but I fear you'd find life so dull you'd get like the other women I know—even though some of them do make a desperate effort to keep up a real interest in life.

A hard worker himself, he believed that "a life of mental toil—plus having to get up in the morning every day to face new and exciting problems—keeps one young." To him, it seemed Elizebeth was thriving where she was.

Perhaps William won her over. Or perhaps it was her own deepest self that convinced her not to quit. It was true that the work sometimes exhausted her, but it also fired her up. As she herself once said about code breaking, "It's a great life if you don't weaken."

The next few months continued to be bumpy, but she decided to stick with the job anyway. Soon she also came up with a solution to her publicity problems.

She decided to disappear.

———

Disappearing was drastic. Yet by the spring of 1938, Elizebeth was willing to try almost anything. As she later explained, the Gordon Lim trial had been the final straw.

At the start of 1938, when the trial had resumed in Vancouver, her testimony helped convict Lim and his gang. Ignoring all her warnings, the Treasury public relations department pushed the story. Not that they needed to push hard. The newspapers already had their eyes on Elizebeth.

Reporters tracked her down at her Vancouver hotel. Photographers chased after her, too. When even the bellhops and waiters started hounding her, she had to escape to another hotel.

"I found that my life was not my own," she wrote.

The press portrayed her as a star, making it sound as if she had won the case on her own. Embarrassed, she wrote to the Mounties to apologize. She knew how much work they had done to track the gang and round up witnesses. She followed up with a letter to her own boss. "I have at no time and to no person . . . claimed the credit for the winning of the Gordon Lim case," she pointed out. She was mortified that the press had made so much of the "mystery-lure of the word code," added to "a woman's name."

To her dismay, the coverage was worldwide. Even worse, it focused on the angle she most wanted to avoid—the fact that she had cracked Chinese codes. Stories about her popped up everywhere, even in places she never expected to see them. Once, while trying to relax on a train, she opened a popular magazine, only to see her own unauthorized portrait staring out at her.

Elizebeth reached her limit when the Treasury forwarded a

LOOK

February 15, 1938

These Women Make Their Hobbies Pay

These women were selected by Durwood Howes, editor of the reference book, "American Women," as outstanding in careers unusual for their sex.

Mrs. Elizabeth Smith Friedman, was the first U. S. woman to become a cryptanalyst (one who deciphers secret code messages). She works at U. S. Coast Guard Headquarters in Washington, D. C.

The article that Elizebeth saw on the train.

telegram from the editor of the *American Magazine*. It was a long litany of nosy questions:

```
WHAT CIRCUMSTANCES LED TO YOU BECOMING THE GOVERNMENT'S
CRYPTANALYST? FOR WHAT DEPARTMENTS DO YOU DECIPHER
MESSAGES? HOW MANY HAVE YOU DONE? WHAT TYPES? HOW DO
THEY FALL INTO YOUR HANDS? PLEASE RECOUNT DETAILS OF SOME
OF THE MOST DIFFICULT, UNUSUAL, AND HUMOROUS CODES AND
CIRCUMSTANCES UNDER WHICH THEY COME TO YOU? WHAT IS MOST
USUAL TYPE OF CODE? WHAT METHODS FOR DECIPHERING USED? HAVE
YOU SPECIAL SYSTEM OR DO YOU PLAY HUNCHES? WHAT RESULT?
CRIMINALS CAPTURED? . . . DO YOU CARRY YOUR DECIPHERING
TASTES INTO PRIVATE LIFE? . . . OUR PHOTOGRAPHER WILL GET
IN TOUCH WITH YOU IMMEDIATELY. PLEASE WIRE WHEN TO EXPECT
DATA. THANKS.
```

"Ad Absurdum!" Elizabeth wrote beneath this. She refused to answer such a silly bunch of indiscreet questions. They would only lead to the kind of ghastly articles that "have sickened me to the point of wishing never to see even my name in print again."

She was angry not only with the reporters, but with the Treasury officials who encouraged them. If she was going to stay in the job, things had to change.

That spring, she told the Treasury officials that from now on she expected them to shield her from journalists. She wanted "no one but no one in the world of the press or radio . . . to get so far as even an interview with me."

After desperate pleading from Ed Meryl, the Treasury public relations chief, she agreed to one last interview with the *American Magazine*. Her conditions? They had to stay off secret subjects, and they had to keep their lips zipped about William and his work.

To keep Meryl happy, Elizebeth also gave him "the bare facts of my life and career" to be used as a sop for reporters. Eager for some kind of human interest angle, Meryl quizzed her about her career high points, her Quaker ancestors, and her Riverbank years. Then he came up with a stock press release. He hyped up the Quaker connection and added a Q&A ("Greatest discouragement?" "Is not discouraged."). Noting that "her figure is small and trim," he finished:

> *She isn't exactly shy, nor modest about her work and its accomplishments, nor is she boastful. She just likes to do the thing that is called her work, and she gets a deal of satisfaction in accomplishing the thing at hand.*

There, at least, Meryl told the unvarnished truth.

After Meryl had his press release, Elizebeth stopped speaking with reporters entirely. There was little she could do about rogue, uncleared articles, but at least no one would get anything more out of her.

Like her husband, she was going dark.

———

That spring, Elizebeth had some unexpected good news. Her old college, Hillsdale, wanted to award her an honorary degree. Their LL.D. would make her a doctor of laws. Elizebeth couldn't have been prouder, and neither could William. She saved and mounted the telegram he sent her on the day of the ceremony:

CONGRATULATIONS, MY DARLING . . . DO YOU REMEMBER ME?
IM THE MAN WHO THINKS YOURE GRAND, IM PROUD AS I CAN BE
OF YOUR RENOWN AND WELL EARNED CROWN OF HILLSDALES LLD . . .
YES. IM THE CHUMP WHO PICKED A TRUMP IN LIFES SWEET LOTTERY
YES, IM THE MAN WHO LOVES YOU STILL—YOUR DOTING HUSBAND
BILL.

It was a red-letter day for Elizebeth, proof that she had lived up to her old dreams of achievement. Speaking for colleagues and friends, William wrote proudly, "*Everybody* is dying to see you."

Elizebeth in her academic robes at Hillsdale.

Diploma in hand, Elizebeth returned to her ordinary routines as the top code breaker at the Treasury Department and the Coast Guard. Perhaps no one but William guessed how close she had come to leaving her job. From the outside, her life looked more or less the same as it had for years, only with fewer reporters.

Appearances, however, were deceiving. The hard winter and the confrontation with the press had given her a new sense of her own strength. And beyond the spotlight, her mission was changing. In 1938, Nazi Germany was a rising threat, and so was Imperial Japan. Global tensions were mounting. With World War II almost on the horizon, Elizebeth's work was about to become more secret—and more demanding—than ever before.

CODE BREAK
CAFÉ CRYPTANALYTIQUE

By the late 1930s, both Elizebeth and William were keeping their working lives under wraps, but they still led a lively social life. They especially loved throwing parties that involved code breaking. These were so elaborate and so much fun that people remembered them for years.

One of their most famous parties took place in November 1938, when the world situation was grim and their own workload was intense. Elizebeth had taken up top-secret duties, and William was about to disappear overseas for a while, preparing for a possible war.

Despite these pressures—or perhaps because of them—they threw themselves into giving a dinner party that no one would ever forget. William called it the "Circuitous Cryptanalytic Comestible Contest," and it took place all over town.

The starting point was "The Café Cryptanalytique"—aka the Friedmans' home. There the guests were divided into teams, then given cipher messages that told them where to seek out the next course. The menus were also encrypted. At each new place, the teams dined on good food and received another cryptic message, pointing them to the next destination. Prizes were offered to the teams that solved the clues first.

William, who had endless energy, did most of the encryptions. Many turned on funny tricks—a silly keyword, perhaps, or a pun. One of the keywords, for example, was YES WE HAVE NO BANANAS. As Elizebeth once said fondly of William, "The whimsy and fun is always carried out to the smallest detail."

Since the Friedmans had many top code breakers in their circle, their party puzzles had to be tough. But they also threw

MESSAGE NO. 2

```
ODDWF   TUSIL   EAREO   KTEPX   AARLF

IENSB   TOATO   REASR   CONHN   SSTTS

BRTNO   CNEUR   ETEXT   RATOA   SNTAX

URWEI   SFHUR   FSIST
```

The "YES WE HAVE NO BANANAS" cryptogram (No. 2).

in some clues that anyone could get—provided they approached the problem the right way.

An opening line on a menu, for instance, was solved by an Army wife who was feeling outclassed by the top talent around her. "The first item was a series of dots done with a blue pen," she remembered. "The 'brains' at the party worked over the number of dots in a group when it occurred to me it had to be 'blue points'—(oysters)—and it was!"

Ten months after the Café Cryptanalytique made its debut, war broke out in Europe. After that, life became bleaker. But Elizebeth saved the party clues and worksheets in her files, as tokens of a happier time.

CHAPTER TWENTY-ONE

The Woman All Spies Fear

In October 1939, a rogue story about Elizebeth appeared under a splashy headline: "The Woman All Spies in U.S. Fear." Showing a chic portrait of Elizebeth at work, it tagged her as "the Amazing Cryptanalyst" that "Uncle Sam" was counting on. Her new job, the article revealed, was to track down "Foreign Spies."

The story drove Elizebeth wild. Her new press policy meant that most reporters left her alone, but a few still concocted glitzy stories that were riddled with fake facts. She loathed these articles, and she especially hated this one. She denounced it as a "hodgepodge of plagiarism pulled from here, a bit from there, the whole misinterpreted and sensationalized to give color to the red-flag word SPIES."

As she well knew, spies were headline news. Nazi spies had been captured on American soil in 1938, and people were worried that more spies were lurking undercover now that World War II had started in Europe. Although Americans had stayed out of the war so far, they were eager to read reports about secret agents and the foiling of foreign plots. If a woman code breaker was part of the story, so much the better.

As the story spread to more newspapers, Elizebeth's fury grew. She told a Treasury official that she wanted to lobby for a law making it illegal to mention government workers by name without their permission. "Forgive the sputtering," she added, "but that's the way I feel about it, just now."

The official suggested a more discreet way to handle the problem. It was time, he thought, to speak with the White House. After all, President Roosevelt had good relations with the press corps. A word from him was often enough to keep newspapers from printing a story that compromised national security.

Elizebeth had not had much to do with FDR, but Eleanor Roosevelt had often invited her to tea and garden parties at the White House. (The First Lady was "very thoughtful and encouraging to us career women," she later wrote.) So maybe she did reach out to FDR. One way or another, the stories about her stopped appearing.

Elizebeth must have been relieved. While it was true that the rogue stories were full of exaggerations and lies, they had also stumbled into the truth. In 1939, she really *was* listening for spies—and Uncle Sam *was* counting on her to uncover their plots.

———

Elizebeth's new mission had started in 1938, when global tensions were high. Hitler's aggressive actions made war seemed almost inevitable, and battleships and submarines started patrolling the oceans and coastlines. At that point, smuggling became such a dangerous occupation that it dropped to almost nothing, so Elizebeth's old job was gone. But the Coast Guard's radio network was still up and running, and it continued to intercept encrypted messages on the airwaves. Elizebeth was told to break them.

She and her team were supposed to keep an eye out for several things. First of all, they had to check for violations of the nation's Neutrality Acts. Passed to keep the United States from getting entangled in another world conflict, the acts forbade Americans to help other countries that were at war. You couldn't supply foreign warships with fuel, for instance, and you couldn't ship guns to foreign armies. By law, it was the Treasury Department that had to enforce these acts, and Elizebeth and her team were the Treasury's "eyes and ears."

Elizebeth also had to search for signs of hostile actions—anything from a foreign warship laying mines to submarines behaving strangely off the American coastline. Above all, she was supposed to be on the lookout for spies. For her, the years from 1938 to 1941 were a time of "exciting, round-the-clock adventures, as we counter-spied into the minds and activities of the agents attempting to spy into those of the United States."

Elizebeth and her unit were not the only Americans trying to uncover spies. Others, including the FBI, wanted to do this, too. But it was the Coast Guard that was best primed to detect so-called clandestine communication, or spy talk.

Most spies used radio to communicate. And the Coast Guard had the most advanced radio interception network in the Americas. Thanks in part to their efforts against the rumrunners, the Coast Guard's network covered the United States from the Atlantic to the Pacific. Not only could it detect radio signals sent from many thousands of miles away, but it used the most up-to-date equipment available. With this, the Coast Guard could pick up weak signals that others missed. They even had High-Frequency Direction Finding (HF/DF, or "huff-duff"), which helped them pinpoint the exact spot that transmissions were coming from. The FBI could not begin to compete with this, nor could any other agency. Even the Navy admitted that the Coast Guard was "10 years more advanced" than its own intercept service.

The Coast Guard's other great asset was Elizebeth herself. In the late 1930s, she was at the top of her game, with exactly the experience needed for the job.

At the time, most high-level American code breakers worked for the Army and the Navy, where they focused on a handful of top-grade military and diplomatic ciphers. Encrypted with machines, these ciphers were so complex that it could take months or even years to figure out how a single type of machine worked. Elizebeth, by contrast, had spent her career cracking a wide variety of messages. Written in a plethora of encryption systems, they ranged from the absurdly easy to the virtually watertight. Bombarded with thousands of intercepts a year, she was used to creating order out of cacophony.

This turned out to be the ideal training for tracking spy talk.

Spies tended to be freewheeling by nature, and they used many different systems to communicate. On the whole, they preferred systems that were simple to memorize. Some spy rings used several code and cipher systems, the way big-time smugglers like Conexco had. They also switched to new encryption systems without notice. For Elizebeth, this was all familiar territory.

Soon thousands of radio intercepts were pouring into her office, just as they had done during the rumrunner days. She was tasked with sorting and classifying them, with her unit's help. "If any text appeared which needed solution, it was our business to solve it if possible," she later said. Once solved, the message could be forwarded to the Army, the Navy, the State Department, or the FBI, which could then act on it.

Many of the secret messages came from British and German vessels. These had to be checked to make sure no one was trying to smuggle out American weapons, or drop off spies, or lay mines in American waters.

Other secret messages were sent by companies in Latin America. While some expressed pro-Nazi sentiments, few companies were prepared to act on them, so actual spies were rare. Still, everything had to be examined.

The turning point came in 1940, when the Coast Guard started detecting new code signals coming from unlicensed wildcat stations like the ones the rumrunners had used. When Elizebeth and her team broke the intercepts, they turned out to be messages from spies.

With each message, Elizebeth and her team learned a little more about these spies. Most were based in South America, in countries that were neutral. They were directed by Nazi handlers in Germany. Handlers and spies were divided into groups called circuits, with each circuit using its own ciphers. Most alarming of all, the number of circuits and spies was growing.

———

Even before this, South America had worried President Roosevelt and his advisors. In 1940, Hitler's sights were firmly set on conquering Europe, but Roosevelt was concerned that South America might be a future target. After all, it was rich in exactly the kinds of resources the Nazis needed. With Argentinian beef, Colombian platinum, and a multitude of raw materials from Brazil, the Nazis could keep their war machine going for the foreseeable future.

And what if the Nazis established air bases in South America? With these in place, German planes could leapfrog their way up the continent and seize the American-controlled Panama Canal Zone, and perhaps even Mexico or Cuba. At that point, their long-distance bombers would be in range of the United States itself.

True, Hitler had shown no pressing interest in South America. At least, not yet. But he had a history of taking over territories he considered German, and he and his ambassadors believed that people of German heritage owed "complete subservience" to their "home country." South America was full of such people.

Since the nineteenth century, millions of Germans had immigrated to the continent, and many maintained strong ties to their fatherland. In Brazil alone, over a million people considered themselves partly or wholly German. Some districts were even known as Greater Germany, where you could go to German schools, shop in German stores, read German newspapers, listen to German radio stations, fly on German planes, and live on streets with German names.

Having German ancestry did not mean you liked the Nazis, of course. Still, across South America, Nazi and fascist sympathizers were commonplace. Paraguay's right-wing national police chief, for example, named his son Adolfo Hirohito, a tribute to Hitler and his soon-to-be ally, the emperor of Japan. In Argentina, the popular movie actress Eva Duarte, better known as Evita, sided with the Nazis. Juan Perón, who later became Evita's husband and the dictator of Argentina, studied Hitler and his Italian sidekick, Mussolini, as role models.

Home-grown fascist movements were even more popular,

especially in Argentina, Brazil, Chile, Bolivia, and Paraguay. Some of these movements echoed the Nazis in their salutes and uniforms, as well as in their attacks on Jews. Many of their leaders and supporters favored a close alliance with the Nazis.

No wonder, then, that Roosevelt feared that South America might fall to Hitler, or at least cooperate with him. To keep that from happening, the United States needed inside information about the plans of South America's Nazi sympathizers and the spies who were working with them. What exactly were they up to? Were they stocking up on guns? Were they plotting coups?

Elizebeth was one of the few people poised to detect such plans. "[T]hat's what I did," she once said about her work. "The spy stuff." She was spying on the spies themselves.

Elizebeth posing with her own portrait, about 1940.

Although the United States was still at peace, Elizebeth's unit was given extra funding and bumped up from five people to seven. While she trained the new recruits, she went on tracking the spy networks herself. The work was demanding. The messages were rising in number, and they were getting harder to crack.

Yet Elizebeth remained unruffled, approaching the job with her trademark energy and élan. If she was worried about anything in 1940, it wasn't her work. It was William.

———

Like Elizebeth, William worked long hours at the office, but by 1940 he had taken to working in the middle of the night, too. He "couldn't sleep," Elizebeth said. "He'd be up until two and three in the morning." Exhausted and tense, he would pad down to the dark kitchen and make himself a huge sandwich and a pot of coffee. Upstairs in bed, Elizebeth could hear him pacing for hours.

Even on good nights, William now bunked in their dressing room, where he'd set up another bed. "Dad used to joke about how they were forced to sleep in separate bedrooms in case they talked about each other's work," their daughter, Barbara, recalled. "It was national security."

William may have joked in front of the children, but the new regime was no laughing matter. In the face of William's insomnia and growing tension, Elizebeth could do little to help, except to keep their home life as normal as she could. For security reasons, she and William could not do what other couples did, and discuss "things at night that worry you and so on," as Elizebeth put it decades later. "My husband never never opened his mouth about anything."

Earlier in her career, she had been allowed to share some details of her Coast Guard work with him, but now that she was tracking spies, she had to keep quiet. And William's own work was so secret that she knew next to nothing about it. It was forbidden for him to confide in her, and forbidden for her to pry.

It was impossible, of course, to hide everything. They knew each other so well that a single word could unlock many layers of meaning. Besides, as any code breaker can tell you, there are times when silence itself speaks volumes, saying as much as any message itself could. And even when Elizebeth and William were silent, their faces talked.

When Elizebeth saw William wearing "a certain grim look that came around his mouth," she would know that something had gone wrong. Likewise, "[a]ny expression on my face he certainly could read." But they both did their best to forget what they saw. "I tried to know as little as possible. I literally did," Elizebeth later said. In the late 1930s and 1940s, security was so tight that "you just hoped and prayed you wouldn't have to know what you didn't want to know."

Her only clue about the source of the strain was a comment William had once made. On a summer evening back in 1939, William had mentioned that his boss had talked to him about the Japanese cipher team. "They aren't getting anywhere," he told William. "You drop everything and take care of it." It was a sign of how disturbed William must have been, even to say that much. Elizebeth knew better than to follow up.

In June 1940, when she went on a long-awaited trip to Mexico, William's letters were doleful but discreet. "Read until 1 a.m. + listened to war news," he wrote. "Have not been feeling any too chipper these days, mostly on account of the news and lack of progress on my problems at the office. But I guess that is only to be expected in these days of time and trial."

Days of trial, indeed. By then the Nazi blitzkrieg had begun in earnest, and Hitler's forces were steamrolling across Europe. Already Luxembourg, Belgium, the Netherlands, and parts of France had succumbed. As William hunkered by the radio, Norway fell to the Nazis, and the British Army struggled to regroup after its defeat at Dunkirk. "We shall never surrender," a grimly defiant Churchill promised, but many expected the British to fold. In France, the German Army was marching toward the capital, backed by Luftwaffe bombers. By the time Elizebeth returned from Mexico, Paris had fallen.

Yet Europe was not the only place of trial that summer. Desperation could be found much closer to hand—as close as the kitchen, where William stood alone in the small hours, brewing his pots of coffee.

Was he still working on Japanese ciphers? Was the group still getting nowhere? These were questions Elizebeth knew she could not ask. Yet as she listened to her husband pace the floor, night after night, she must have wondered. Perhaps she guessed the truth, that William was wrestling with a problem so profound it was almost impossible to solve.

Whatever Elizebeth suspected, she must have been certain that William would triumph. Her faith in his genius was absolute.

What she never saw coming was that the victory would nearly destroy him.

CHAPTER TWENTY-TWO

The War Within

I n his debonair suits, two-toned shoes, and stylish ties, William did not look like a warrior. Yet since 1939, he had been fighting one of the hardest battles of World War II. His fearsome opponent? A machine called Type B.

Machines had always fascinated William. As a teen in Pittsburgh, he had studied electronics. Later, he tinkered with wires, switches, and radios in his spare time. When inventors created new machines that could be used for encryption, William's gift came into its own.

Before encryption machines came along, people had to compose their own ciphers, writing them out letter by letter. Known as *hand ciphers*, these encryptions could be very complex, which made them more secure. But complexity had some big drawbacks. The more steps a cipher had, the more time it took to encrypt. Each step also opened the door to more mistakes.

Cipher machines changed that equation. Provided you knew

Portrait of William.

the correct settings, the mechanics did most of the work, making it speedy to compose and read even very complex ciphers. Known as *machine ciphers,* these encryptions also had fewer mistakes, since a machine could process millions of letters without a single error.

Because machine ciphers were so complicated, and because they had fewer mistakes, they were hard to break. Yet William conquered a number of them in the 1920s and 1930s, using only paper, pencil, and brainpower. He then took the insights he had gained and built cipher machines for the Army that were even more secure.

In the mid-1930s, he and his assistant Frank Rowlett designed a machine called SIGABA. Heavy, costly, and temperamental, it was nevertheless ahead of its time. In World War II, both the Army and the Navy would use SIGABA machines to transmit high-level secret messages. Not only did the system allow Roosevelt and

Churchill to communicate in perfect security, but it remained in use and unbroken into the 1950s—an astonishing record.

The one great downside to SIGABA was that it pulled William away from the day-to-day grind of Army code breaking. So, too, did his many departmental duties and interagency meetings. He kept a close eye on his handpicked SIS unit as they fought to crack German, Italian, and Japanese systems, but for the most part he let them get on with the job by themselves. It was a routine that worked well until February 1939, when Japan introduced the Type B cipher machine.

Later given the code name Purple, the new machine baffled William's team. This was why William was ordered to take charge and become directly involved in breaking it. Yet even with his help, cracking Purple seemed almost impossible.

Purple was used by Japanese diplomats, which meant it carried the very highest-grade secrets. To protect those secrets, Japan's coding chiefs had outdone themselves. For a start, Purple didn't use rotors, the motorized gears inside most cipher machines. Instead, it used stepping switches, electronic devices that scrambled the message in baffling ways. In addition, the machine encrypted six letters of the alphabet with one cipher, then used an entirely different cipher for the other twenty. To make the challenge even greater, the Japanese changed the settings of Purple machines daily, and used them sparingly. Most days, Purple carried only a single, short message.

These brief Purple messages, following no known pattern, were an almost impossible riddle. No other country could crack them, in part because no one could guess how the machine was built. But William refused to give up. He went over and over the work his team had done, searching for new strategies to test. Night after night, he strained to see patterns that seemed just out of sight. But a year rolled around, and the team was still stuck.

Purple would not yield.

―――――

As William and his team struggled to break Purple, the world around them grew darker. After World War II began, the news grew steadily worse. By the summer of 1940, the Nazis had conquered most of Europe, and they were unleashing their bombers on Britain. In the newly occupied countries, Jews were forced to sew yellow Stars of David on their clothes. Many were deported to concentration camps. In a small town in Poland, a new camp was opened, known as Auschwitz.

For William, who had dreaded the coming of evil times ever since he was a small child, it was like watching a nightmare become real.

Worrying things were happening at home, too. As William battered at Purple with all his might, Jewish refugees were being turned away from the United States, on the grounds that they were not the kind of citizens America wanted. Vigilante groups like the Silver Shirts and Ku Klux Klan were openly anti-Jewish and actively recruiting. Soon the aviator Charles Lindbergh, perhaps the most famous man in America, would claim in a speech that Jews had too much influence over "our motion pictures, our press, our radio, and our government." His audience of thousands applauded.

No wonder William paced around at night, unable to sleep. While he could talk to Elizebeth about the Silver Shirts and Lindbergh, she still knew nothing about Purple, the problem that worried him most. All day long, and sometimes all night, he turned the problem around and around in his mind. He was determined to find a way in.

———

Over time, William's team ended up with a stash of about a thousand Purple messages. These included a handful of cases where two messages had been sent on the same day with the same machine settings. Gradually, William became convinced that these messages were the only way into Purple.

The team made complex tables of the letter distributions in these messages. Then they searched for subtle repetitions that would reveal the pattern of the switches that drove the Japanese machine. Day after day, they spent long hours at their desks, going over worksheets of jumbled letters.

For a long while, no one saw anything. But on the afternoon of September 20, 1940, a young code breaker named Genevieve Grotjan approached some of the senior team members. Shy but "obviously excited," she said she had something to show them.

Grotjan was one of William's newest hires. Born in 1913 in Buffalo, New York, she had been a prizewinning graduate student in math. Yet like many women before her, including Elizebeth, she had struggled to find a good job. Fortunately, William was an early believer in the value of a diverse workforce, and he sought out talent wherever he could find it. In 1939, when Grotjan got a high score on a civil service exam, he offered her a place in his unit. Since then, she had been part of the Purple team, where she was known as Gene.

On that September afternoon, Gene brought her immediate supervisor, Frank Rowlett, to her desk. There, as Frank told the story, she "lays out worksheets, points to one example, then another, then a third. She stands back, with eyes tranced behind her rimless glasses."

She had found the pattern that was the key to breaking Purple.

The men started cheering. The rest of the team came running. William came, too, asking, "What's all the noise about?"

"Gene's found what we've been looking for," Frank told him. "Look here, and here, and here."

They now had the pattern they needed.

William looked "suddenly tired." It had been a long battle, and it wasn't over yet.

The rest of the team was relieved, exhilarated, shaky with hope. They celebrated with Cokes, then got back to work.

———————

William and his team spent the next week working hard—"almost day and night," he later said, trying to wedge open the crack in the cipher that Gene Grotjan had found. Then the United States intercepted a sudden burst of Purple messages. The reason for the leap in activity was ominous: Japan, Germany, and Italy were signing an alliance pact. But that same day, William and his team decrypted two Purple messages in full.

They had broken Purple.

It was a stunning achievement, with wide-ranging impacts. During World War II, Purple gave the United States and its allies a secret edge in the Pacific. It helped them in Europe as well, thanks to Japan's ambassador in Berlin, who used Purple to relay Hitler's detailed war plans to Tokyo. It even turned out to be crucial for the D-Day invasions. The entire operation was so valuable that its insights were code named Magic, and over the course of the war it saved many American and Allied lives.

To work, however, Magic had to remain secret. So when William came home on those triumphant September days in 1940, he said nothing to Elizebeth. She had no idea something special had happened.

"Now wouldn't you have thought that any being that was human . . . would have said something that day?" Elizebeth marveled over thirty years later, after she learned the truth. "Never said a word to me. I didn't know anything about it."

———

At first, Purple was completely solved for one indicator setting only. All through the autumn of 1940, William and his team continued to push hard. After several weeks, they had worked out solutions for a third of the possible settings. Soon their insights allowed them to build their own working copy of a Japanese Type B machine—even though they had never seen one, or even any designs for one.

In a top-secret report, William gave the entire team credit for every major advance. Only by "cooperation and close collaboration of all concerned could the solution possibly have been reached," he wrote. All true—yet, as the team's leader, he knew that ultimately he was responsible for the team's success or failure.

It was a crushing weight to bear. "It put a lot of psychological pressure on him," a team member later said.

The pressure became all the greater after William was selected for a new secret mission. Although the United States was still officially neutral, it was lending aid to Britain, then under Nazi assault by air and sea. The Purple machine was selected as the next gift, and William was instructed to deliver a copy to Britain.

Heavy, bulky, and fragile, with banks of switches carefully wired together, Purple was not a natural traveler. The best chance of getting it safely to Britain was to pack it in huge crates and send it by sea. And that meant a voyage across the icy North Atlantic, where Nazi submarine "wolfpacks" were sinking ship after ship.

On December 23, William was commissioned as a lieutenant colonel and told to prepare for the trip. He could not tell Elizebeth any details about the mission. He may not even have known himself when it would take place—only that it would be soon, and that everything had to be ready in time. Yet Elizebeth must have seen that his anxiety and insomnia were reaching unbearable levels. Just before the voyage, in January 1941, the unthinkable happened.

William's mind broke down.

CHAPTER TWENTY-THREE

Heebeegeebees

The "crash," as Elizebeth called it, came on Saturday, January 4, 1941. Neither she nor William ever set down in words what happened that day. Evidently, it was a nightmare that they both wanted to forget. "Fight, flight, or neurosis" was how William described the general symptoms to himself later on, struggling to make sense of them on paper. "[H]eebeegeebees" or "hbgbs" was his shorthand for it. By this, he meant a feeling of "nervousness, depression, even despondency," combined with extreme insomnia.

William ended up at the Army's flagship medical center, Walter Reed General Hospital. There they offered him a bed in the Neuropsychiatric Section. At the time, it was thought to be an ideal place to recover from a mental breakdown. But for William, it was anything but.

William never described in detail exactly how he was treated there. The reality of that grim period stayed locked inside him, like a code that could not be broken. But from what we know of Walter

Reed at that time, and from a few things that he and Elizebeth let drop, we can piece together some of what happened.

Opened in 1930, the section of Walter Reed that William found himself in had 104 beds on five locked wards. The hospital's previous building for mental illness had burned down when an inmate set it on fire, so patients were closely watched to make sure they didn't cause trouble. Cut off from the rest of the hospital, the unit was patrolled by security guards.

Actual psychiatrists were few and far between. William shared a ward with up to twenty other men who were also battling mental illness. "There was only one psychiatrist for them all," Elizebeth remembered painfully. William was not offered any one-on-one sessions. Instead, treatment was group-based, and patients were encouraged to talk over their cases with each other. For William, burdened with secrets that involved the nation's security, the treatment was wildly unsuitable. But at Walter Reed, it was all that was on offer.

At the time, psychiatry was still a relatively new field. Private, one-on-one therapy was unusual. More common was the approach of Walter Reed's chief psychiatrist, Colonel William Clare Porter. Less interested in healing minds than in observing the ways they could go wrong, Porter saw it as his job to keep mentally ill people out of the Army. In milder cases, he sometimes counseled that a soldier be discharged from his normal duties and given desk work instead.

In such a scheme, William was an oddity—a man who already did desk work but found it too stressful. Because his job involved one of the most secret projects of the entire war, he couldn't even state exactly what he did all day. What were the psychiatrists of Walter Reed to do with such a man?

Observe him was the answer. For week after week after week.

Elizabeth must have been beside herself. Despite her demanding job, she visited William daily, for as many hours as she could spare, and she could see that the hospital stay wasn't helping him. But Army rules did not allow her to bring him home. Having entered Walter Reed, William was required to remain there until he was diagnosed.

To Elizabeth, the diagnosis seemed self-evident. She knew nothing about Purple, but she knew how hard her husband had been working. To her, William's breakdown "was nothing more or less than exhaustion."

Exhausted William most certainly was. But there was more to his breakdown than that.

————

Later in life, Elizabeth and William admitted that 1941 wasn't the first time that William had come close to unraveling. Even before he had met Elizabeth, he had sometimes struggled with what he called "dark moods." In 1920, when they were trapped at Riverbank, he had grown thin and listless under the strain.

After a few good years in Washington, the problem cropped up again. In 1927, William sought a psychiatrist's help, a very unusual move at the time. Elizabeth insisted that this was merely an experiment, with the young doctor "trying out his training" and William "trying out a patient's role." But William was experimenting because he needed help.

In the early 1930s, he again found himself "on the verge of nervous exhaustion." This time he told no one about it and simply hoped it would pass. Making time for golf and other hobbies helped, and he started to feel better. But he found he had "to be careful" not to get too wound up by his work.

Staying well was a tightrope act for William, and breaking Purple destroyed his balance. Locked in the noisy ward at Walter Reed, he felt worse than ever before.

Although neither he nor Elizebeth knew it yet, even harder times were coming. For the rest of his life, William would go through cycles when his mind would race, insomnia would take hold, and he would fall into a deep depression. Elizebeth blamed these episodes not only on overwork, but also on "the military and its antisemitism."

Antisemitism was everywhere in American life, but at work William saw its ugly face up close. Joseph Mauborgne, his immediate boss in the Signal Corps, was an open-minded man and a good friend. William also had several Jewish colleagues in the SIS, most of whom he hired himself. Yet elsewhere in the Army, antisemitism was common, and sometimes extreme.

Many officers in the Army's Military Intelligence Division (MID) were obsessed with the idea that Jews were a threat to America. After World War I, MID spent years building up a massive internal file on the "Jewish Question." It included lists of prominent American Jews, whom the MID kept tabs on. In addition, the file contained a report called "The Power and Aims of International Jewry."

The Army also endorsed eugenics, making it part of the official curriculum for Army officers. In 1921, they even invited William's old Cold Spring Harbor supervisor, Charles Davenport, to teach them. Davenport's racist and antisemitic theories then became part of the Army War College course for nearly two decades.

William had to work closely with officers who believed in these theories. Some of the sharpest reprimands he ever received were from General George Strong, a man who made antisemitic jokes in private, and who pushed Roosevelt to clamp down on "militant"

Jews. In stinging rebukes, Strong questioned William's loyalty and friendships, and at one point limited his contact with British officers. William suspected that his own Jewish background made officers like Strong treat him differently. To face such constant prejudice, year in and year out, was a heavy burden.

But if antisemitism contributed to William's breakdowns, there was another factor at work, too. Elizebeth and William may have suspected as much, since two of his brothers also developed severe mental illness. Like him, both were treated at mental hospitals. In the language of the day, they had "psychosis" and "severe neurosis"—terms that were sometimes applied to William, too.

Near the end of Elizebeth's life, she learned that one of William's doctors, Zigmund Lebensohn, had given his "hbgbs" a more precise label. Whether Lebensohn ever shared this with William is not clear. But having treated him through many ups and downs, Lebensohn believed that William was "an extraordinarily intelligent man" with "Manic Depressive Illness." In other words, he was certain that William had what we now call bipolar disorder.

In the 1940s, the condition was not well understood, and the doctors at Walter Reed did not recognize it in William. Even if they had, there was no effective treatment on offer. Later on, lithium would revolutionize the treatment of bipolar disorder, but the drug would not be licensed in the United States until 1970.

In 1941, there was nothing.

———

After eleven long weeks, Dr. Porter and his colleagues finally settled on a diagnosis for William. Their verdict? He was suffering from an "anxiety reaction" due to "prolonged overwork on a top secret project." On March 22, he was sent home. He was told to go back to work as soon as possible.

"I began to recover the day I left Walter Reed," William later wrote. By April 1, he was back at his desk. Yet full recovery was a long time in coming, in part because his breakdown changed the way his colleagues saw him. That April he was taken off high-pressure code breaking and discharged from active duty in the Army. For the rest of the war, he served essentially as a senior civilian advisor and administrator.

It was a demanding post in its own way. Not only did William help oversee a massive expansion of Army code breaking, but he also played a key role in several high-level Allied missions. But he was cut to the quick by the official discharge. He protested, but it wasn't until 1946 that the Army restored him to his previous rank.

During the war itself, William had to stand by and watch as his colleagues and assistants became military officers, then rose in rank. "[E]verybody went into uniform," as one person put it. Meanwhile, William had to wear street clothes. The contrast was obvious to everyone and stood out in every photo. Although he dressed as carefully as ever, his trim suits now served as a constant reminder of his breakdown.

It was left to Elizebeth to help him heal—and in ways large and small, she did exactly that. Trying not to let her own anxiety show, she did her best to restore him to himself. Both then and later, whenever the "hbgbs" returned, she was his rock.

Knowing that his job was essential to his self-respect, she did everything she could to help him keep it. During some of the darkest times, when William could barely function, she quietly "took him to work every morning and put his pen in his hand to get him started."

At a time when mental illness carried a deep and almost ineradicable stigma, Elizebeth refused to let it create a chasm between her and her husband. She never stopped loving William, then or later. If anything, she loved him all the more for what they had endured together. In her unshakable opinion, he was the smartest and most attractive man she had ever met—and she made sure he knew that.

To William, she was a constant beacon. He never stopped feeling lucky that she was his wife. Her "indomitable spirit helped me climb up out of a psychological morass that was pretty deep and distressing," he later told their son.

A Friedman family snapshot.

To their relief, William continued to recover throughout the summer. Soon he was taking his usual delight in wordplay and jokes. In October, he wrote a funny letter, full of puns and one-liners, to Barbara, at college in Minnesota. He still had nights when he went downstairs to the kitchen, unable to sleep. But now he could describe his snacks to Barbara in a lighthearted way, as "my usual quadruple-decker sandwich (constructed according to secret patent number 3,975,884, a license to which I gave you in a moment of weakness)."

Soon he and Elizebeth were up to having friends over. They even made new ones. Among them were several British intelligence officers who appreciated the Friedmans' warm welcome and friendly wit. Some of these new friendships would be lifelong.

By the fall of 1941, then, Elizebeth and William had achieved a measure of hard-won peace. Yet in the wider world, the war was drawing closer to American shores—and it would push both Elizebeth and William to their limits.

CHAPTER TWENTY-FOUR

Elizebeth's War

In late 1941, as the United States teetered on the edge of joining World War II, code breakers were in huge demand—especially top talent like Elizebeth. Although her main job involved tracking spies and ships for the Treasury Department and the Coast Guard, others in Washington sought her help, too. Among them was a man known as "Wild Bill" Donovan.

A free-spirited World War I hero and Wall Street lawyer, Donovan had been chosen by the president to head up a brand-new agency, later known as the Office of Strategic Services (OSS). The dull name cloaked the agency's glamorous mission. In essence, the OSS was the nation's spy program—the forerunner of the CIA. To make it a success, Donovan needed the best possible encryption systems, and that was why he turned to Elizebeth.

To get her, Donovan had to push hard. No agency wanted to give up its code breakers, especially one as good as Elizebeth. But Donovan was friendly with the head of the Coast Guard, which likely helped. Donovan's right-hand man—James Roosevelt, the president's oldest son—did some arm-twisting, too. The result? Elizebeth and some of her staff were loaned to Donovan's office.

Elizebeth did not care for her new bosses. Bill Donovan and James Roosevelt kept demanding the impossible, and she felt they condescended to her. Both were fond of high society and preferred to spend time with the social elite—a category that didn't include Elizebeth. But she set her feelings aside and gave the new job her full attention.

While code breaking was Elizebeth's forte, she was also a top-notch code *builder*. Her gift for spotting weaknesses in codes and ciphers made her good at creating strong ones. In the 1920s, she had helped William build codes for the Army and for million-aire Edward McLean. In the 1930s, the Treasury had asked her to create one, too. Now she started on state-of-the-art systems for Donovan and his spies.

She was halfway through the assignment when Japanese fighter pilots bombed the American naval base at Pearl Harbor in Hawaii. The surprise attack—at dawn on Sunday, December 7, 1941—killed over twenty-four hundred Americans and put most of the Pacific Fleet out of action.

The next day, the United States went to war.

———

When the news about Pearl Harbor reached Washington, William was devastated. He had broken his health to break Purple, but his efforts hadn't kept his country safe. Eighteen-year-old Barbara Friedman remembered him "practically sobbing" on the phone that Sunday afternoon. "They knew, they knew, but they knew," he said, distraught.

Had Purple given the United States a warning of the attack—a warning that was ignored? William was not closely involved in Purple operations at the time, so he couldn't say for sure. But that was what he feared. Close to another breakdown, he went into the office and tried to piece together what had gone wrong. Later, Congress would investigate, too.

Both Congress and William reached the same conclusion. It was true that Purple had warned that Japan might attack the United States. But there was no clue—via Purple or anything else—stating when or where the attack would occur, except that it would likely be very soon, in December.

Sadly, a series of mistakes, bad decisions, and red-tape snafus between the Army and the Navy meant that even this general warning was ignored. For William, and for the nation, Pearl Harbor was a painful lesson in human error—and the limits of even the most brilliant cryptanalytic machinery.

———

For Elizabeth, the impact of Pearl Harbor was immediate and personal. She saw William slip into another cycle of sleepless nights, anxiety, and depression. As before, the secrecy of his work meant that he could not tell her what was the matter. Refusing to enter Walter Reed again, he remained at home, where she tried to help him as best she could.

Meanwhile, she was having to cope with Donovan's urgent and ever-growing demands. Working nights and weekends, she finished the job in late December. Rather than create a single code system, she had built several, to be used as field circumstances allowed. The most secure system was based on a one-time pad.

As she later noted, one-time pad systems are "really the only unbreakable cipher in existence." They require the use of long, random, nonrepeating keys that only the sender and receiver know. Each key must be used only once and then destroyed. In Elizebeth's day, huge numbers of these keys were often printed on pads of paper, but they could also be hidden on film, tapes, or parachute silk. Agents would tear off each key after using it and then burn or otherwise demolish it. Since the key was too long and random to memorize, it could not be extracted from them, even under torture.

Germany and Russia were already making use of one-time pad systems, and at one point William and the Army took an interest in them, too. Overall, however, the United States was slow to adopt this type of system, so Elizebeth did Donovan a big favor by setting him up with one. Thanks to her, America's spy handlers enjoyed highly secure communication links—far safer, for instance, than those used by America's diplomats.

Elizebeth's systems worked well, and Donovan relied on them for the rest of the war. To her frustration, however, she and her team received little credit for their work. Perhaps as a result, her last report to Donovan detailed exactly what that work had involved, as well as the long night and weekend hours her team had put in. Aware by now of his reputation for recklessness, she reminded him again of basic security precautions. In a bid for the respect she knew she deserved, she signed off with the honorary title that she rarely used—"DR. E. S. FRIEDMAN."

With the job for Donovan finished, Elizebeth could go back to her own unit. That should have been a relief, but it wasn't, because big changes were afoot at the Coast Guard. With war approaching, the entire service was being transferred to Navy control.

The prospect of reporting to the Navy made Elizebeth "very rebellious and gloomy." So rebellious, in fact, that she tried to put a stop to her unit's transfer.

———

Why did Elizebeth balk at being assigned to the Navy?

First of all, she knew that the Navy never allowed a civilian to run anything. Once her unit was shifted over, an officer would be put in over her head, and she would have to follow his orders. Even if he decided to split her unit up, she couldn't stop him.

Elizebeth was also wary of Laurance Safford, a key intelligence director at the Navy. "My personal opinion," she once admitted, ". . . is that Safford is a nincompoop." She thought he had poor code-breaking skills, and he often sent half-baked "flubdedubs and gadgets" to her Coast Guard unit, wasting everyone's time. But nincompoop or not, she would have to report to him if she worked for the Navy.

Elizebeth also knew that the Navy was not a welcoming workplace for women. The sad fate of Agnes Meyer—now Agnes Meyer Driscoll—was a case in point.

For almost two decades, Driscoll had been the Navy's star code breaker. Although she had briefly left the Navy in the early 1920s (when Elizebeth filled in for her), she soon returned. At a time when women were a rarity at the Navy, Driscoll's career flourished. Then she had a bad car accident in 1937. As Driscoll struggled to recover, her male colleagues started to undermine her. Some of these Navy men had been trained by her, but that didn't stop them from playing tricks on her and calling her a "witch" and a "hag."

Elizebeth had probably heard how far Driscoll's star had fallen. While she had never warmed to Driscoll herself, it was not a story that boded well for any woman who worked for the Navy.

When Elizebeth protested the Navy transfer, she was powerful enough to get a hearing. She also had a good case. While it was true that everyone in the Coast Guard had to accept Navy control, her own contract was actually with the Treasury Department, which was only *loaning* her to the Coast Guard. That meant that the Treasury had to agree to the transfer.

The top men at the Treasury knew how good Elizebeth was at her job, and they wanted to keep her happy. With war in the offing, however, the Navy was growing more powerful, and its demands trumped everything else. In the end, the Treasury could only arrange better terms for her.

On the weekend of Pearl Harbor, after a tense phone call, an agreement was reached: Elizebeth would report to the Navy. In return, the Navy promised that she and her unit would be kept together.

It wasn't the outcome Elizebeth had wanted. But with the United States headed into a full-scale war, it was the best she could get.

At first, everything stayed more or less the same. Although Elizebeth's unit was now part of the Navy, it took more than a year for the Navy to get around to changing its name—from Coast Guard Unit 387 to OP-20-GU. In the meantime, the unit remained in its longtime home in the Treasury Annex on Pennsylvania Avenue. For the first few months of 1942, Elizebeth also remained the unit's acting head.

In April, she was even asked to represent the Coast Guard at a high-level meeting of U.S., British, and Canadian

Elizebeth at work in 1940.

intelligence officials. She was the only woman at the table. A female presence at this level was such a rarity that a British record keeper later corrected the minutes of the meeting, whiting out the "s" of "Mrs." so that she became "Mr. Friedman." At the meeting itself, her practices were praised as a model for others to follow.

Yet change was on the way. As she had expected, a male officer was named the new head of the unit. Captain Leonard T. Jones—soon to be Lieutenant Commander Jones—was actively in charge by the summer of 1942. From then on, Elizebeth had to follow his orders.

A radio expert with the Coast Guard, Jones had been trained by William in the early 1930s. Elizebeth had worked with him before—most recently on the code system for Donovan's spy agency. Back then, however, Elizebeth had been in charge, and Jones assisted her. Now Jones ran the show.

For Elizebeth, it was a frustrating setup. She got along with Jones personally, even having him over to dinner with his wife, but it was hard to have him put in above her. She had far more experience and skill in code breaking than he did, and she had created the unit. Yet now it was Jones who gave the orders and determined what their mission should be. She tried to keep the unit running smoothly, but she questioned whether he was making the best use of her team.

She was right to worry. Jones wanted the unit to focus closely on South American spies. But in 1942, those spies were using the same straightforward ciphers over and over again. For Elizebeth and her team, most of these ciphers were easy to break—and once they were broken, even a trainee code breaker could read other messages sent using the same system. Elizebeth believed that she and her highly skilled team should be working on other, more difficult problems.

What sorts of problems did she have in mind? It's not clear, but perhaps she was thinking about Japanese naval codes. These had features in common with codes she had solved before, and they were more crucial to the war effort than the chatter of South American spies. It would have been logical for the Navy to ask Elizebeth and her team to help break them.

Logic, however, lost out to Navy hierarchies and power games. For Jones, it made no sense to let Elizebeth move on to other duties and another boss. Having been lucky enough to be assigned some of the best code breakers in America, he was not about to let them slip through his fingers. Nor would he allow them to dictate terms. When she debated the unit's mission with him, he always overruled her. It was his unit now, and it would focus on South American spy talk.

Elizebeth was exasperated by Jones and what she saw as his "excessive concern as to what was best for him professionally." Nevertheless, she gave her all to the job. Jones might be the boss, but she was still the unit's best code breaker, and she knew the others looked to her for guidance. She was not going to let them down, or offer them anything less than her best.

———

During the war, Elizebeth worked a standard nine to ten hours a day, with only Sundays off. So did William. "They were gone long before I came down to have breakfast," their daughter, Barbara, recalled. Extra duties, like breaking the open code in the Doll Woman letters in 1944, made her working days even longer.

Office conditions were far from ideal. In 1943, the Navy moved Elizebeth's unit into a "grubby, ramshackle temporary building with [a] flat roof and thin walls." In the sticky Washington summers, it became an oven. Stuck on the second floor, Elizebeth sweltered in hundred-degree temperatures. Once, the thermometer hit 114. In peacetime, heat like that would have shut down the office, but in the middle of a war, they had to carry on. She and her team put in full days at their tables and desks, breaking codes in the stifling heat.

Because household help was in short supply in wartime Washington, Elizebeth did a second shift when she got home. It was a time of shortages and limited labor-saving devices, and housework could take hours. As a farmer's daughter, Elizebeth had the skills to be self-reliant, but it was hard to find the time—and the supplies. "It would be a cinch to make the blouse [I need]," she wrote once, "if I ever had five minutes—plus the *hours* it would take to find the material." At one point, she had a local restaurant drop off daily dinners for her teenage son, just to be sure he got fed.

Under pressure at work and at home, Elizebeth often worried about her family. William was at the top of her list. After his Pearl Harbor relapse, he had recovered quickly. For the rest of the war, however, he had to shoulder heavy burdens. Noting William's rapport with his British counterparts, the Army made him a point man in U.S.-U.K. intelligence relations, twice sending him on long trips overseas. Yet that very same rapport also got him into trouble. At one point, the head of military intelligence—who distrusted Jews on principle—decided William had loose lips and ordered him "to refrain from technical and social contacts with the British," as well as with the U.S. Navy. Taken literally, the ban included Elizebeth herself, since she worked for the Navy. Although the order was soon rescinded, its sting lingered. Still prone to insomnia, William often felt "tense," and he worried that the "hbgbs" were never far away.

Elizebeth was concerned about their children, too. Both

Barbara and John were coming of age in a society in which anti-semitism was common. Although they had been allowed to make their own decisions about religion, and neither identified as Jewish, their background still made them the target of prejudice. Barbara felt this most keenly. Like her father, she also suffered from bouts of insomnia and anxiety.

Monday through Saturday, when Elizebeth was at work, she had to push all these worries to the back of her mind. The Nazi spies in South America might be using relatively simple codes and ciphers, but reading their messages still required focus and care. If a single letter or digit was copied out wrong, it could waste hours of everyone's time.

Each message her unit cracked was another window into the spies' world. Over the course of the war, her team would break into dozens of spy networks, including thirty-seven circuits linked to Hamburg, and a further twenty-four that were handled from Berlin.

As early as 1941, Elizebeth and her team had even started to identify some of the key players in those networks, at least by their code names. The one who called himself Sargo seemed to be more important than most. Elizebeth became intent on tracking him down.

She didn't know it yet, but she was on the trail of South America's most dangerous Nazi spy.

CODE BREAK

CODE NAMES AND CRIBS

Like many undercover agents, South America's Nazi spies used code names—like Sargo, Humberto, Alfredo, Luna, Guapo, and Utz—to keep themselves safe. But sometimes these code names made it easier for Elizebeth to track them.

"Humberto" and "Alfredo" were cases in point. Because these names were long, and because they used uncommon letters and combinations like F and MB, they stood out. They also cropped up frequently in the spies' messages, creating a pattern for Elizebeth to spot.

In one spy circuit, Elizebeth discovered that almost all the messages ended with either HUMBERTO or ALFREDO. Sometimes she would detect a letter, like B or F, that told her which name was being used. Otherwise she would try each name in turn. The code names were the weak points that gave Elizebeth a pathway into the messages.

British code breakers called this kind of word a *crib*—slang for "cheat sheet." Later on, some Americans started using the term, too. In code-breaking terms, a crib is any word or phrase that is known (or likely) to be in a message and that can be used to solve it. The formal name for this method is *known-plaintext attack*.

The basic idea was one that Elizebeth and her team had often used before, so they knew it was crucial to harvest as many cribs as they could from the South American messages. For example, they noticed that one spy circuit always started their messages with one of the following words: SUDAMERIAT, WEDEKIND, SUDAMERO,

EGMARSUD. Another always signed the messages with the word SCHOEN, the code name of the German ambassador to Chile.

By repeating code words and code names so often, the spies were opening the door to Elizebeth and her team.

CHAPTER TWENTY-FIVE

Sargo

The spy known as Sargo was an SS officer, part of the Nazis' elite Schutzstaffel force. On his left hand, he wore a ring with the SS death's head—a sign of his loyalty to Hitler. His real name was Johannes Siegfried Becker, but he had dozens of aliases and more than one false passport. Blond and vain, he often dyed his hair, and he was known as a ladies' man. He had a string of girlfriends, even though his fingernails were so long that they curled.

Born in Germany in 1912, Becker was an early convert to the Nazi Party. Able to speak four languages, he was a natural recruit for overseas assignments. From 1936 to 1939, he spied for the Nazis in Brazil and Argentina. When World War II began, the SS spy agency in Berlin made him their top man in South America. At the time, Becker was still in his twenties.

At first, Becker's handlers wanted him to serve as both spy and saboteur. They supplied Becker with a partner—but no training—and then gave him explosives to attack British ships in Argentina's harbors. When Becker showed up with the bombs in the port of Buenos Aires, the German diplomats there were outraged. They complained to their bosses in Berlin, saying that Germany needed to court friends in South America, not start bombing campaigns. Becker had to get rid of his explosives.

If sabotage did not work out for Becker, spying did. He was good at milking contacts and finding recruits. Wherever he went, he drew more people into his web. Over the course of the war, as many as 250 agents ended up connected to him in some way. Within these networks, he became best known as Sargo.

Johannes Siegfried Becker, aka Sargo.

Like other spies, Sargo used radio to keep his spy circuits connected with Germany, sending all messages in code or cipher. Getting a signal all the way across the Atlantic was a challenge, especially in stormy weather. Sometimes it was more reliable—though much slower—to use letters or human messengers instead. Then in 1941, the SS sent Sargo a young German radio expert, who built powerful transmitters and radio networks that could reliably reach Berlin, Cologne, and Hamburg. The system must have seemed like high-tech wizardry to some recruits. But radio was actually the spies' weak spot, because it allowed Elizebeth to find out what they were up to.

Via radio, Sargo and his recruits often disclosed plans for fascist uprisings and coups to their Nazi masters. They also passed along embassy gossip and whatever secrets they could glean about the American war effort, such as the number of bombers U.S.

factories were producing and how many planes the U.S. had in total. The spies sent the Nazis many shipping details from South American ports, too—long lists of vessel names, cargoes, and departure dates.

Elizebeth was alarmed when she saw these lists, because she knew that the Nazis would use them to ambush Allied ships, often by submarine. Germany was sinking over a thousand Allied merchant ships every year, killing many sailors and destroying a vast tonnage of Allied supplies. By 1942, the Nazi subs were so successful that Britain, which had to import much of its food, was in danger of starvation.

Elizebeth and her team took note of every ship that was listed, as well as everything else the spies said and did. Once they broke a message, it was sent on to other agencies, which decided what was to be done about it. At times, ships were warned to change their courses. That's what happened in March 1942, when Elizebeth discovered that the Nazis were planning to ambush the RMS *Queen Mary,* which had over eight thousand American servicemen on board. The ship was ordered to change direction, saving all their lives.

Yet each action had to be weighed carefully. If all Allied ships were saved, the Nazis would grow suspicious and guess that someone had broken their codes. Then they would change them, leaving the United States and its allies in the dark about their plans. While the Allies eventually wanted to destroy the Nazi spy networks, for now it was more useful to keep them talking—and to have Elizebeth listen in.

There was a name for what she was doing, a word that had just been invented: *counterintelligence.* It was another way of saying that she was spying on the spies—a job that required both skill and restraint.

After years of practice, restraint came easily to Elizebeth. Her team, too, was utterly trustworthy. But some of the agencies who received her intelligence were not so reliable. The FBI, in particular, was eager to take action and make a splash, even at the risk of giving the game away.

For Elizebeth, the FBI's initials spelled nothing but trouble.

―――――――

Elizebeth and the FBI ought to have been natural allies. But in the mind of the FBI's domineering director, J. Edgar Hoover, they were rivals.

A native of Washington, DC, Hoover had started out as a messenger boy at the Library of Congress. By 1924, when he was in his late twenties, he was already well on his way to building the Feds into his own loyal empire. A powerful figure in Washington, he was allowed to shape the agency as he wanted. For Hoover, that included getting his agents—often called G-men—to monitor left-wing activists. It also meant getting rid of female agents. There would be no more G-women until after his death in 1972.

In Hoover's world, only men were supposed to fight crime and keep their country safe. So it must have rubbed him the wrong way to see Elizebeth winning battles against smugglers and gangsters in the 1920s and 1930s. To add insult to injury, she then turned out to be better at counterspy operations than the FBI was.

Even before World War II, Hoover had wanted his G-men to become the chief spy hunters in the Americas. Yet when the United States captured its first Nazi spy in 1938, the FBI bungled the case. Not only did the agency let most members of the spy ring escape, but the leading FBI agent sold his side of the story to the newspapers. The FBI became a laughingstock.

Hoover was not amused. Desperate to restore the FBI's reputation, he did whatever was necessary to make the agency look good. That included playing dirty tricks on Elizebeth and her unit.

It took Elizebeth a while to grasp what was happening. The FBI was expert at covering its tracks, and its agents were willing to lie when confronted. But long before the Doll Woman case—when the FBI took credit for her work, rubbing her out of history—Elizebeth learned that the agency could not be trusted.

Here's an example of the kind of game they played. In January 1941, Elizebeth and her team started decoding messages from an unlicensed radio station. It appeared to be based on Long Island, New York, and its messages were alarming. The station was broadcasting vital details to Germany about New York shipping traffic. The FBI told Elizebeth's team not to worry. Their agents were monitoring the signals and had the situation in hand.

Six months later, when the Long Island station was finally shut down, Elizebeth learned that the FBI had actually been *running* it as part of a sting operation to catch Nazi spies. When the spies were arrested, Hoover trumpeted the news to the papers. He did not add that his decoy station had supplied vital information to the Nazis. Experts now believe that the FBI-run station likely gave the Germans better intelligence than they got from their actual spies in South America during the entire rest of the war.

As a direct result of the station's broadcasts, the Nazis sank at least one Allied ship and its crew. Elizebeth and her unit were keenly aware of this, but they could say nothing. Since the Espionage Act made it illegal to disclose the details of their work to the public, they fumed in silence while Hoover strutted around like a hero.

Elizebeth had other reasons to distrust the FBI as well.

In the summer of 1941, the FBI had demanded that she train the head of their brand-new code-breaking unit. She spent more than a month working with him, but there was only so much he could learn. The FBI still depended on her to handle the brunt of their code breaking.

She and her team worked fast, passing their hard-won decrypts, keys, and code books back to the FBI. But the FBI did not return the favor. When the G-men arrested spies and got hold of their code books, no one shared those books with Elizebeth—not even when her team had made the arrest possible.

To add insult to injury, the FBI claimed in public that their success was due to their own code breakers. They never once credited Elizebeth or her team for anything. Even within their own agency, they did their best to disguise who had done the actual work. They filed Elizebeth's decrypts under new index numbers, making them look like their own.

All this was bad enough. But in 1942, the FBI did something worse.

From Elizebeth's decrypts, the FBI knew she was listening to spy networks in Brazil. That was where Sargo was, as well as other key agents. Thanks to their radio chatter, she was picking up valuable insights into their partners and plans. Rather than shut down the network, it made more sense, for the moment, to keep milking it for details.

The FBI, however, disagreed. Spoiling for more action, it wanted to shut down the spy networks then and there. It pushed for Brazil to arrest the spies right away. When the arrests didn't happen fast enough, the FBI went rogue. It passed hundreds of exact copies of Elizebeth's decrypts to the U.S. State Department so they could be shared with Brazil's officials. In March 1942, Brazilian police arrested many suspects and showed them the decrypts. The suspects then got word to their Nazi handlers that the networks were compromised.

For the United States, it was a complete screwup. The arrests netted only a few small fry, but the Nazis now knew that their codes had been broken. Suddenly, their networks went dark. Sargo and other key spies remained at large, but there was no longer any easy way to track them. Where Elizebeth had once picked up useful chatter, there was now near silence.

She and her team were incensed, and so was their boss. The trigger-happy FBI had just made their job much more difficult. To Elizebeth, it seemed that the "South American stuff" was "dying." She wanted "something to do."

That "something" came along in October 1942. By then, many spy rings were broadcasting again, but they were using new codes. Some of these were easy to break, but soon it became clear that the Nazis had made a game-changing decision. To improve security, they had given their top South American spies a present—a coding machine called Enigma.

The Nazis believed Enigma was unbreakable. Elizebeth's next big challenge? To crack it.

CHAPTER TWENTY-SIX

Cracking Enigma

A t first glance, an Enigma machine looks like a boxy, heavy-weight typewriter. Its letter keys are in German "QWERTZU" order, and you press them to type out your message.

At second glance, you might notice something strange about this machine. For one, there is a second set of "QWERTZU" indicators above the keyboard. Stranger still, if you press the "Q" key, it isn't the "Q" indicator that glows, but perhaps an "A" or a "J" or a "Z." If you strike the "Q" key a second time, another letter lights up.

Unlike a regular typewriter, an Enigma also has removable gears,

A three-rotor Enigma machine in its wooden case.

known as rotors. In most models, there's also a plugboard at one end. If you tinker with these, you might work out that the rotors and plugboard link up the letter keys and the indicators. You might also notice that each keystroke changes exactly what those links are. By then, you might guess that you're typing on a very sophisticated cipher machine.

As you type, Enigma encrypts your message—and the number of ways it can do this is mind-boggling. Between the rotors and the plugboard, a typical Enigma machine has almost 159,000,000,000,000,000,000 (159 quintillion) possible settings. Even for an expert code breaker, this is daunting. If you try each combination in turn, it will take far more than a lifetime to get through them all.

The only quick way to break Enigma messages is to use another Enigma machine with the exact same initial settings. Nazi Enigma operators were told which settings to use—the key could be changed each day—but outsiders wouldn't know where to begin. For this reason, the Nazis considered Enigma unbreakable.

What the Nazis didn't know was that a Polish team had cracked an early Enigma machine in 1932. As Enigma became more complex, the Poles created a decoding device that helped decrypt the messages. They passed their insights to the French and the British just before Germany attacked Poland in 1939. British code breakers then made more breakthroughs. Thanks in part to a young mathematician named Alan Turing, they came up with new ways to tackle Enigma, including much more powerful decoding machines.

But the Nazis, too, kept leaping ahead. When they added new rotors to some Enigmas, the British were locked out for months on end. The Nazis also created different types of Enigmas and unique daily setting tables for various branches of their forces. Sometimes the Nazis added a secret twist to the tables, which further confused the code breakers.

In short, Enigma was so complex that it could not be solved once and for all, even by the British experts. Every day, there were new settings to unlock and new complications to unravel. It was a continual pursuit, one puzzle following another. And now Elizebeth was joining the hunt.

———

The very first time that Elizebeth tried to solve an Enigma message was back in January 1940, before the United States had entered the war. That winter, her team saw some strange intercepts that followed no known pattern. Once they had more than sixty of these odd messages, they started to puzzle out what they might be.

The cipher was so complex that it took days to break it. On worksheet after worksheet, Elizebeth and her team fought for each letter. Gradually, they saw signs that the messages were in German. It also looked like no letter was ever encrypted as itself—that is, an "A" was never an "A." That was a known trait of Enigma.

Finally, they found their way to a full solution. But to their chagrin, the mysterious messages turned out not to be from the Nazis. Instead, they were harmless bulletins from the Swiss Army, written on a simple, commercial version of Enigma. It was nowhere near as complex as the top-secret Enigma machines the Nazis had developed. In fact, Elizebeth herself had a commercial Enigma machine in her office so that her team could study it.

Still, even simple Enigma was hard to break, and Elizebeth was proud that she and her team had been up to the job. What's more, they had gone a step further, using the messages to figure out how the Enigma rotors were wired up. This would give them a head start in solving future messages. As far as they knew, it was the first time Americans had recovered an Enigma wiring from messages alone.

If these 1940 Enigma messages were a practice round, the ones that Elizebeth saw in October 1942 were the real thing. Written on Nazi Enigma machines, they would be much harder to crack.

Because the United States and Britain were now fighting together, Elizebeth turned to British code breakers for help. The world's experts in decrypting Enigma, the British had created banks of powerful electric machines—called bombes—to help with the work. But bombes were costly and time-consuming to run, and there were nowhere near enough of them, so British code breakers were also solving many Enigma messages—fully or in part—with pencil, paper, and know-how. Elizebeth hoped they could offer her some tips.

One of her key contacts was F. J. M. Stratton, a famous English astronomer, so short and round and jolly that he reminded people of Santa Claus. Another was Oliver Strachey, a British cryptologist who ran a code-breaking unit in Canada that tracked spies, just as Elizebeth's team did.

These British experts knew that most Nazi spies used their own version of the Enigma machine. It was often called Abwehr Enigma—after the Abwehr, the main Nazi spy division. Also known as Enigma G, it was the machine Elizebeth's spies were likely to be using.

Designed to be lightweight and easy to carry and set up, Abwehr Enigma was a medium-security model. Instead of a plugboard, it had four rotors with unusual rotation patterns. These had been designed to make Abwehr messages harder to crack, but the British had picked up on the patterns, which they called "lobsters" and "crabs." Elizebeth and her team took note and adopted the same terms.

Although Abwehr Enigma was easier to break than the highest-grade Enigmas, it still had over 48 billion possible settings. That meant it could still take days, weeks, and sometimes even months to crack its messages.

While the British knew a lot about how the machines operated, neither they nor anyone else could tell Elizebeth which of the many billions of Enigma settings the South American spies were using. It was up to her to uncover them.

———

At the start, Elizebeth had too few Enigma intercepts to draw any clear conclusions. But by December 1942, her team had a total of twenty-eight messages. That was enough to begin trying to solve them—or so she hoped.

To break them, she and her team looked at the messages *in depth*. This was a process that involved lining up messages to detect new patterns that could unlock the cipher. If the Enigma operators had followed orders and used a unique key setting for each message, solving in depth might not work. Even if it did, it could take days or even weeks to complete. But Elizebeth and her team had a lucky break. The spies had used the same settings for all twenty-eight messages. That made it easy to line them up correctly and spot the patterns they needed. Letter by letter, the plaintext emerged.

Once they had the plaintext, Elizebeth could see how each

letter had been encrypted. She then used that to work out what kind of Enigma wiring would produce those results. Sitting at her desk, many thousands of miles away from the machine itself, she mapped its inner circuits.

It was a remarkable feat. Bletchley Park, the U.K.'s secret code-breaking center, was staffed with hundreds of mathematicians, linguists, and professors, and it had dedicated units that could solve Abwehr Enigma with pencil and paper alone. Working far away from Bletchley, with minimal Enigma experience, Elizebeth and her small team had managed to achieve the same goal. And as more Enigma messages kept coming in, they soon became as fast as the British themselves.

Even before this, the British had spotted how good Elizebeth was at code breaking. In late 1942, some officers had talked about recruiting her and her team to work with the U.K. on "outstanding problems"—which perhaps included Enigma. They had wanted her to visit Bletchley, but nothing came of this plan. In any case, Elizebeth's boss was never going to allow her to travel overseas to work with someone else.

When Elizebeth forged her own path to Enigma, the British were impressed. They were also alarmed. Britain's ability to read Enigma was a vital war secret, and they had gone to great lengths to protect it. Now they had to worry about potential leaks from Elizebeth's work. What if a loose-lipped American bragged about cracking Enigma? Word might get back to the Nazis, who would change the system. Then the Allies' secret Enigma advantage would be gone.

The British trusted Elizebeth and her team to keep quiet. But they did not trust the FBI. To their relief, Elizebeth's unit felt the same way about J. Edgar Hoover and his men—and so did the U.S. Navy and the Army. For safety's sake, they all agreed that Hoover would be told only what he needed to know about Elizebeth's results. He would not receive actual decrypts, and Enigma itself would never be mentioned.

The plan worked. Hoover had no idea that he was being left out of the loop.

Meanwhile, Elizebeth and her team kept working away at the Enigma messages. They were learning more and more about what South America's top spies were up to. And they did not like what they saw.

CODE BREAK

SOLVING IN DEPTH

When Elizabeth and her team solved Enigma *in depth*, what exactly were they doing? And why did it work?

Let's start with this cipher: PXODLOBXIIVFPYBZHBO.

This is a simple substitution cipher. If you make a table of how often each letter appears, and you compare it to how often letters appear in normal English, you can work out that the message is based on this cipher alphabet:

A	B	C	D	E	F	G	H	I	J	K	L	M	N	O	P	Q	R	S	T	U	V	W	X	Y	Z
X	Y	Z	A	B	C	D	E	F	G	H	I	J	K	L	M	N	O	P	Q	R	S	T	U	V	W

This cipher is *monoalphabetic*. That is, it uses a single cipher alphabet that never changes. So if you discover that O = R, that rule holds true for the entire message. Every time you see an O, you know it is really an R.

Enigma is a *polyalphabetic substitution cipher*. That means that it uses *many* cipher alphabets. Enigma shifts to a new one with every keystroke. So if you discover that O = R at the start of the message, you still don't know what O means later on. That is part of why Enigma is so hard to break.

But there is a weakness to the system. If multiple messages are sent on the same Enigma settings, the first letter in each message will use the same cipher alphabet (which we'll call Alphabet 1). The second letter in each message belongs to another cipher alphabet (which we'll call Alphabet 2). The same is true of the third letter (Alphabet 3), and so on.

If you can collect enough messages sent on the exact same settings, you can line them up. Looking down each column, you will see letters that come from the same cipher alphabet. The pattern of those letters can help you break the cipher.

Imagine, for instance, that you had messages that started like this, all sent on the same settings:

Message 1: O X Z T B Q . . .
Message 2: K A S R Q J . . .
Message 3: O E J M D W . . .

Stacked up like this, Column 1 is from Alphabet 1, Column 2 is from Alphabet 2, and so forth.

With just three messages, the columns are shallow, and you can't learn much. But if you have many messages, you have *depth*, and you can start to see patterns.

When Elizebeth and her team stacked up the twenty-eight Enigma messages they had in December 1942, they discovered that the first column had far more O's in it than anything else. They knew that B is a letter that very often appears at the start of German words, so they guessed that O might stand for B. In Enigma, letters were always paired, so that would mean that B stood for O. And that would be true for every B and O that appeared in the first column. The team penciled those guesses in, looked at other frequent letters, and made more guesses.

Enigma operators were supposed to change their machine settings daily, plus make other minor changes for each message. That made solving in depth a challenge, but top code breakers figured out other ways of aligning messages with statistics and other insights. If Enigma operators slipped up and used the same settings more than once, breaking the cipher was much easier.

When messages were lined up properly, and a code breaker made enough good guesses, German words would eventually appear. That's what happened in this case—but only because the team had enough messages to solve in depth.

CHAPTER TWENTY-SEVEN

A Spy at Sea

The first Nazi Enigma messages that Elizebeth broke came from a spy network with the code name GREEN. Over time, as more messages came in, she and her team got a clear picture of the GREEN network's efforts to build up a Nazi presence in Argentina. She also had a front-row seat when Berlin sent this revealing message on November 6, 1943:

> *The new Enigma which arrived together with trunk transmitter is for RED. It is a birthday surprise for LUNA.*

Elizebeth had already been tracking the RED network for some time. She knew LUNA was the code name of the radio operator who had worked with Sargo in Brazil. She had reason to believe Sargo was part of the RED network, too. And thanks to this message, as well as others sent from Berlin that week, Elizebeth had advance notice that RED was about to start using an Enigma machine.

In a blow for Elizebeth's team, RED's Enigma messages turned out to be doubly encrypted. First, the network put them through the lower-grade cipher machine, known as a Kryha, that they had used before the Enigma arrived. Those results were then typed into an Abwehr Enigma with new settings, different from those used by the GREEN network. Because of this layered approach, it took Elizebeth and her team many weeks to break the messages and work out the wiring on the new machine. They persisted, however, because they knew that Sargo and his sidekick Luna were worth tracking.

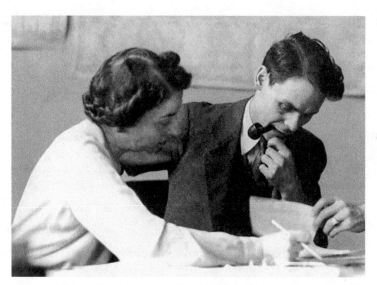

Elizebeth with Robert Gordon, one of her assistants.

In time, Elizebeth and her team penetrated the ciphers—their most impressive achievement yet. They kept reading what other spy rings sent, too. They soon uncovered a wide range of Nazi plots.

In Argentina, a new pro-fascist government had come into power, and Sargo and other spies were pushing the country to cooperate more closely with Germany. Sargo was also working to overthrow the governments of Bolivia, Paraguay, Chile, and Brazil, so that pro-Nazi leaders could be installed across South America. He and his agents were looking for ways to attack the United States and its allies, too.

Some of these plans were no more than pipe dreams. Others, however, were scarily close to realization.

The question now was: How could they be stopped?

————

Even before Elizebeth and her team broke into the RED network, the United States and its allies were searching for a way to smash Argentina's spy rings. To get Argentina's government to cooperate, they had to confront its officials with proof of what the spies were up to. But if they shared Elizebeth's Enigma decrypts with Argentina, they feared that the country's many pro-Nazi officials might share them with the spies.

If that happened, it would be like Brazil all over again, only with higher stakes. The Nazis used Enigma everywhere, and if they switched the way it worked—or, still worse, switched to another machine—the Allies would lose their secret advantage. They might even lose the war.

Was there any way forward? In October 1943, Elizebeth found one.

While breaking messages from Sargo's spy rings, she learned that one of his top recruits, Osmar Hellmuth, was heading to Germany. With the blessing of both Sargo and Argentina's president, Hellmuth was going to seek closer ties between his country and

Hitler. He also intended to do a deal with the Nazis to get weapons for Argentina.

The plan was more than wishful thinking. Hellmuth was only a minor Argentine diplomat, but thanks to Sargo, he had contacts at the highest level. Once he reached Europe, he was due to meet with Heinrich Himmler, the leader of the SS. He might even meet with Hitler himself. And if Hellmuth's mission succeeded, the Allies would face a stronger and more dangerous partnership between Germany and Argentina.

But what if the Allies could capture Hellmuth before he reached Germany? That would give them two big wins. First, it would put an end to Hellmuth's mission. Second, the Allies could say that they had learned about Argentina's spy rings from him, rather than from Enigma messages. The Nazis would be angry with Hellmuth, but they would continue to trust their cipher machines—and the Allies could go on milking Enigma.

To capture Hellmuth, the Allies needed the name of the ship he would sail on. Elizebeth and her team uncovered it: the *Cabo de Hornos*. Other American and British agents were tracking Hellmuth, too. After putting together all their leads, the Allies swung into action, with Britain taking charge. When the *Cabo de Hornos* made a routine stop in Trinidad, British authorities boarded the ship and arrested Hellmuth.

At Camp 020, a secret interrogation center near London, Hellmuth spilled everything he knew, including the true identity of Sargo. He even gave them a detailed description of the spy behind the code name. From that point on, Sargo was a marked man.

Two months later, after a fascist coup in Bolivia, the United States decided it was time to round the spies up. With Hellmuth's confession in hand, American officials told Argentina to break off relations with the Nazis or face the consequences.

Argentina crumpled. In January 1944, the country renounced its diplomatic ties with Germany, Japan, Italy, and their Axis allies. It also directed its police to hunt down Nazi spies, with help from the FBI.

Hounded and harried by forces on the ground, the spy rings of Argentina collapsed. Although the master spy Sargo remained elusive, his networks were quickly destroyed, and so were his radio stations and power bases. After Luna, his radio expert, was captured, Sargo's reach was even further diminished. He tried to hatch new plans, but soon it was all he could do merely to keep himself alive. He was a spent force long before he was finally caught in Buenos Aires near the end of the war.

Sargo had been the linchpin in Nazi spy networks not only in Argentina, but also across all of South America. Once he was on the run, the Nazis' influence over the continent dwindled. As the United States continued to apply pressure, South America tilted toward the Allies. By the spring of 1944, it was clear that the Nazis had lost their chance of taking the continent.

Elizebeth had played a big part in that invisible battle, and she could now declare victory. But she had no intention of resting on her laurels. World War II wasn't over, and she had more code-breaking battles to win.

Overkill

By the spring of 1944, with the Nazis' South American spy networks all but crushed, Elizebeth was eager for a new challenge. That spring, D-Day was approaching, and the United States was still fighting, island by island, for the Pacific. Top-notch code breakers were desperately needed on all fronts.

She was more than ready to take on any new job she was given—the tougher, the better. There was, however, a big obstacle in her way: her boss, Leonard Jones.

To her dismay, Jones saw no reason for a change in mission. He continued to insist that she and her team focus on the dwindling South American spy intercepts, which provided little useful intelligence. "[T]he problem was worked to the point of overkill," Elizebeth maintained, both then and long afterward. She believed the "talents of the unit could have been better used on more important projects."

It wasn't until the fall of 1944 that Jones at last conceded that perhaps the team should be doing more on other fronts. From then on, Elizebeth sometimes had a chance to deal with new kinds of traffic, including messages from occupied China. But it was a case of too little, too late. The new ciphers were not as demanding as those she had cracked earlier in the war, and they did not yield much in the way of vital intelligence. Overall, she and her team remained an underused resource.

Mired in low-level tasks, Elizebeth must have longed to do something more to help win the war—especially since her own children were headed into harm's way. In 1942, Barbara had transferred from Carleton to Radcliffe, but in 1944, she signed up to serve in the Panama Canal Zone. When John finished high school that same year, he joined the Army Air Corps. Calling Elizebeth from flight school in the spring of 1945, he told her that he had been ordered to an undisclosed location: "I will let you know where I am, when I am," he added—hard words for a wartime parent to hear.

As the war flung her family apart, Elizebeth spent hours writing letters to hold them together. She shared John's news with Barbara, let John know how Barbara was doing, and told William how proud she was of them both. She advised on Christmas presents ("any little *inexpensive* lighters"), fussed about their diets ("you probably need Vitamine B"), and worried they might be drinking too much ("There now, forgive the lecture").

Her letters also kept her family up-to-date about what was happening on the home front. When President Roosevelt succumbed to a stroke in April 1945, leaving the nation bereft of its leader, Elizebeth wrote to Barbara in Panama:

Oh, my darling—
I wish I could talk to you by telephone—just as on that

catastrophic day of Pearl Harbor you called us from far away Minnesota—There is too much in my mind and heart to say it all.

Without Roosevelt, Elizebeth was afraid that America would be vulnerable to "evil influences like . . . the Klan" and home-grown fascism. Perhaps worrying that her letter had become too sad, she ended by saying to Barbara, "I can imagine the ferment that world-conscious mind of yours is in. It is for us to fight all the more for a truly *international* post war world. A universe-full of love to you!"

A few weeks later, after the Nazis surrendered, Elizebeth wrote to Barbara about "a thrilling sight:—Lights on again in Washington. The Capitol. The Monument." She and William saw them at dusk, when "the sky was so very lovely, too, maroons, lavenders, blues." The war wasn't over yet, but it was clear that the end was near.

That week, Elizebeth and William took a "glorious three days" of vacation together. Summing it up for their children, she wrote that they both stayed home and "loafed," then celebrated their anniversary in style. They had cocktails and went dancing past midnight. They bought new clothes ("I have not bought either any dresses or shoes since two years ago last spring"), took in a stage show ("Guy Lombardo"), and ate at Ruby Foo's famous Chinese restaurant. "It was one of the nicest interludes we have ever, ever had."

In August, during the last days of the war, Elizebeth was the only one at home. Barbara and John were far away, playing their parts in the war effort. William was in Europe, part of a high-level Allied mission to scour Nazi strongholds for intelligence secrets. Suffering from an attack of nausea, Elizebeth crept around the house alone—and then she heard the news that Japan was about to surrender.

"Now I can sleep, this night," she wrote to William. "I certainly have been busy—driven, in fact, with the stillion things to do, but I'm getting all tired now of all chores and no play with my sweetheart." It made her happy to imagine "a long vacation in that dream island I'm always talking about!" She signed off, "Love forever and ever—Elsbeth."

The dream island never materialized, and there wasn't much in the way of vacation, either. But in September, something even better happened: William finally came home. It took longer for the kids to return, but in time Elizebeth had her whole family together again, safe and sound.

———

After the war ended, Elizebeth's work offered no more moments of nail-biting suspense, just endless tedium. She was asked to help record the unit's history. That meant detailing every spy circuit they had tracked and how each kind of code had been broken. The final account came to more than three hundred pages.

She also had to sort through the unit's massive backlog of paperwork. "Reams of 'work-sheets' were destroyed in the desire not to bury completely all posterity under a mammoth paper mausoleum," she later joked. The remaining papers had to be "grouped, described, labeled, indexed, and reverently dispatched to their sealed tombs in the government vaults."

As she worked, Elizebeth had to come to terms with the fact that her own vital role in wartime code breaking was vanishing from sight, too. Bound by oaths of secrecy, she could tell no one what she had accomplished during the war, not even her husband.

Anyway, who would believe her? The FBI had been quick to claim full credit in the newspapers for capturing South America's spies, as well as for breaking the Doll Woman's codes. J. Edgar Hoover had even starred in a short film that celebrated the FBI's great victory against Nazi spies in the United States and South America. The public was impressed, and the FBI came out of the war stronger than ever.

The public knew nothing about the part Elizebeth had played. Within military circles, however, her unit received a measure of praise, and even some awards. They went to her boss, however, not to her. Leonard Jones became the proud possessor of the Legion of Merit, the World War II Victory Medal, the American Campaign Medal, the National Defense Service Medal, the Navy Unit Commendation Ribbon, and the Order of the British Empire.

There were no medals for Elizebeth.

Instead, she was told to vacate her Navy quarters and return to her old office at the Coast Guard. As she left the Navy precincts for the last time, she had to sign "the pledge that was exacted of all departing"—a lifelong vow of secrecy. It banned her from ever discussing the work she had done during the war. She had long since accepted that this was part of the job, that she had entered "a vast dome of silence from which I can never emerge." But it meant that there was no way for her to claim her wartime achievements as her own.

By the time she returned to the Coast Guard, the government was slashing jobs right and left. Never one to flinch from hard facts, she knew it was only a matter of time before they shut down her unit, too. Given the rise of machine code breaking and the general decline in smuggling, the "usefulness of my section was therefore in my opinion ended," she stated. "I wrote the letter abolishing the positions, including my own." When her job ended in September 1946, she was more than ready to move on.

"It was the end of a Period, an Era," she once said of this time. Yet it was also a new beginning. More code-breaking adventures lay ahead of her—and from now on, she would do her best to set the terms.

CODE BREAK

PROCEDURE 40

For over sixty years, the official history of Elizebeth's World War II unit was buried deep in the "sealed tombs" of the government archives. It was a highly classified document, with every page stamped TOP SECRET ULTRA, the code name for Enigma. Almost no one even knew it existed, except for the archivists who looked after it in secret.

In 2008, the *History of Coast Guard Unit #387, 1940–1945* was finally declassified. It is the key that unlocks Elizebeth's secret wartime life. Pore over its 329 oversized pages, and you can learn the details of dozens of spy circuits that she and her team tracked. You can also discover how they broke each type of encryption, from the simplest commercial code systems all the way to Enigma.

It's a weighty tome, in more ways than one. But every so often, you glimpse the pure fun of ciphers and codes. Take this cipher grid, for example:

D	O	N	E	M
S	P	I	A	L
T	B	R	C	F
G	H	K	Q	U
V	W	X	Y	Z

This was the first step of what was known as Procedure 40, a cipher used by spies broadcasting from fascist Spain. It was based on a Spanish proverb: *Donde menos se piensa salta la liebra.* ("Where one least expects it, the hare jumps out." It's a way of saying, "Be alert for the unexpected." Not a bad motto for a code breaker.)

Here's how it worked:

(1) To make the 5 x 5 grid, you wrote out the Spanish keyword, letter by letter. You skipped any letters that had already appeared (so DONDE became DONE). You also skipped the letter J. You then filled in the leftover letters, in order, starting with C and ending with Z.

(2) Next, you took your message and broke it into groups of five. *"Necesito dinero"* ("I need money") would look like this, with an X filling out the last group:

NECES ITODI NEROX

(3) To encipher the first letter of each group, you replaced it with whatever letter was above it in the grid. (The last line is treated as if it were "above" the first line.)

(4) To encipher the second letter, you replaced it with whatever was to the right of it in the grid. (The first column is treated as if it were "right" of the last one.)

(5) To encipher the third letter, you replaced it with whatever was below it in the grid. (The first line is treated as if it were "below" the last one.)

(6) To encipher the fourth letter, you replaced it with whatever was to the left of it in the grid. (The last column is treated as if it were "left" of the first one.)

(7) The last letter of the group stayed the same.

If you followed all these steps, you ended up with:

XMQNS NBPMI XMKDX

This was a clever cipher, yet it was only the first step of Procedure 40. Those other steps were even more challenging.

Complicated though it was, Procedure 40 takes up only four pages of the huge *History of Coast Guard Unit #387*. Covering more than fifty encryption systems, the book testifies to the doggedness and ingenuity of Elizebeth and her team.

CHAPTER TWENTY-NINE

Secrets

A few years after the war ended, Elizebeth made a surprise visit to one of her neighbors—a woman she barely knew, who was ill. "A knock at the door brought me out of bed," the neighbor later wrote, "to find her standing there holding a tray for my dinner . . . roast lamb, roast potatoes and gravy . . . and a bud vase with a yellow rose."

"A good meal will make you feel much better," Elizebeth said.

The neighbor was touched by Elizebeth's quiet generosity. "I am not certain whether it was the food or the rose that made me have a quick recovery from my cold, or just the knowledge that someone cared," she later wrote. "She stayed and talked with me while I ate, then left quietly to return to their own apartment where Mr. Friedman was engrossed in his . . . research."

As far as the neighbor was concerned, it was William who was the distinguished member of the family. It never occurred to her that the woman who had cooked the dinner was also a top code breaker—and Elizebeth saw no reason to tell her.

Elizebeth was not one to brag, but that was not the only reason she kept quiet. After all, if most people saw her as ordinary, it made it easier to keep her secrets. And in the postwar years, Elizebeth had a growing number of secrets to hide.

In her professional life, she was so good at lying low that it is difficult to discover exactly what she was up to during this period. Her employment record is sketchy, even downright mysterious at times. Sometimes there are no clues at all about what she was doing—the equivalent of radio silence.

Elizebeth in the 1950s.

Here's what we know: In November 1946, a mere two months after Elizebeth left the Coast Guard for good, she was snapped up by another Washington agency, the brand-new International

Monetary Fund (IMF). Working as a consultant for $40 a day, Elizebeth created and managed their secure communications system.

It was a crucial job. After World War II, most of the world's financial systems were on their last legs. Even countries that had won the war, such as Britain and France, had crippling debts. Many feared economic collapse. Experts worried that the world was about to fall into yet another Great Depression.

It was the IMF's job to prevent that from happening. To keep the world's economies and trade running smoothly, it oversaw international exchange rates and payment systems. That meant that the IMF dealt with highly confidential data about each country's economy, assets, and currency. When France needed to devalue its currency, for example, they told the IMF in advance. But if speculators got hold of that inside information, they could use it to enrich themselves—and, in the process, they might send France, and possibly the world, into financial free fall.

Elizebeth was the person who protected that information. The IMF no longer has any trace of her in their records, but their secure channels worked well from the start, and that was thanks to her. She stayed at the IMF until August or September 1949.

After that, we reach the most baffling chapter in Elizebeth's working life. The only evidence for it comes from a few memos in her files, showing that she was recruited for another government job in November 1949. But what was the job, exactly? We know that the title was "Chief of the Cryptographic and Physical Security Unit," and that the position was graded G.S. 12—a high level at the time. The starting salary was $6,400, which was more than Elizebeth ever earned at the Coast Guard or the Navy.

From that point on, however, the trail goes cold. Other critical details have been censored in the memos, making it unclear who was offering her the job and exactly what it entailed.

Since the job never appeared in her personnel file, she must have turned it down. But why did she apply, and what made her step back? Did she instead take up work as a consultant elsewhere, as she had at the IMF? Or did she simply stay home? All we know for sure is that she had retired from work completely by the early 1950s. The rest remains obscure.

Of all the secrets Elizebeth kept, however, there is one that stands out from the others. It was both painful and personal, and it had to do with William.

———

Unlike Elizebeth, William was recognized for his wartime achievements, receiving a rare Medal for Merit from President Harry S. Truman in 1946. He then became a top advisor at the military's new joint intelligence agency in 1949. Later, the National Security Agency (NSA) became the nation's secret center for communications intelligence and code breaking, and he played a key role there, too. Yet peacetime brought no permanent relief from his inner war.

As early as 1947, William's tension and insomnia again reached a high pitch. He also experienced a "psychic giddiness" that made it difficult for him to walk a straight line. Seeing a psychiatrist helped at first, but in the winter of 1949–1950, William plunged into a deep depression. That January, he was desperate enough to check into a hospital again. But over the next few weeks, he continued to get worse.

In March, his doctors decided to try a fairly new and radical treatment: electroshock. Known today as electroconvulsive therapy, this involved sending electrical current through the brain and inducing seizures. For William, it worked miracles. Within two weeks, he was himself again. When he left the hospital, he was so happy and elated that "he kissed the nurses good bye."

Even two years later, he was still in good spirits. "I am in better health than I have been for a dozen years in the past," he wrote to a friend in 1952, and "enjoying it immensely." He was so well that Elizebeth left him on his own for three months while she traveled in Europe. She had "an itchy foot," William joked, "and the cash to assuage the itch."

To their distress, however, the cure was not permanent. Later in the 1950s, William slipped into depression again—and not for the last time.

Elizebeth, as always, was his lifeline. To her way of thinking, they were a team, pure and simple, and she gave without counting the cost. Nevertheless, it was a hard time for her.

Part of the strain was that William's ongoing troubles had to be kept quiet. Many of his colleagues knew that he'd had some kind of breakdown during the war, and that he was still somewhat fragile, but they didn't know much more than that. For William and Elizebeth, full disclosure was risky. His job was on the line, and so were his influence and the income they both depended on. Elizebeth trusted only a few close friends with the bleak truth.

Yet even if Elizebeth shied away from disclosure, she refused to become isolated. She kept up with old friends, and she also made plenty of new ones, some decades younger than she was. She was good at drawing people out. "I doubt that she ever was bored," one friend marveled, "she had such interest in everyone and the world about her."

Elizebeth also found comfort in her kitchen. Now that she had more time on her hands, she enjoyed making elaborate foreign dishes. Like code breaking, it was a pursuit that required patience, precision, and attention to detail, and she was good at it. When

William was well, they loved throwing dinner parties that show-cased her talents. On bad days, cooking allowed her to focus on something besides her problems.

She also continued to take an interest in progressive politics. In 1947, she warned of the dangers of atomic warfare and campaigned for global efforts to ban nuclear weapons. In 1951, during a keynote speech about code breaking and the rumrunner years, she spoke up about the general problem of addiction. She didn't think that either banning or legalizing drugs was a good response. Instead, she said that "your duty and my duty . . . is to see that every young person has security and a healthy environment." She wanted every child to be "made to feel wanted and respected as a human being, no matter what his race, creed or color."

Elizebeth also made time for another absorbing pursuit—writing a book.

As a young woman, Elizebeth had dreamed of being a writer. Now she was determined to fulfill that dream. The project she had in mind was a book about Shakespeare and ciphers, like the one she had started during World War I. And Riverbank would be part of the story.

To her delight, William wanted to work on the book with her. For decades, they had been required to keep their professional secrets locked away from each other. Now, at long last, they had a project they could share.

It was a joyful collaboration, and it reshaped their lives. At the end of 1952, they bought a run-down house on Capitol Hill, chiefly because it was a short walk to the Library of Congress and the Folger Shakespeare Library. The house was "a jewel," a friend recalled, "but made so by her." Elizebeth threw herself into its restoration, "finding lights/flooring/doors/you name it." It became their sanctuary, their "cherished home."

Up on the second floor, they installed their own private library. Assembled over many years, it was their most precious possession. Elizebeth and William guarded its resources carefully. A treasure trove of materials on cryptography, the library included both rare books and modern photocopies. The Friedmans also housed some of their own papers in the library, as well as various cipher machines and coding devices. No item could be removed without being signed out, not even by their own children.

To outsiders, the library must have seemed a curious hodgepodge. It had a huge range, everything from serious academic tomes to a "Sky King Spy Detecto Writer," found in a box of breakfast cereal. Experts knew, however, that it was one of the finest private cryptology collections in the country.

Elizebeth and William in their library, with some of their coding devices.

This library became the base camp for their new Shakespeare project. Determined to do the job thoroughly, they covered every angle of the problem. Elizebeth, for instance, might go to the Folger Library to research early printing presses. Meanwhile, William took photographs of old folios and enlarged them. Then, just as they had done during the first heady days of their courtship at Riverbank, they both discussed what they saw in Shakespeare's work—and what they didn't see.

In 1954, they learned that the Folger Library was holding a contest for the best unpublished manuscript about Shakespeare. The winner would get a whopping $1000 prize. Although the deadline was close, they raced to meet it. They finished their thousand-page treatise just in time—and it won the prize.

They celebrated, but disaster followed. On the same Sunday that the newspapers proclaimed their surprise success, William had a heart attack. "I stood in the front hall," Elizebeth wrote, "and watched my husband being carried on a hospital cot out the door."

William survived, but he spent three months in the hospital. Even then, his heart remained weak, and he had to retire early from his top-secret job at the NSA. Knowing how much this upset him, Elizebeth was glad to receive an offer from Cambridge University Press for their Shakespeare manuscript. The hitch? The editor wanted them to cut two-thirds of it. A tall order, but they got down to work.

It was hard to know what to leave out, but Riverbank stayed in the book. Fabyan and Gallup had both died

William and Elizebeth at a book party.

in the 1930s, so there was no reason not to be honest about their failures, but the Friedmans were inclined to be generous, too. In most senses, Riverbank's cipher project had been a waste of time, yet it had yielded two great results: It had brought the two of them together, and it had led them to their life's work.

In 1957, their book, *The Shakespearean Ciphers Examined*, came out to great acclaim. Reviewers praised the "cool, surgical, irrefutable analyses of two of the world's leading cryptologists." With insight and humor, Elizebeth and William had proved, once and for all, that Shakespeare's plays contained no ciphers or codes.

Elizebeth and William were cheered by the book's reception. They were profiled in the *New Yorker,* and they clipped reviews and answered enthusiastic letters. "I've always bragged about you two as being the 'greatest pair of brains ever wedded in holy matrimony,'" an old Army friend wrote after reading the book, "and I never was wrong."

Elizebeth and William started to consider what other books they might write together. For years, they had both been fascinated by the Mayan glyphs, the script of the ancient Maya of Mesoamerica. Plenty of other experts were also intrigued by the potent drawings and had tried to decipher them, without success. Now Elizebeth and William hoped to have a crack at them, too.

There were other code-breaking mysteries that called to them as well. One was the enigmatic Voynich Manuscript, written in a language no one could read. Then there were the Beale ciphers, which claimed to lead to a lost treasure in Virginia. The Friedmans even considered writing a history of cryptography itself.

They were in their sixties, but in many ways the world was opening up for them. For years, they had been able to say next to nothing about cryptology in public. Now that they were retired, they were free. It was a relief to know they could finally write books and appear in newspapers without angering security-minded officials.

Or could they?

It turned out that not everyone was happy with their newfound fame. Already, in certain circles, discreet alarm bells were ringing. Although Elizebeth and William did not know it, their lives were about to be turned upside down.

CHAPTER THIRTY

The Raid

On December 30, 1958, a truck lumbered to a stop outside Elizabeth and William's Washington row house. Several men hopped out and rapped the elephant-head knocker at the front door. They were on a mission for the National Security Agency—the hush-hush government intelligence agency where William had worked before his retirement, and which he still sometimes served.

The NSA's target? Elizabeth and William's personal library.

Elizabeth and William knew the men were coming, and they knew they had to answer the door. Anything else would only turn the NSA further against them, and they couldn't afford to do that.

In retirement, William had completed secret missions for the NSA, but even so, his ties with the agency had become fraught. Although he was highly valued by the NSA's first director, William had little common ground with the blunt general who succeeded him in 1956. He did not get on well with the agency's new deputy director, either.

The tensions grew when the Department of Defense tightened security after several spy scandals. Under the new rules, access to information about code breaking became more restricted. Some documents that had been made public were classified all over again. The NSA's new director was in favor of the new policy, taking the hard line that "All official cryptanalysis is a type of activity that should be protected no matter how old it has become." To William, that seemed like overreach.

As William saw it, many of the newly restricted documents had only historic value. They gave no vital secrets away. If people wanted to learn about old codes and ciphers, why stop them? But the NSA was not swayed by this. Instead, its top officials insisted in 1958 that William turn over any such documents in his possession—even the ones that he himself had written.

At first, William stalled. Most of the papers dealt "with the history of cryptography and should belong to the American people," he argued. In fact, copies of some of them were available at the Library of Congress—and to William, that was just how it should be. Why should he surrender them?

Unmoved, the NSA decided to take back the documents anyway. Which was why the truck was parked by the Friedmans' house that December morning, and why the men were knocking at their door.

After William and Elizebeth let them in, the men went up to the library—the most treasured room in the Friedmans' house. They seized William's government-issue safe and the materials inside it. They took books, manuals, and index cards, many of them dealing with old ciphers from World War I and the 1920s. They even confiscated letters that William had written, some dating back to the Riverbank years.

Elizebeth and William did not dare protest. But they were outraged.

Only a small fraction of their library was carted away, about six boxes of materials in all. The rest they were allowed to keep. But that did not lessen the shock of having their books, papers, and letters seized by the government.

As a power grab, the raid startled even some of the higher-ups at the NSA. Rumors spread at their headquarters. According to one story, William "went berserk" when the men turned up. He was said to have thrown the documents at them.

The truth was quieter and sadder. "He was obviously upset by the action being taken," said Donald Coffey, one of the NSA men who carried out the job. Yet to Coffey it was clear that William was too much of "a gentleman" to shout or lash out.

As for Elizebeth, Coffey remembered that she was "a very nice lady." She did, however, "let it be known, I think, that she was unhappy with this decision because it made her husband unhappy. And she thought, especially in the view of his contributions, that this was a wrong decision to have been made."

"Wrong" was an understatement. Elizebeth was livid about the raid. She told a later director of the NSA that it was a "search-and-seizure act," a violation of their rights under the Constitution. More than a decade later, she told a confidant that the raid "was what one might have expected of Nazi Germany, but not of the United States."

The raid forced both Elizebeth and William to ask painful questions about the tensions between security and freedom, and to reconsider the path their country was now on.

Almost as long as they had been code breakers, Elizebeth and William had been concerned about the impact of secrecy on democracy. They knew, none better, that the nation's safety depended on keeping some things under wraps. Yet they were also aware that secrecy could be misused. What if the government hid its wrongdoings? What if it pursued a hidden agenda against the wishes of the people? What if it secretly hounded its political opponents?

Long before the NSA came after their library, Elizebeth and William knew that these were not theoretical questions. Experience had taught them that their own government could not always be trusted. In the 1920s, during the Teapot Dome scandal, William had helped unmask the corruption in President Harding's cabinet. Later, Elizebeth had seen firsthand how the FBI played fast and loose with the truth.

In the 1950s, they both watched the rise of Senator Joseph McCarthy with dismay. They abhorred McCarthy's witch hunts for communists and his attacks on civil liberties. In their eyes, he was a danger to democracy—"a man who flouted the authority of the Senate, who overrode the Constitution while his followers cheered."

Although Elizebeth didn't know it, William had other reasons for mistrust. During his long career as a code breaker, he had been privy to many secrets. As early as the 1930s, for example, his unit covertly read the telegrams of private citizens. He had always had mixed feelings about this, but he had come to accept it as the price of keeping his country safe. But at the NSA, he had seen secrecy running rampant, and it troubled him.

Secrecy is a form of power, and power corrupts. That was a lesson

William already knew. But it seemed to him that the NSA was ignoring it.

At the time, hardly any Americans knew about the NSA. Insiders joked that its initials stood for "No Such Agency." Yet behind the scenes, the NSA was quietly growing more and more powerful. It had nothing like the surveillance capability it has today, but its networks were widening, and it was gathering large amounts of intelligence with little democratic oversight. It also resorted to covert action when it thought this was justified—and during the Cold War, justification was easy to find.

The agency's initials were also said to stand for "Never Say Anything." It was tough on security leaks and wary of potential whistleblowers. Employees and even ex-employees were expected to keep a low public profile. But for William, this was a challenge. Reporters had started calling him the Army's code-breaking genius in the 1920s. Although he had gone dark after that, he was later identified in congressional hearings as the man who broke Purple. He was news.

"He was always being approached," a colleague remembered. "When people thought about cryptography, Pearl Harbor or anything else, he was the man that a lot of the government agencies or . . . the newspapers thought about." To many people, William *was* the NSA—or at least the closest the agency had to a semipublic face. And although he always refused to discuss secret matters, even his refusals could attract attention, further angering the NSA.

The NSA worried about William in part because few people knew as many of their secrets as he did. Even after his official retirement in 1955, the NSA had continued to send him on covert missions to Europe. Despite his fragile physical and mental health, William still had an unequaled breadth of cryptographic experience, as well as close and long-standing friendships with key people in European intelligence circles. Both were vital for the work the NSA had in mind.

William was barred from telling Elizebeth anything about these missions. For her, the European trips were simply pleasure jaunts, during which her husband took the chance to catch up with old friends. For William, they were high-stakes, high-stress encounters. The NSA had instructed him to patch up fraying relations with Britain's intelligence community—and also to lay the groundwork for spying on America's enemies, as well as some of its closest friends.

William did what was asked of him, but he knew the work raised ethical issues. When was it okay to eavesdrop? What did you owe your allies? If you were protecting your country, did the end always justify the means?

William and Elizebeth in Sweden, 1957—a relaxing trip for Elizebeth, a challenging mission for William.

These questions had troubled William for much of his career. Often he had felt torn by a tug-of-war between duty and honor—a tension, he thought, that might account for "a good portion of my psychic difficulties over the years." But his work with the NSA in the mid-1950s brought his concerns to the fore, and the ethics of secrecy started to consume him. He soon would start to ask whether "the collection of secret intelligence" could be reconciled "with the democratic ideals of a free and open society."

For the NSA, a man who asked questions like that was a problem. Increasingly, the higher-ups at the agency came to see William as a loose cannon. After using him for one last, vital mission, they clamped down on him. The library raid was part of that clampdown, and to the NSA it seemed justified.

The NSA insisted—then and always—that the raid was merely a routine matter, but Elizebeth and William believed it had been intended to humiliate and intimidate. How else could they explain the NSA not trusting them with their own correspondence, or with documents available at the Library of Congress?

Whatever the truth of the matter, the raid was a turning point for Elizebeth and William—and the start of a downward spiral.

CHAPTER THIRTY-ONE

Fallout

I f William and Elizebeth saw the library raid as a humilia-
tion, it was not the only one. William was soon required to
surrender additional documents to the NSA, and his talks and
lectures were censored. When he asked for permission to publish articles about the early history of code breaking, the NSA
forbade him to do any such thing. He was not even allowed to
republish an article about literary ciphers in Edgar Allan Poe's
nineteenth-century short story "The Gold-Bug." In 1960, when
the NSA restricted his access to top-secret materials, William
was crushed.

They were "clamping down on *every* thing that he did,"
Elizebeth later wrote. Although William tried to find acceptable
projects, he could never predict what the NSA might censor. In
1962, for instance, when he was asked to write a basic book for
teenagers about cryptography, he had trouble getting clearance:

They seem to think that this whole subject is taboo, a private
preserve, and poachers thereon will do so at their peril. And they
have the laws and the means to enforce their views. . . . I am sure
that their attitude is indefensible, but I do not wish to jeopardize
my liberty in proving that it is.

Over the years, the uncertainties wore him down. "Even at this
moment, I do not know what they regard as 'classified,'" William
confided to a close friend in 1966. "They—the 'authorities'—
change their minds from time to time. And I just do not have the
strength to fight so I am 'left up in the air.'"

Unable to guess what the NSA would accept, and not wanting
further trouble, Elizebeth and William abandoned their plans to
write more books together. Even so, they lived with the fear that
the NSA might raid them again.

What most chipped away at their happiness, however, was the
way the conflict with the NSA affected William's health. Conclud-
ing that a "secrecy virus" had taken over the NSA, William saw
no chance of recovering the position of respect and trust he had
once enjoyed. The rapid fall from grace unmoored him. Brooding,
he became convinced, at times, that "the NSA considers me their
greatest security risk." In secret notes written only for himself, he
confessed that he found the "feeling of being 'has-been' unendur-
able," and that he had "suicidal thoughts."

Soon he had to be hospitalized again. This time, however, he
was judged too frail for doctors to apply electric currents to his
brain. In the absence of effective treatment, his recovery was ach-
ingly slow—and soon followed by another depression.

He and Elizebeth had talked about moving to Europe, where
they would be farther away from the NSA. They had even planned

to bring their library with them. But now William no longer had the health to travel, and he worried that such plans would displease the NSA, anyway. Instead, they stayed home, right in the heart of Washington.

For Elizebeth, as well as for William, these were hard years. The winters were especially bleak. William's depression was always worst then, and he sometimes drank too much and grew "irritable" with Elizebeth. This was so out of character that she went to see his doctor about it, but there was no real help on offer.

Their finances were a constant worry, too. As inflation ate away at their modest government pensions, Elizebeth spent long hours going over their checkbooks, bank records, and tax forms. It upset her that they had served their country for most of their working lives, and yet now they had to fear for their future. In 1967, she wrote:

> *I used to say and meant it, when in the old days friends yipped about taxes, "Now look,* some*body has to pay taxes, and I am glad to pay my share." Well, no more. Not when oil well millionaires and timberlands owners and god-knows-who-else get away with murder and pay nothing.*

William and Elizebeth were also worried about their daughter, Barbara, who was locked in a brutal divorce and custody battle in the early 1960s.

Elizebeth helped in every way she could, but her own health was not good. She had serious bouts of shingles and diverticulitis, and she became painfully thin. At times, she was overwhelmed by all that both William and Barbara needed from her.

Yet there were good days, too. In the summers, when William

usually felt best, they relaxed in lawn chairs on the brick patio. Their children came to visit, and there were now grandchildren to enjoy. Old friends liked to drop by as well.

Now and then, they dressed up for these gatherings and took photos. Leaning on his cane, William would sport a bow tie and a natty black beret. Elizabeth wore tailored dresses, her salt-and-pepper hair softly curling.

At one end of the garden, William had planted a Talisman rose. Now it bloomed for each anniversary, cascading in a shower of pink and gold. And when the garden palled, Elizabeth and William had another retreat to sustain them—their library.

———

For the Friedmans, their library was a place of solace, an escape from a world that was not always kind. It was also their greatest treasure, in more ways than one. In 1968, its many books, pamphlets, and cryptographic curiosities were valued at $49,500—an amount worth at least $370,000 today.

What would happen to their collection when they were gone? For a long time, William hoped to build a museum to house it. But as his health worsened, they lowered their sights, planning instead to leave it to the Library of Congress. By the 1960s, however, they were having second thoughts. On a visit there, Elizabeth was shocked to find an important collection of papers "scattered higgledy-piggledy over those iron shelves. . . . I went home and told my husband. We sort of cried on each other's shoulders."

Wherever their collection went, they wanted it to be kept together in good condition. So they struck the Library of Congress off their list. But now where could they turn?

The NSA's newest director was eager to offer their collection a home. But his colleagues told him that William would never agree. "No way," they said. "Friedman doesn't like NSA."

It was an oversimplification, but not much of one. The Friedmans were not about to trust their library to the same agency that had ransacked it. Besides, they wanted their collection in a place where ordinary citizens could consult it. If they left it to the NSA, it would be locked away, out of reach.

William had always taken the lead in building the collection. Now he took the lead in finding a caretaker for it. In 1966, he settled on a surprise choice: the Marshall Library in Lexington, Virginia.

Small, new, and not well known, the Marshall Library was three hours from Washington, so it was not easy for Elizebeth and William to visit. But it had been founded by a man they both admired—General George C. Marshall—and it had the policies they needed. Open to the public, the Marshall Library was also being certified for the storage of classified documents. That meant that even if some of William's papers were later reclassified, the collection could be kept together.

William handled the terms of the transfer, and legally the gift was in his name only. In reality, however, the gift was a joint one. The collection would later include Elizebeth's books and papers as well as his, and the transfer had her full backing.

The one hitch? The Marshall Library wanted them to catalogue the collection before they turned it over. It was a reasonable request, but an overwhelming one, too. By late 1966, Elizebeth and William were spending several hours a day indexing their library, at least when they were well enough. In 1967, a typist from the Marshall Library started coming in to help them once a week.

It wasn't enough. Their book collection was vast, ranging from their college textbooks to the latest scholarship on cryptography.

Their personal papers were even harder to collate. And William's health was going further downhill.

When the end came, it was swift. Shortly after midnight on November 2, 1969, William's heart stopped, and Elizebeth could not revive him.

Later that night, still in shock, she picked up her daybook and wrote: "My beloved died at 12:15." Perhaps the writing steadied her. Perhaps it just made her loss more unbearable. Like an open code, the brief words hid a world of grief within them.

Within hours, friends and family rallied around her. Soon hundreds of letters, telegrams, and cards poured in. Elizebeth was touched to see that "my beloved Bill, or Billy as you like, was known, admired, and loved practically all over the world." She kept her favorite cards, including a note from historical novelist Herman Wouk. "His effect on world history was incalculable, greater than that of kings & captains," Wouk wrote. "Yet what a modest man!"

The Army saw to it that William was buried in Arlington National Cemetery with full military honors. Elizebeth was glad to see her husband recognized in this way, but she remained angry about how he had been treated in his last years. She also feared that the full breadth of his achievements might never be publicly acknowledged, due to government secrecy. She wanted the record to be set straight so that William would be remembered for generations to come.

She was seventy-seven, but her last important battle was still in front of her. Within a few weeks, she was back at her desk, working to save her husband's legacy. In the process, she would save her own as well.

She started with their library.

CODE BREAK

THE LAST WORD

William and Elizebeth's tombstone.

Although the Army was in charge of William's funeral, Elizebeth had to decide what should be put on his tombstone. She sketched out the design on graph paper, and the stonecutter went to work. Carved into the top are the flags of the Signal Corps, the branch of the Army that William had served. Beneath that came his name, rank, and years of birth and death.

It was simple and fitting, but there was more. After leaving a long gap so that her own name could be added later,

Elizebeth put one more line: KNOWLEDGE IS POWER. As long as she had known William, it had been one of his favorite sayings.

If you visit the grave, you might notice something curious about the lettering of that last line. Some letters have serifs on them. Others do not. The arrangement is roughly like this:

KNOWLEDGE IS POWER

If you divide those letters into groups of five and throw away the leftover R at the end, the pattern looks like Bacon's cipher. In this case, the sans-serifs are Type "a." (If you guessed the sans-serifs were Type "b" and you tried to solve it that way, you would see combinations like **bbaba**, which don't exist in Bacon's cipher. That would tell you to try it the other way.)

The pattern here is **babaa / aabab / aabab**. These are William's initials: WFF.

The lettering was no accident. As Elizebeth later explained, "Since WFF had used that phrase so much, I decided (along with his associates and our son and daughter) to have the message 'WFF' carved thereon."

It was a secret message—the perfect memorial for a code breaker.

CHAPTER THIRTY-TWO

The Library

W hen William died, the Friedmans were still cataloguing their library collection. Before it could go to the Marshall Library, everything had to be indexed. Elizebeth committed herself to seeing the job through.

"It is now 2½ months since my beloved so suddenly departed this life," she wrote to family and friends in late January 1970.

"I have been working very steadily and hard—some days 8 to 10 hours a day— right here at his desk in our library." She made notes about books they had bought together and puzzles they had shared. Now and then she had help, but often she worked alone.

Elizebeth at William's desk.

Glancing down at William's desk, she could see snapshots arranged under the glass. John as a solemn toddler. Barbara dancing under blossoms. William in his dapper bow ties. Elizebeth herself gazing up at the sky.

Among the photographs was a postcard of the *Rokeby Venus,* her face looking uncannily like Elizebeth's. There was also a small card in Elizebeth's handwriting, sent to William in 1936:

> *"Friend of my soul, forever true,*
> *What do we care for flying years [. . .] ?"*
> *To my sweeter-than-ever Lover*
> > *Your*
> > *Elsbeth*

The years flew by no longer. For Elizebeth, the road ahead seemed long and empty. "Washington . . . is anything but a happy place for me to be right now," she wrote. She wanted to sell the house and go. Instead she stayed put and kept indexing the collection, determined to preserve William's place in history.

———

It took Elizebeth about a year to get the books and papers ready for the Marshall Library. She was told that the "Government" would ensure that they were transported there safely. Behind her back, the NSA secretly took charge, overseeing the pickup and delivery of the collection on December 17, 1970.

Perhaps Elizebeth suspected something was up, because she trailed the movers down the highway in her ailing Plymouth. It was a long trip for her, but she knew that the collection was valuable, and she wanted to ensure that it reached Lexington without any trouble. After her seventy-four cartons of material were delivered, she went home.

Perhaps her presence made the NSA hold back from examining the collection that day. But the next month, before most of the boxes had even been opened, NSA agents went to the Marshall Library to trawl through the Friedmans' papers. At some point, either then or later, the agency quietly removed items from the collection. The NSA also took the index cards linked to them. Roughly two hundred cards disappeared.

Elizebeth never protested because she never knew it happened. But she remained incensed by the NSA's 1958 raid, and she continued to press for the government to return the books and papers it had taken then. The NSA ignored her.

It took more than forty years for the NSA to loosen its grip. In 2015, the agency declassified over fifty thousand pages of Friedman materials, including some of the items taken from the Friedmans' library. Yet even then, there were limits. Some lines were inked over, and a small number of Friedman documents remained secret in full. More than half a century after William's death, those documents are still judged too sensitive for release.

During the early 1970s, Elizebeth continued to worry that William might be forgotten. To keep this from happening, she often made the long drive down to the Marshall Library. She spent many hours helping to get their papers and books in order, and her devotion to William's memory impressed the community there.

As Elizebeth worked with the collection, she kept adding notes to it. Her comments could be terse, and sometimes funny. A lively letter from a friend described William as "the epitome of the dapper and dangerous man." Elizebeth set down her verdict in shaky green ink: "Save this to read over when I get the blahs."

In the 1970s, the NSA was reluctant to say much about William in public, but it did at least recognize him within its own circles. It named its main auditorium after William in 1975, complete with a bronze sculpture of his head. Delighted to see him honored, Elizebeth attended the dedication ceremony. It pleased her that it took place on their wedding anniversary.

During these same years, Elizebeth searched for a biographer to write the story of William's life. The hunt was a long one. Code breaking, it turned out, was not everyone's cup of tea. Dismayed, Elizebeth noted that some writers were "*afraid* of the technicality of the subject."

An English writer, Ronald Clark, finally took the job, but he found it hard to write about a man with so many secrets. To make the work easier, Elizebeth granted Clark exclusive access to the records in the Marshall Library. She also agreed to be interviewed, and she enlisted the help of her children. Barbara took time out from her work as a labor activist to set down her memories. So did John, who was building a career for himself in film production.

Clark's book, *The Man Who Broke Purple,* disappointed them all. Elizebeth did not see "the man I knew and loved" in its pages. She comforted herself that at least it made William better known to the public.

Looking for other ways to keep William's name alive, Elizebeth recorded interviews with the Marshall Library and NSA historians. Like the men on her doorstep in the 1920s, some interviewers started with a focus on William, only to become interested in Elizebeth. Although Elizebeth was happy to put William front and center, people increasingly wanted to talk about her own career.

British producers from the BBC came calling, and she appeared on television, sharing tales from her rumrunner days.

Just before her eightieth birthday, a reporter from the *Houston Chronicle* visited. She found Elizebeth "lounging in a turquoise silk robe from China, a gift from her husband in 1928." Tiny and lively, Elizebeth spoke of the days when code breaking could be done with pencil and paper. Although she knew that computers were now essential, she had never become reconciled to them. "Everything is so damn big today," she told the reporter. "It's a curse. The problem with machines is that nobody ever gets the thrill of seeing a message come out."

It was a pleasure to remember the old days, in part because the current ones were hard. The Friedmans' valuable collection had gone to the Marshall Library as a gift, and Elizebeth had to pinch pennies. She fretted about inflation, and the stock market crash of 1974 made her "shake and despair."

According to her youngest grandson, Elizebeth still had "a voice like a lion." Yet the rest of her was fading. Her last days were spent in a nursing home near her son in New Jersey.

On October 31, 1980, when she was eighty-eight, Elizebeth's heart gave up. Her last words were "love you."

––––––––

Elizebeth's ashes were buried in William's grave. Her name was added to the stone:

BELOVED WIFE
ELIZEBETH SMITH FRIEDMAN
1892 . . . 1980

She had seen no need for a funeral ceremony. But on November 5, exactly eleven years to the day after William's funeral, a small crowd of family and friends gathered for a memorial service.

Together, they celebrated Elizebeth. They remembered her favorite poems. They spoke of how she had loved her family. They honored what she had accomplished.

"A dynamo in low heels" was how one old friend described her. Having worked in intelligence himself, he marveled at the thought of this "wispy, gentle, self-effacing woman knocking off, one by one, some of the nastiest pieces of business then existing." What's more, she had seen off these "Calibans of brute strength, enormous bankrolls and stupendous power" using only "Nature's greatest resource, a radiant intellect."

It was a remarkable story. And yet it nearly died with her.

———

Elizebeth's family wanted the world to know about her. They always hoped that someone would write her biography, but for years nothing quite came together. Part of the problem was that much of her work was secret, and some of it was still hidden in classified files. As a result, she soon was all but forgotten, except by those who had known her best.

Even so, her legacy was powerful. Through her example and efforts, she already had opened up opportunities for other women. In doing so, she forged a path for the female code breakers who came after her.

One woman who followed Elizebeth's lead was Wilma Zimmerman Davis. Born twenty years after Elizebeth, Davis had studied math in West Virginia during the Great Depression, then struggled to find a job that used her talents. In the mid-1930s, she spotted an article about the Friedmans in the Sunday paper, covering Elizebeth's Coast Guard work in detail. Amazed, Davis drank in every word.

Until then, the idea of being a code breaker had never occurred to Davis, but afterward she signed up for a course in the subject. When she completed it, William Friedman recruited her for his Army unit in the late 1930s. Davis cracked Italian, Japanese, Chinese, and Russian ciphers during World War II. Later, she served in the NSA, working on Russian intercepts. Her career as a code breaker spanned more than three decades—and it all started because of Elizebeth.

Davis was part of a wave of women who broke codes in the late 1930s and 1940s. To win World War II, the United States needed to recruit thousands of new code breakers, and the majority of the hires were female—about eleven thousand women in all. Often called "Code Girls," these women were critical to Allied victory, and some remained in the job long after the war. One was Juanita Moody, who monitored Cuba for the NSA during the 1962 Missile Crisis. Another was Gene Grabeel, who broke Soviet messages during the Cold War. Yet another was Ann Caracristi, who became the first female deputy of the NSA.

A few of these lifelong female code breakers became friendly with Elizebeth. To others, she was simply a legend—only dimly remembered but still discussed. Yet as more and more women followed in Elizebeth's footsteps, taking jobs in intelligence, technical analysis, and law enforcement, she began to be remembered more often. Remembrance led to research, and to the recovery of buried secrets.

Though long gone, Elizebeth herself helped unlock some of these secrets. Needled by the way the FBI had grabbed credit for her work, she had wanted the real story to be documented somewhere.

Barred from telling the full truth, she instead left clues in the massive catalogue of books and papers she gave to the Marshall Library. On a handful of index cards related to the FBI, she jotted short notes warning that the agency's claims were exaggerated and that the Coast Guard and the Treasury knew the truth. She added that some of what the public knew about the Doll Woman case was "Not True." Her notes were coded signals that were designed to lead researchers deeper into her own files, where they could start to piece together what had really happened. But the signals needed the right receiver, and it took years before they finally were spotted by historian Colonel Rose Mary Sheldon.

When more government records were declassified, they confirmed that Elizebeth had played a major role in pursuing Nazi spies. The true scope of her achievements was finally becoming visible.

At long last, she started to receive her due. In the 1990s, the NSA gave her a place in their Cryptologic Hall of Honor. Soon her name began to appear on government buildings. In 2014, a federal intelligence award was named for her. People began to write books and articles about her. In 2019, the United States Senate passed a resolution in her honor.

Admired as a pathbreaker, Elizebeth is now regarded as a role model—a woman who excelled in a technical field through her courage, smarts, and grit. The young woman who wanted "to 'achieve'" would have been delighted.

Yet if Elizebeth always hoped her story would be told someday, she wanted the account to be an honest one. "Hero worship," she once wrote, "has . . . never been something I enjoyed when directed at me personally." She wanted her record to reflect not only her triumphs, but also her hidden struggles. She made that kind of story possible with the library that she and William left behind.

In 1916, Elizebeth's adventures in code breaking began in the Newberry Library, with a phone call to an oddball millionaire. Now, more than a century later, another library ensures that those adventures can be remembered as she lived them.

At the Marshall Library, her papers are held in twenty-two gray archival boxes. They are the code that Elizebeth left behind her—the cryptic dots and dashes of her life. If you pierce their mysteries, you start to uncover the truth of who she was.

April 22, 1913.

To be born a Smith; to under-go all the worn-out jokes and mirth-less hoaxes perpetrated over that name; to see the senseless smile and the empty remarks *the same forth* every time one must be introduced to a stranger; to have it flung in one's face that one's name is "so common so easily remembered, don't you know": these were my heritage. "Smith"! Worse still, plain "Miss Smith!" Was there ever phrase more pregnant with do-littleness, insignificance and ordinariness, than plain "Miss Smith"? To my fancy, disliking as I do

A page from Elizebeth's diary.

Open the boxes, and you see Elizebeth at her most confident and her most vulnerable. Writing a love letter. Receiving a telegram. Confronting her boss. Holding a child. Testifying at a trial. Scribbling in her diary.

Turn the pages of that diary, and her inky scrawl rewinds the clock, to a time when her story is just starting. As her words spill across the page, she senses that she stands on the brink of something great. "Is it possible I am to have them, after all," she writes—"Youth, and Love, and Life?"

A note flutters between two pages of the diary, as it once fluttered down to her: "My dearest—I sit here studying your features. You are perfectly beautiful!!"

"The goal is set," Elizebeth writes. "Will we win?"

In the hush of the library, she reveals her hidden story.

ACKNOWLEDGMENTS

When I was nine, my family moved into an old house that was full of secrets. Only one other family had ever lived in it, and they left a lot behind. Wheatback pennies hid between the floorboards. Dusty amber bottles lurked in the root cellar. A broken china doll lay buried in the garden. What intrigued me most, though, were the old magazines in the attic.

I was the kind of kid who read whatever I could get my hands on, including all six sides of the cereal box, so I read those magazines cover to cover. My favorites were the *Reader's Digest*s from the 1930s and 1940s. As rain beat down on the old slates above me, I paged through them. And when I reached the September 1937 issue, I made the acquaintance of "The Key Woman of the T-Men," Elizebeth Smith Friedman.

Even back then, she amazed me. As I've uncovered more of her story, I've only become more impressed.

Libraries and librarians were important in Elizebeth's life, and they are in mine, too. Without them, I could not have written this book. I owe an especially profound debt to Paul Barron, Jeffrey

Kozak, and Melissa Davis, the librarians at the George C. Marshall Foundation, where Elizabeth's papers are kept. Their generosity was and is astounding. Paul Barron let me pore through the photo files, took me to lunch at the VMI canteen, and kept the archive open late so that I could get to everything. When Covid-19 lockdowns made it impossible for me to return, Melissa Davis cheerfully answered my emails and tracked down documents and photos for me. I can say for certain that the Friedmans picked the right library. Elizabeth's records are in excellent hands.

Many other librarians deserve my thanks, too. I'm grateful to the Manuscripts and Archives Division at the New York Public Library, including Kyle Triplett and Meredith Mann, who made sure I had everything I needed during my visit there. My thanks also go to the staffs of the Bodleian Library and the Vere Harmsworth Library at the Rothermere American Institute, and to Paul Johnson of the National Archives Image Library in the UK. I also tip my hat to Colonel Rose Mary Sheldon, who wrote the invaluable annotated guide to William Friedman's collection at the Marshall Library.

The NSA deserves a round of applause for making it so easy to access many Friedman papers and other materials online. So does Jason Fagone, author of an earlier biography of Elizabeth, who has generously shared many original documents at archive.org. The Marshall Library and the UK National Archives have also made many items available online. These resources have been a great gift to researchers like me, especially during the pandemic.

Melba Edwards knows Elizabeth's birthplace as few others do, and I thank her for sharing local knowledge, documents, and photos with me. Chris Atchison, Elizabeth's grandson, and Steve Thomas, her great-nephew, kindly shared family stories. Barbara M. Lewandrowski, Director of Public Affairs at Arlington

National Cemetery, answered questions about Elizebeth's burial. Paul Reuvers of the Crypto Museum helped with details about Abwehr Enigma.

I'm grateful to Jeremy Fleming for inviting me to speak at GCHQ and to the people there who gave me insights into the operations of a modern-day signals intelligence agency. I would especially like to thank GCHQ historian Tony Comer, not only for giving me a tour of the museum there, but for advising me on the byzantine details of the agencies overseeing clandestine communications in WWII. He also deserves thanks for introducing me to former NSA historian Betsy Rohaly Smoot, who welcomed me into the fold of cryptologic history and helped with questions I had about one of Elizebeth's better-kept secrets. Betsy was also kind enough to ask Joseph Frechette of INSCOM and David Sherman and David Hatch, her former colleagues, to weigh in on those questions. Another of Elizebeth's biographers, Gregg Smith, responded to a query on the same issue. I am grateful to them all.

I had just finished the first draft of this book when Hilary Steinman asked if I would talk with her about the Friedmans for an *American Experience* documentary. I'm glad I said yes, because the many hours I spent with her and Chana Gazit were a delight. My thanks to them both and to Sarah Keeling, Richard Pinches, and the entire team at Meadows Farm Studios, who made our filming day run so smoothly (wasps notwithstanding).

My agent, Sara Crowe, believed in this project from the beginning and through all its drafts. I'm grateful for her support and that of the rest of the amazing Pippin team.

It's a pleasure to work with an editor as warm and welcoming as Lee Wade. Her perceptive questions helped me crack the puzzle of how to tell this story. I'm grateful as well to Andrea Lau, Alison Kolani, Charlotte Roos, Jennifer Baker, Renni Johnson, Nancee

Adams, and the many other people at Random House who have worked on this book.

Heartfelt thanks to Jenny Turner and Jenka Sokol, two wonderful historians and friends who read the entire draft with great care. Their enthusiastic comments and thoughtful criticism helped me find my bearings. I'm also indebted to Jenny for listening to me talk about this book on countless Skype calls, and for constantly cheering me on. I'm grateful to my parents, Barbara and Crispin Butler, who read a late draft for me, and to Tori Turner, who commented on a number of chapters. I owe a lifetime of chocolate chip cookies to David Greenfield, who recovered and restored images that seemed beyond saving.

My thanks to everyone who offered help and support in other ways, particularly Carolyn Colton, Kathi Fisler, Karl Galle, Charlotte Guillain, Emma Huxter, Hannah Nyala, Kit Sturtevant, Laurel Turner, Annika Vanlandingham, Katia Vanlandingham, Nancy Werlin, and the Oxford Crit Group. I'm grateful as well to the Oxford Center for Life Writing, especially the Tuesday seminar and lunch group. Special thanks to Kirsten and Jon Howard and Rebecca Sokolovsky and Franco Bassegio (and their super kids!) for hosting me during research trips.

Above all, I send loving thanks to my two favorite code breakers, David and Tessa. Who else would read so many drafts of this book and check countless code and cipher details, just to make sure I got everything right? AQW CTG CNYCAU KP OA JGCTV.

BIBLIOGRAPHY

Archive Collections

BCC Bacon Cipher Collection, Manuscripts and Archives Division, New York Public Library.

ESFP Elizebeth Smith Friedman Papers, George C. Marshall Research Library. (Numbers separated by a colon indicate box and file numbers.)

NAUK The National Archives, UK.

> Osmar Helmuth Case File. KV 2/1722.

> Siegfried Becker Case File. KV 2/89.

WFC William F. Friedman Collection of Official Papers, National Security Agency. nsa.gov/news-features/declassified-documents/friedman-documents/.

WFFP William Frederick Friedman Papers, George C. Marshall Research Library.

Unpublished Papers and Manuscripts

Friedman, Elizebeth Smith. Diary. ESFP Box 21. George C. Marshall Research Library.

Friedman, Elizebeth Smith. Memoir [unpublished]. George C. Marshall Research Library. marshallfoundation.org/library/wp-content/uploads /sites/16/2015/06/ESFMemoirComplete_opt.pdf.

Friedman, William F. "Bletchley Diary," 1943. Edited and annotated by Colin MacKinnon. colinmackinnon.com/attachments/The_Bletchley_Park_Diary _of_William_F._Friedman_E.pdf.

History of Coast Guard Unit #387, 1940–1945. 1946. National Archives and Records Administration (NARA), College Park, MD. archive.org/details /HistoryOfCoastGuardUnit387.

Jones, Leonard T. "History of OP-20-GU." 16 Oct 1943. NARA, College Park. archive.org/details/HistoryOfOP20GU.

Jones, Leonard T. "Memorandum to OP-20-G on Clandestine Radio Intelligence." 7 Sep 1944. NARA, College Park. archive.org/details /MemorandumToOP20GClandestineRadio.

Elizebeth Smith Friedman Interviews

ESF/BBC ESF. Interview with the BBC. Transcript. ESFP 5:15.

ESF/FP ESF. Interview with Forrest Pogue. 16–17 May 1973. Transcript.

ESF/ML ESF. Interview with Marshall Library Staff. 4–6 Jun 1974. Transcripts (5 Parts).

ESF/MS ESF. Interview with Margaret Santry. NBC Radio. 25 May 1934. ESFP 11:15.

ESF/RLB Benson, R. Louis. "Summary of Interview of Mrs. E. S. Friedman." 9 Jan 1976. NSA-OH-1976–22. ID 4237384.

ESF/RWC ESF. Interview with Ronald W. Clark. ("A little while with Elizabeth [sic] Friedman.") 1975. ESFP 12:1 and ESFP 16:22. archive.org /details/ElizebethFriedmanInterviewWithRonaldClark.

ESF/VV ESF. NSA Oral History Interview with Virginia T Velaki. 11 Nov 1976. Transcripts 16, 17, 18. NSA-OH-16, ID 4237384; NSA-OH-17, ID 4229028; NSA-OH-18, ID 4229013.

Additional NSA Oral History Interviews

Caracristi, Ann. OH-15-82. 16 July 1982. ID 4222264.

Carter, Marshall. OH-15-88. 3 Oct 1988. ID 4245881.

Coffey, Donald F. OH-23-82. 4 Nov 1982. ID 4143315.

Currier, Prescott H. OH-38-80. 14 Nov 1980. ID 4234888.

Davis, Wilma. OH-25-82. 3 Dec 1982.

Kullback, Solomon. OH-17-82. 26 Aug 1982. ID 4235410.

Rowlett, Frank. OH-71-(1-10). [n.d.]. ID 4223202.

Sinkov, Abraham. OH-79-(02-04). May 1979. ID 4241364.

Tiltman, John. OH-04-78. 1 Nov 1978. ID 4234882.

Other Sources

Arch, Paul Antony. "Geneva's Incredible Fabyan Estate." NorthwestQuarterly
.com, Summer 2015. northwestchicagoland.northwestquarterly.com/2015/07
/genevas-incredible-fabyan-estate.

Army-Navy Screen Magazine #42, "Battle of the United States," 1944.
https://collections.ushmm.org/search/catalog/irn1003973.

Atchison, Chris. Phone interview with the author. 19 Jan 2021.

Bamford, James. "The NSA Is Building the Country's Biggest Spy Center
(Watch What You Say)." *Wired,* 15 Mar 2012. wired.com/2012/03/ff
-nsadatacenter.

Bamford, James. *The Puzzle Palace.* London: Sidgwick & Jackson, 1982.

Bard, Gregory V. "Module 10.1: Exploring Steganography with the Baconian
Cipher." discrete-math-hub.com/modules/Baconian.pdf.

"Battle of the Atlantic Statistics." American Merchant Marine at War.
usmm.org/battleatlantic.html.

Bellovin, Steven M. "Vernam, Mauborgne, and Friedman: The One-Time Pad
and the Index of Coincidence." Technical Report CUCS-014-14, 13–15.
mice.cs.columbia.edu/getTechreport.php?techreportID=1576.

Bendersky, Joseph W. *The Jewish Threat: Anti-Semitic Politics of the U.S. Army.*
New York: Basic Books, 2000.

Bennett, Michael E. "Guardian Spies: The Story of Coast Guard Intelligence
in World War II." *American Intelligence Journal* 27(1) (Fall 2009): 16–22.

Biographical Memoirs of Huntington County, Indiana. Chicago: B. F. Bowen,
1901.

Burke, Colin. "What OSS Black Chamber? What Yardley? What 'Dr.'
Friedman? Ah, Grombach? Or, Donovan's Folly." userpages.umbc.edu/~burke
/whatossblack.pdf.

Calamur, Krishnadev. "A Short History of 'America First.'" *The Atlantic,* 21 Jan
2017. theatlantic.com/politics/archive/2017/01/trump-america-first/514037.

"Captain Leonard T. Jones, USCG." Cryptologic Hall of Honor. NSA.
nsa.gov/about/cryptologic-heritage/historical-figures-publications/hall-of
-honor/Article/1620386/captain-leonard-t-jones-uscg.

Chambers, John Whiteclay. *OSS Training in the National Parks and Service Abroad in World War II.* A Wartime Organization for Unconventional Warfare. nps.gov/articles/a-wartime-organization-for-unconventional-warfare.htm.

Clark, Ronald W. *The Man Who Broke Purple.* London: Weidenfeld & Nicholson, 1977.

Cooney, Tory. "Cracking the Code: Hillsdale Alum Aided U.S. Intelligence During World Wars." *The Collegian.* 21 Mar 2014. hillsdalecollegian.com/2014 /03/cracking-the-code-hillsdale-alum-aided-u-s-intelligence-during-world -wars.

Coplen, Dan. "Crooked Roads and a Long-Gone School." *Huntington Herald-Press,* 28 Oct 1985, 52.

Corera, Gordon. "The Crypto Agreement." BBC Radio 4, 28 Jul 2015. bbc.co.uk/programmes/b0639w3v.

Cornell Alumni News. Ithaca, NY. 60:18. 15 Jun 1958.

"Deciphers Intricate Chinese Code." *Star-Phoenix* [Saskatoon], 9 Feb 1938, 8.

DeFerrari, John. "The Magnificent Raleigh Hotel." www.streetsofwashington .com/2010/03/magnificent-raleigh-hotel.html.

Department of Commerce. *Report of Investigating Board,* 16 Nov 1937. rosap.ntl.bts.gov/view/dot/32997.

"Doll Woman Gets Ten Years for Espionage." *New York Daily News,* 15 Aug 1944, 32.

Dominion of Canada. *Report of the Royal Canadian Mounted Police for the Year Ended March 31, 1938.* Ottawa, 1938.

Dunin, Elonka. "Cipher on the William and Elizebeth Friedman Tombstone at Arlington National Cemetery Is Solved." 17 Apr 2017. elonka.com/friedman /FriedmanTombstone.pdf.

Edwards, Melba. Phone interview with the author. 27 Dec 2019.

Edwards, Melba, Rosemary Kumfer, and Velma Harden. *Zanesville, Indiana History 1849–1976.* 1976. plainofsharon.org/scott/gramps/src/c/c /d11e6de2334519a08cc.html.

Ensign, Eric S. *Intelligence in the Rum War at Sea.* Joint Military Intelligence College, 2001.

Fagone, Jason. *The Woman Who Smashed Codes: A True Story of Love, Spies, and the Unlikely Heroine Who Outwitted America's Enemies.* New York: Dey Street, 2017.

"FBI Nabs Woman for Code Notes." *New York Daily News,* 22 Jan 1944, 112.

"Fewer Books Used in 1918." *Huntington Herald,* 11 Feb 1919, 2.

Figes, Orlando. *A People's Tragedy: The Russian Revolution, 1891–1924.* London: Bodley Head, 2014.

Friedman, William [and Elizebeth Friedman]. *An Introduction to the Methods for the Solution of Ciphers.* Riverbank Publication No. 17. Geneva, IL: Riverbank Laboratories, 1918.

Friedman, William, and Elizebeth Friedman. *The Shakespearean Ciphers Examined.* Cambridge: Cambridge University Press, 1957.

Funderburg, J. Anne. *Rumrunners: Liquor Smugglers on America's Coasts, 1920–1933.* Jefferson, NC: McFarland, 2016.

"The Gentleman's Agreement: Secret Deal Between the NSA and Hagelin, 1939–1969." Crypto Museum. cryptomuseum.com/manuf/crypto/friedman.htm.

Gentzke, Ann Whitcher. "An American Hero." *At Buffalo,* Spring 2018. buffalo.edu/atbuffalo/article-page-spring-2018.host.html/content/shared/www /atbuffalo/articles/Spring-2018/features/an-american-hero.detail.html.

Glasser, Ellen. "Voices of the First Women Leaders in the Federal Bureau of Investigation." Ph.D. diss., University of North Florida, 2016.

Goldin, Claudia, and Lawrence F. Katz. "Education and Income in the Early 20th Century: Evidence from the Prairies." *Journal of Economic History* 60(3): 782–818.

Gould, Nathan. "The Jew in the Oil Investigation." *Jewish Advocate,* 24 Apr 1924, 2.

Guise-Richardson, Catherine E. "Protecting Mental Health in the Age of Anxiety: The Context of Valium's Development, Synthesis, and Discovery in the United States, to 1963." Ph.D. diss., Iowa State University, 2009.

Hagan, Carrie. "The Coast Guard's Most Potent Weapon During Prohibition? Codebreaker Elizebeth Friedman." *Smithsonian Magazine,* 28 Jan 2015. smithsonianmag.com/history/coast-guards-most-potent-weapon-during -prohibition-codebreaker-elizebeth-friedman-180954066/.

Hannah, Theodore M. "Frank B. Rowlett: A Personal Profile." *Cryptologic Spectrum* 11 (Spring 1981): 5–21.

Hatch, David A. "From the Archives: Friedman Takes the Stand." *Cryptologia* 32 (2008): 180–183.

Helmick, Leah Stock. "Key Woman of the T-Men." *Reader's Digest,* Sep 1937, 51–55.

Hinsley, F. H., and Alan Stripp, eds. *The Codebreakers: The Inside Story of Bletchley Park.* Oxford: Oxford University Press, 1993.

Hoehling, Adolph A. *Women Who Spied: True Stories of Female Espionage.* New York: Dodd, Mead, 1967.

"How Secret Codes and a Secret Love Tracked Down the Big Dope Ring." *Spokesman-Review* [Washington], 3 Dec 1933, 33.

Huntington County, Indiana: History & Families, 1834–1993. Paducah, KY: Turner Publishing Co., 1993.

Janssen, Marian. *Not at All What One Is Used To: The Life and Times of Isabella Gardner.* Columbia: University of Missouri Press, 2010.

"John R. Friedman." Obituary. *Boston Globe,* 26 Sep 2010. legacy.com/obituaries /bostonglobe/obituary.aspx?n=john-rfriedman&pid=145611711.

Kahn, David. *The Codebreakers.* London: Weidenfeld & Nicholson, 1974.

Kruh, Louis. "A Cryptological Travelogue: Riverbank – 1992." *Cryptologia,* 17(1) (Jan 1993): 80–94.

Lawrence, Cera R. "The Eugenics Record Office at Cold Spring Harbor Laboratory (1910–1939)." *The Embryo Project Encyclopedia,* 21 Apr 2011. embryo.asu.edu/pages/eugenics-record-office-cold-spring-harbor-laboratory -1910-1939.

League of Nations. Advisory Committee on Traffic in Opium. *Summary of Illicit Transactions and Seizures,* C. 135 M. 80. Geneva, 1938.

Lindbergh, Charles. Des Moines Speech, 11 Sep 1941. charleslindbergh.com /americanfirst/speech.asp.

Lunnen, Connie. "She Has a Secret Side." *Houston Chronicle,* 24 May 1972 (ESFP 11:14).

Lyle, Katie Letcher, and David Joyner. *Divine Fire: Elizabeth Friedman, Cryptanalyst.* drive.google.com/file/d/0B-Z_E7dFXRF _VlJWR01GemM4dDA/view.

Martin, Paul. "Hitler's Favorite American: 'Biological Fascism' in the shadow of New York City." Salon.com, 23 Mar 2014. salon.com/2014/03/23/hitlers _favorite_american_biological_fascism_in_the_shadow_of_new_york_city.

"Mask Order Is Issued." *Huntington Herald,* 10 Dec 1918, 1.

McConahay, Mary Jo. *The Tango War: The Struggle for the Hearts, Minds, and Riches of Latin America During World War II.* New York: Macmillan, 2018.

McDonnell, Francis. *Insidious Foes: The Axis Fifth Column and the American Home Front.* Oxford: Oxford University Press, 1995.

Molnar, Courtni E. "'Has the Millennium Yet Dawned?': A History of Attitudes Toward Pregnant Workers in America." *Michigan Journal of Gender and Law* 12:163 (2005), 163–187.

Mowry, David P. "Cryptologic Aspects of German Intelligence Activities in South America During World War II." *United States Cryptologic History,* Series IV, Vol. 11, Center for Cryptologic History, NSA 2011, 15. nsa.gov/Portals/70 /documents/about/cryptologic-heritage/historical-figures-publications /publications/wwii/cryptologic_aspects_of_gi.pdf.

Mowry, David P. *Listening to the Rumrunners: Radio Intelligence During Prohibition.* NSA: Center for Cryptologic History, 2014.

"Mrs. J. M. Smith Passes Away." *Huntington Herald,* 1 Mar 1917.

Mucklow, Tim. *The SIGABA/ECM II Cipher Machine: "A Beautiful Idea."* NSA: Center for Cryptologic History, 2015.

Mundy, Liza. *Code Girls: The Untold Story of the American Women Code Breakers of World War II.* New York: Hachette Books, 2017.

Munson, Richard. *George Fabyan: The Tycoon Who Broke Ciphers.* CreateSpace, 2013.

Murphy, Royse P., and Lee B. Kass. *Evolution of Plant Breeding at Cornell University: A Centennial History, 1907–2006.* hdl.handle.net/1813/23087.

Penkower, Monty Noam. "The Kishinev Pogrom of 1903: A Turning Point in Jewish History." *Modern Judaism* 24(3) (2004): 187–225.

"Photos Taken of Martian Signals." *New Britain Daily Herald,* 27 Aug 1924.

Roos, Dave. "How Prohibition Put the 'Organized' into Organized Crime." History.com, 9 Mar 2021. history.com/news/prohibition-organized-crime-al -capone.

"Scientist Weds Elizabeth [sic] Smith; Groom is Noted." *Huntington Press,* 26 May 1917.

Sears, David. "The Spy in the Doll Shop." *Smithsonian Magazine,* 2 Mar 2016. smithsonianmag.com/history/spy-doll-shop-180958251/.

Sheldon, Rose Mary. *The Friedman Collection: An Analytical Guide.* marshallfoundation.org/library/wp-content/uploads/sites/16/2014/09 /Friedman_Collection_Guide_September_2014.pdf.

Sheldon, Rose Mary. "William F. Friedman: A Very Private Cryptographer and His Collection." *Cryptologic Quarterly,* 2015-01, 34: 4–29. nsa.gov/about /cryptologic-heritage/historical-figures-publications/publications/cryptologic -quarterly/assets/files/cryptologic-quarterly-2015-01.pdf.

Sherman, David. "The National Security Agency and the William F. Friedman Collection." *Cryptologia* 41(3) (2017): 195–238.

Sherman, David. "William Friedman and Pearl Harbor." *Intelligence and National Security,* 33(3): 309–323.

Smith, G. Stuart. *A Life in Code: Pioneer Cryptanalyst Elizebeth Smith Friedman*. Jefferson, NC: McFarland & Co, 2017.

Smoot, Betsy Rohaly. "Pioneers of U.S. Military Cryptology: Colonel Parker Hitt and His Wife: Genevieve Young Hitt." *Federal History*, Issue 4 (2012): 87–100. shfg.org/resources/Documents/FH%204%20(2012)%20Smoot.pdf.

Spetter, Allen. "The United States, the Russian Jews and the Russian Famine of 1891–1892." *American Jewish Historical Quarterly* 64(3) (Mar 1975): 236–244.

Standlee, Mary W. *Borden's Dream: The Walter Reed Army Medical Center in Washington, DC*. Washington, DC: Borden Institute, 2007.

"Strange Case of the Talking Dolls." *St. Louis Post-Dispatch*, 3 Sep 1944, 1.

Stripp, Alan. "The Enigma Machine: Its Mechanism and Use." In *The Codebreakers: The Inside Story of Bletchley Park*, edited by F. H. Hinsley and Alan Stripp (Oxford: Oxford University Press, 1993), 83–88.

Sweeney, Michael S. *Victory of Secrets: The Office of Censorship and the American Press and Radio in World War II*. Chapel Hill and London: University of North Carolina Press, 2001.

Tagg, Lori. "Army's First Cipher Office Broke the Code on Modern Cryptology." 7 Jul 2017. army.mil/article/190449/Armys_first_cipher_office _broke_the_code_on_modern_cryptology.

"They Make News Here and There." *Charlotte Observer*, 15 Feb 1938, 3.

Thiesen, William H. "The Long Blue Line: Hurricane Hero, Founder of USCG Intelligence." Posted 24 Sep 2015 by Diana Sherbs. coastguard.dodlive .mil/2015/09/the-long-blue-line-hurricane-hero-founder-of-uscg-intelligence.

Twinn, Peter. "The *Abwehr* Enigma." In *The Codebreakers: The Inside Story of Bletchley Park*, edited by F. H. Hinsley and Alan Stripp (Oxford: Oxford University Press, 1993), 123–131.

U.S. Congress. *Pearl Harbor Attack: Hearings Before the Joint Committee on the Investigation of the Pearl Harbor Attack*. 1946.

"U.S. Woman Expert Deciphers Chinese Code, Traps Opium Ring." *Boston Globe*, 9 Feb 1938, 6.

"Velvalee Dickinson, the 'Doll Woman.'" fbi.gov/history/famous-cases/velvalee -dickinson-the-doll-woman.

Walton, Calder. *Empire of Secrets: British Intelligence, the Cold War, and the Twilight of Empire*. London: Harper Press, 2013.

Weinberg, Gerhard L. *Hitler's Foreign Policy: The Road to World War II, 1933–1939*. Enigma Books, 2005.

Welchman, Gordon. *The Hut Six Story.* Cleobury Mortimer: M & M Baldwin, 1997.

"William Friedman and Miss Elizebeth Smith Were Married Monday." *Geneva Republican,* 23 May 1917.

"Wilma Davis." Women in American Cryptology. NSA. nsa.gov/about /cryptologic-heritage/historical-figures-publications/women/Article/1620898 /wilma-davis/About-Us/EEO-Diversity/Employee-Resource-Groups/About -Us/EEO-Diversity/Employee-Resource-Groups.

Winona [Yearbook]. Hillsdale, MI: Hillsdale College, 1915.

NOTES

CHAPTER ONE The Doll Shop Spy

1 *"I have been so very busy"*: "Velvalee Dickinson, the 'Doll Woman,'" fbi.gov, fbi.gov/history/famous-cases/velvalee-dickinson-the-doll -woman.

1–2 FBI and the Dickinson case: "FBI Nabs Woman for Code Notes," *New York Daily News*, 22 Jan 1944, 112; "Strange Case of the Talking Dolls," *St. Louis Post-Dispatch*, 3 Sep 1944, 1; Smith, 143, 146–148, 157–159; Sears, "The Spy in the Doll Shop"; "Velvalee Dickinson, the 'Doll Woman,'" fbi.gov.

2 FBI was worried: Smith, 148.

2–3 Edward Wallace: Smith, 148–149; Fagone, 293–294.

3 FBI and ESF: Fagone, 206, 293–294. The FBI worried the credit might go to ESF's husband as well.

3 "Confidential Informant T4": Smith, 149; Fagone, 293–294.

3 "open code": ESF to Edward C. Wallace, 1 Apr 1944, ESFP 7:1; Smith, 149.

4 *"The only new dolls"*: Hoehling, 106.

4 ESF's analysis of the Doll Woman letters: ESF to Edward C. Wallace, 1 Apr 1944, ESFP 7:1. See also Smith, 152–154; Fagone, 295.

5 August 1944: "Doll Woman Gets Ten Years for Espionage," *New York Daily News*, 15 Aug 1944, 32.

5　"the War's No. 1 Woman Spy": "The FBI vs New York Spies," *New York World-Telegram,* 22 Jun 1945, ESFP 7:2.

5　FBI website: "Velvalee Dickinson, the 'Doll Woman,'" fbi.gov.

CHAPTER TWO　Starting Out

7–8　"odious name": ESF, Diary, 22 Apr 1913, ESFP Box 21.

8　Family legend: Smith, 15; Fagone, 7.

8　Smith family and farm: Edwards, et al., 206.

8　wavy brown hair, hazel eyes: Lyle and Joyner, 31.

8　"as one continual period": "Family Anecdotes," ESFP 12:11.

9　John Marion Smith: Smith, 14–15; *Biographical Memoirs,* 408–410; ESF, Memoir, 45.

9　"wonderful little Mother": ESF, Diary, 8 Jan 1918, ESFP Box 21.

9　Sopha was . . . student days: ESF to WFF, n.d. [Jan/Feb 1917], ESFP 2:1; "Mrs. J. M. Smith Passes Away," *Huntington Herald,* 1 Mar 1917; *The WPA Guide to Indiana,* 313; United States Census, 1870, *FamilySearch* (familysearch.org/ark:/61903/1:1:MXXB-X35), B J Strock.

9　"My mother encouraged me": ESF/VV 17:16.

10　Antioch School: Melba Edwards, phone interview with the author, 27 Dec 2019; Coplen, 52.

10　German and Latin, "rare force": Smith, 15; "Miss Smith and Darwin Hamer Win," *Daily-News Democrat* (Huntington, IN), 20 Mar 1909, 1.

10　never even graduated: Goldin and Katz, 784.

10　father refused to pay, Wellesley, Swarthmore, Earlham: ESF, Memoir, 1–2.

10　Quaker: ESF, Memoir, 1–2; *Huntington County, Indiana: History & Families, 1834–1993,* 371; Genealogical Material, ESFP 11:21. ESF occasionally said that her father had once been a Quaker, presumably before he went off to war as a teenager. Yet ESF's own records suggest that the family may have left Quakerism long before then, when her great-grandfather was expelled by the Quakers for fighting in the War of 1812.

10　GPA, college plans: *Daily-News Democrat* (Huntington, IN), 19 May 1910, 2; ESF, Memoir, 1–2.

10　she spent the next year at home, playing piano: *Daily-News Democrat,* 9 Sep 1910, 2; *Huntington Herald* (Huntington, IN), 9 Dec 1910, 5.

10–11	subtract one year: ESF did this for decades, beginning sometime before 1917. Likely she started to lie during college, embarrassed about being a year older than most of her classmates and angry about her year spent at home. See chapter 16.
11	College of Wooster, loan: ESF, Memoir, 2; *Huntington Herald,* 26 Jul 1911, 4.
11	English, Greek, philosophy, poetry, Shakespeare: Fagone, 8.
11	"I am never quite so gleeful," "I should have been born a man.": ESF, Diary, 2 Jul 1913, ESFP Box 21.
11	"indigo," "make dresses": ESF, Diary, 27 Feb 1913, ESFP Box 21.
12	plain speaking: ESF, Diary, 20 Mar 1913, ESFP Box 21.
12	"I hate the place": ESF, Diary, 22 Jun 1913, ESFP Box 21.
12	misunderstood, bad attitude: ESF, Diary, 8 Jul 1913, ESFP Box 21.
12	sleep "out under the stars": ESF, Diary, 30 Jun 1913, ESFP Box 21.
12	row, paddle a canoe: ESF, Diary, 25 Jul 1913, 11 Aug 1913, ESFP Box 21.
12	"heart was carried completely away": ESF, Diary, 14 Jul 1913, ESFP Box 21.
12	"romance gone wrong": Lyle and Joyner, 19.
12	"I wanted," "worthless and useless": ESF, Diary, 14 Oct 1913, ESFP Box 21.
12	hit her stride: *Winona,* 1915, 39.
12–13	Harold Van Kirk: [Harold] Van Kirk to ESF, Jun–Sep 1920, ESFP 1:45; *Battle Creek Enquirer,* 18 Apr 1926, 7; *Ft. Wayne Journal Gazette,* 17 Dec 1922, 34; ESF, Memoir, 1.
13	$600: Smith, 15.
13	was business: *Winona,* 1915, 39.
13	substitute high school principal: ESF Personnel File, "Personal History Statement," 1 Jul 1930, ESFP 7:3; ESF/VV 16:7.
13	"I had broken my engagement": ESF, Memoir, 1.
13	"fiancé–gone astray": ESF, note on Letters, [Harry] Van Kirk to ESF, Jun–Sep 1920, ESFP 1:45.
13–14	Van at Huntington, Hillsdale; lucky escape: *Huntington Herald,* 27 Jul 1915, 3; *L'Anse Sentinel,* 2 Oct 1915, 6; Janssen, 46–48, 58–60.
14	desolate, "run-of-the-mill": ESF, 20 Jun 1917, ESFP Box 21; ESF/VV 16:7.
14	"a long stretch": ESF, Diary, 20 Jun 1917, ESFP Box 21.

14   "wish[ing] passionately": ESF, Diary, 20 Jun 1917, ESFP Box 21.

14   May 1916: ESF remembered it as "May or June," but it must have been late May because she was working full-time at Riverbank by June 5, 1916, after an interview there about a week earlier (ESF/VV 16:7–8, BCC Box 15, "Elizebeth W. Smith" [sic] file).

CHAPTER THREE What Do YOU Know?

15   "Hog Butcher": Carl Sandburg, "Chicago" (1914).

15   Chicago job search: ESF, Memoir, 1; ESF/FP, 1.

15   "I thought of myself as sitting down at a desk": ESF/RWC, 3.

16   "I did not even know," "an archaeologist would have": ESF, Memoir, 1.

16   "It was something so startling": ESF, Memoir, 2.

16   But she let the librarian call: ESF, Memoir, 2.

17   "In came this whirlwind" and following dialogue: ESF/VV 16:8.

17   Fabyan's appearance: ESF/FP, 2; ESF/ML 5:2.

17   barely more than five feet tall: Winifred Mallon, "Woman Wins Fame as Cryptanalyst," *New York Times*, 1937, ESFP 17:2; "Statement of Personal History," Nov 1946, ESFP 11:16. ESFP sometimes claimed to be 5'2" or 5'3", but photos suggest Mallon was closer to the truth.

17   "Will you go out," "knocked kind of breathless," and following dialogue: ESF/VV 16:8.

17   "lifted me," Union Pacific: ESF/VV 16: 7; ESF/FP, 3; ESF, Memoir, 2.

17–18 "white Puritan collar," "simplest kind of hat": ESF/FP, 3; ESF/VV 16:7.

18   "Where am I?": ESF/VV 16:8.

18   "WHAT DO *YOU* KNOW?" and following dialogue: ESF, Memoir, 3. See also ESF/FP, 3; ESF/VV 16:8.

18   turned her head: ESF/ML 5:2.

18   Elizebeth let Fabyan talk: ESF/ML 5:3.

18   car and chauffeur waiting: ESF/FP, 3.

CODE OR CIPHER?

19   codes and ciphers in college: ESF, Interview by Ed Meryl, 1939, ESFP 17:14; ESF/MS, 1, ESFP 11:15.

20   *cryptanalyst:* WFF to John Manly, 8 Jan 1922, 4 Feb 1922, 13:22.

20   "we don't make 'em": ESF/FP, 43.

CHAPTER FOUR Riverbank

21 the private estate: Fagone, 22.

21 "colonel": Munson, 2.

21–22 Fabyan: ESF, Memoir, 3, 10–11; Fagone, 22–24; Munson, 4–10; Arch, "Geneva's Incredible Fabyan Estate."

22 the estate, Riverbank, on the porch: ESF, Memoir, 5–6, 8–9, 38–40; Smith, 16; Fagone, 32, 50; Munson, 2; Arch, "Geneva's Incredible Fabyan Estate."

22 "You never get sick": Munson, 2.

22 Riverbank Laboratories: Fagone, 26–28, 31.

22 "Be spectacular.": ESF/VV 18:10.

22–23 Elizabeth Wells Gallup: EWG biographical notes, n.d., BCC 13:11; Friedman, *Shakespearean Ciphers*, 188–197, 224.

24 "Queene Elizabeth": Friedman, *Shakespearean Ciphers*, 191.

24 reminded her of her father: ESF, Memoir, 45.

24 "The world began to pop": ESF/FP, 5.

24 $30: ESF/ML 5:6.

24 "We swam," "engineer": ESF, Memoir, 7.

24–25 "We used to go": ESF/VV 16:5.

25 Riverbank guests: ESF, Memoir, 24; Fagone, 51.

25 fine meals, "always had pitchers": ESF/FP, 5.

25 "He gave orders": ESF, Memoir, 9.

25 "hell chair," web of rope: ESF, Memoir, 6; ESF/RWC, 2.

25 "Whenever he wanted to bawl anybody out": ESF/ML 5:3.

26 "give them hell": ESF, Memoir, 6.

26 At first . . . to decrypt: 5 Jun 1916, BCC, Box 15 ("Elizebeth W. Smith" [sic] file).

28 chosen to explain: ESF, Memoir, 6–7.

28 "My admiration": Friedman, *Shakespearean Ciphers*, 211.

28 But this simply wasn't true: See *The Shakespearean Ciphers Examined*, the book that thoroughly disproved the theory, coauthored by ESF herself.

29 Before the summer was over: ESF, Memoir, 13.

FROM BACON TO BINARY

30–31   Bacon, bilateral, binary: Bard, "Module 10.1: Exploring Steganography with the Baconian Cipher," discrete-math-hub.com /modules/Baconian.pdf.

CHAPTER FIVE A Dear Good Friend

32   "I was sitting there," "attire at all": ESF, ESF/FP, 5–6.

32   hazel eyes: WFF, "Statement of Personal History, ca. 1955, WFC/ NSA, ID A335508.

32   "strongly intellectual face": ESF, Memoir, 8.

32–33   Russia: Spetter, 236–244; Figes, 52–53, 80–81, 157–162.

33   Friedman family, American citizen: Clark, 1–4, 6; Sheldon, "William F. Friedman," 4–5. Clark says that Rosa's father later joined them in Pennsylvania, and records show that her mother did, too: geni.com /people/Meril-Trust/6000000001386581889.

33   "the wolf always": BF to Ronald Clark, 26 Sep 1976, ESFP 14:14.

33   "hoard": BF to Ronald Clark, 26 Sep 1976, ESFP 14:14.

33   Kishinev: Penkower, 187–225; Clark, 2.

33   marked by fear: Zigmond M. Lebensohn, M.D., to Ronald W. Clark, 10 May 1976, ESFP 13:30.

34   chess, athlete, speech contest, high school: Clark, 4–5; ESF/FP, 6; Kahn, 184.

34   Erie City Iron Works: WFF, "Statement of Personal History, ca. 1955, WFC/NSA, ID A335508.

34   "scratching a living": Clark, 5.

34–35   Cornell: Clark, 5–6.

35   "Eugenics Bill," corn hybrids, Cold Spring Harbor: WFF was enthusiastic about plant breeding, but there are no records of his supporting human eugenics, and he was not involved in the work of the Eugenics Record Office (ERO) at Cold Spring Harbor. *Cornell Alumni News*, 60:18 (15 Jun 1958), 639; Carnegie Institution of Washington, *Year Book No. 11* (Washington, DC: Carnegie Institution, 1912), 93; Carnegie Institution of Washington, *Year Book No. 12* (Washington, DC: Carnegie Institution, 1913), 97; WFF, "Statement of Personal History, ca. 1955, WFC/NSA, ID A335508.

35   Davenport: Murphy and Kass, 32; Lawrence, "The Eugenics Record Office"; Martin, "Hitler's Favorite American."

35	another advisor: This was A. W. Gilbert. See WFF to H. H. Love, 24 Jun 1949, WFC/NSA, ID A70009; Murphy and Kass, 13.
35	Riverbank offer: Clark, 7–9; Murphy and Kass, 32.
36	WFF's working conditions, duties: ESF, Memoir, 8, 12; ESF/ML 5:5; Fagone, 47, 49; Clark, 16.
36	"The Gold-Bug,": Clark, 4–5.
36	shared her doubts: ESF, Memoir, 13; Fagone, 61–62.
36	Billy Boy and Elsbeth: ESF to WFF, 20 Jan 1917, 31 Jan 1917, ESFP 2:1; Smith, 19–20; Lyle and Joyner, 60.
36	William had fallen in love before: Clark, 6; Kahn, 184.
36	as if each were a cipher: Fagone, 90–91, elaborates on this.
37	"mangled and torn," "never *feel* again": ESF, Diary, 20 Jun 1917, ESFP Box 21.
37	introduced him to her mother: ESF to WFF, 31 Jan 1917, ESFP 2:1.
37	Edna: Lyle and Joyner, 57.
37	"I think that E cares": Edna Smith Dinieus to WFF, n.d., ESFP 4:3.
37	appendicitis: *Huntington Herald,* 14 Dec 1916, 3.
37	"Flame which we kindled": WFF to ESF, 20 Jul 1918, ESFP 2:14. See also ESF to WFF, 31 Jan 1917, ESFP 2:1. In ESF to WFF, 20 Jan 1917, ESFP 2:1, ESF refers to a promise she made in mid-December to write WFF a letter "within forty days." This suggests both that she hadn't seen him since around the time of the surgery, and that something significant happened then.
37–38	"It seems so hard to be thinking": ESF to WFF, 31 Jan 1917, ESFP 2:1.
38	"Mother-kins": ESF to WFF, 6–7 Feb 1917, ESFP 2:1.
38	"hours pacing": ESF to WFF, 31 Jan 1917, ESFP 2:1.
38	"Comforter": ESF to WFF, 20 Jan 1917, ESFP 2:1.
38	"It is so awful": ESF to WFF, 31 Jan 1917, ESFP 2:1.
38	"battle of wills": ESF to WFF, 31 Jan 1917, ESFP 2:1.
38	"I cannot afford": ESF to WFF, 6–7 Feb 1917, ESFP 2:1.
38	"I try to make myself work": ESF to WFF, 31 Jan 1917, ESFP 2:1.
38	"dear good friend," "one of the truest friends": ESF to WFF, 6–7 Feb 1917, ESFP 2:1; "Dear boy": ESF to WFF, 31 Jan 1917, ESFP 2:1.
38	"rocking": ESF to WFF, 20 Jan 1917, ESFP 2:1. See also WFF to ESF, 18 Aug 1918, ESFP 2:15.

38   "North Star": ESF to WFF, 6–7 Feb 1917, ESFP 2:1.

38   "I think of you": ESF to WFF, 6 Feb 1917, ESFP 2:1.

39   "I want, oh, so much": ESF to WFF, 6–7 Feb 1917, ESFP 2:1.

39   Sopha died: Sopha Smith, Certificate of Death, Indiana State Board of Health.

39   no longer willing to waste time: Fagone, 65.

39   Fabyan lost his temper: ESF, Memoir, 13–14.

39   that month . . . new orders: Letter, GF to "The Intelligence Office, War Department," 15 Mar 1917; ESF, Memoir, 13–14.

CHAPTER SIX The Skeletons of Words

40-41   radio in World War I: Kahn, 298–299; Fagone, 66–67.

41   Zimmermann telegram: Kahn, 282–297.

41   "possibly three": ESF, Memoir, 14–15.

42   Fabyan, the Army, Mauborgne, code-breaking center: ESF, Memoir, 14; Letter, GF to "The Intelligence Office, War Department," 15 Mar 1917; Telegram, GF to R. H. Van Deman, 6 Apr 1917; all in WFFP, Item 734; Capt. Mauborgne to Chief of the War College Division, 17 Apr 1917, WFFP Item 734; R. H. Van Deman to GF, 18 Apr 1917, Item 734; Clark, 24.

42   secret messages at Riverbank, mail sacks: ESF, Memoir, 16; Kruh, 83.

43   messages in many languages: ESF/ML 2:8; ESF, Memoir, 21–22.

43   Parker Hitt, Genevieve Young Hitt: ESF/ML 5:6; ESF/VV 16:12; Smoot, 90–92, 96–97.

43   "became the learners": ESF, Memoir, 15.

43   basic working practices, "to use the eraser," "different minds": WFF [and ESF], *An Introduction to the Methods for the Solution of Ciphers*, 3–4.

44   within two hours: ESF/ML 2:7.

44   "The skeletons of words": ESF, Codebreaking Book MS, 42, ESFP 9:12.

45   "magic," "beautiful," "in a passionate embrace": WFF to ESF, 9 Sep 1918, ESFP 2:16.

45   "wrestling with myself": WFF to ESF, 9 Sep 1918, ESFP 2:16.

45   "I believe in an all-wise": Booklet 3, Cosmology Exam, 27 Jan 1915, EFSC 12:8.

45   "Spring spells God": ESF, Diary, 30 Jun 1913, ESFP Box 21.

45   "the Painter": ESF, Diary, 23 Mar 1913, ESFP Box 21.

46   "Smith-Friedman Alliance": Edna Smith Dinieus to WFF, n.d., ESFP 4:3.

46   "talked over the impossibility": WFF to ESF, 9 Sep 1918, ESFP 2:16.

46   In early May: ESF to WFF, 8 May 1917, ESFP 2:1.

CHAPTER SEVEN   Will We Win?

47   "sudden," local paper: Lyle and Joyner, 62; "Scientist Weds Elizabeth [sic] Smith," *Huntington Press,* 26 May 1917.

47   "You would have thought," first time: Clark, 21.

47   "Oh, Billy, Billy": ESF to WFF, 8 May 1917, ESFP 2:1. (The second half of this letter was later misfiled in a Jan 1917 envelope.)

48   On May 21, 1917: "William Friedman and Miss Elizebeth Smith Were Married Monday," *Geneva Republican,* 23 May 1917, 1; Wedding photographs, F-108, F-109, ESFP.

48   not sure she could ever love William: The fear of not being able to love went deep. Later that summer, she noted down an idea for a "story of a girl and a man who had loved her through a close comradeship of six years. She constantly had to lament the fact that she *could not love.* The homing instinct absent . . ." ESF, Diary, 38, ESFP Box 21.

48   "compassion": ESF, Diary, Poem, 46, ESFP Box 21.

48   "no happy marriage": ESF, Diary, 8 Jan 1918, ESFP Box 21.

48   "good" man: ESF, Diary, 46, ESFP Box 21.

48   "the Miracle": ESF, Diary, 8 Jan 1918, ESFP Box 21.

48   "To fall in love": ESF, Diary, 8 Jan 1918, ESFP Box 21.

48   "Youth, and Love, and Life": ESF, Diary, 20 Jun 1917, ESFP Box 21.

49   "He became my all in all.": ESF, Diary, 46, ESFP Box 21. See also WFF to ESF, 23 Sep 1918, ESFP 2:16.

49   "My dearest": ESF, Diary, 13 Aug 1917, and WFF note, ESFP Box 21.

49   "Tonight my Lover-Husband": ESF, Diary, 13 Aug 1917, ESFP Box 21.

49–50   book cipher case: ESF, Memoir, 24–31; WFF, Account, ESFP 6:13. Fagone, 80–83, places the case in early 1917, but WFF testified that they first saw the messages in the fall of 1917. Hatch, 180–183, believes the visitor was likely from British intelligence. He also suggests that the Friedmans had help from the British, but this contradicts ESF's and WFF's accounts. Possibly the British had cracked the code but needed Americans to do this independently so that they would not appear to be interfering in U.S. affairs.

51   "someone had to stay behind": ESF, Memoir, 31.

51   "I was never able to decide which": J. Rives Childs to Vanessa Friedman, 28 Sep 1981, ESFP 12:14.

51   said to be unsolvable, "Of course," "I unlocked": ESF, Code-Breaking Manuscript, ESFP 9:12.

51   "shrewd 'guess,'" "painstaking labor": WFF [and ESF], *Introduction*, 3–4; Fagone, 84–86.

52   Pletts, Riverbank: ESF, Memoir, 32–34; Clark, 36–38.

52   "*I took one look*": WFF, "Communications Security Lecture," 48, WFC/NSA, ID A63403.

52–53   "sitting across from him," "*He asked me to lean back*": ESF, Memoir, 33–34.

53   "absolutely indecipherable": WFF, "Communications Security Lecture," 49, WFC, NSA, ID A63403.

THE KEY TO THE CIPHER

54   Pletts Cryptograph: WFF, "Communications Security Lecture," WFC/NSA, ID A63403, 47–50; WFF, "The Friedman Lectures on Cryptography," WFC/NSA, ID A2119475, 143–144; Clark, 36–38.

CHAPTER EIGHT Underlings

55   "the supreme commander," "underlings": ESF, Memoir, 18–19.

55   they received no replies: Lyle and Joyner, 74.

56   Fabyan was reading their mail: ESF/FP, 62; Lyle and Joyner, 74–75.

56   bugged, not out of the question: ESF/VV 18:4–5; Fagone, 99.

56   Army stopped writing, made other plans, security risk: ESF, Memoir, 21; ESF/VV 18:14.

56   MI-8: Kahn, 351–352; ESF, Memoir, 21–22; Tagg, "Army's First Cipher Office."

56–57   officer training: ESF, Memoir, 23; Kruh, 86.

57   Elizebeth as coauthor: ESF, "Personal History," 21 Oct 1927 and 3 Jul 1931, Personnel File, ESFP 7:3; Fagone, 77–78.

57   the answer may lie, with nothing: Fagone, 78–79.

57–58   Riverbank Publication No. 17: "Riverbank Book on Ciphers," BCC, 14:2. The draft has a note in WFF's hand saying the "Appendix I Historical and General" is "by Elizebeth [sic] Smith Friedman." Overall, the draft has many substantive corrections from WFF, and fewer, largely stylistic, ones from ESF.

58   "Even in those days": ESF/VV 18:8.

58   "our R-K pamphlet": WFF to ESF, 20 Jul 1918, ESFP 2:14.

58   "He felt like a draft evader": ESF/RWC, 10.

59   By June, William was a first lieutenant: WFF, "Statement of Personal History," ca. 1955, WFC/NSA, ID A335508.

HIDING IN PLAIN SIGHT

60   In front of them sit: ESF/ML 2:11.

61   William kept a copy of this photo under glass: marshallfoundation .org/library/photographs/photographs-glass-william-f-friedmans -desk-many-years.

CHAPTER NINE   Don't Be Afraid to Take a Step

62   the Army did not allow female code breakers: WFF to ESF, 14 Jul 18, ESFP 2:14; Smith, 30.

62   "I, a mere woman": ESF, "Pure Accident," *The Arrow* (Feb 1930), 400, ESFP 12:9.

62   jobs in the Navy: Lyle and Joyner, 96; WFF to ESF, 7 Oct 1918, ESFP 2:17.

63   "Darling," etc.: WFF to ESF, Jun to Dec 1918, ESFP 2:13–19.

63   "Sixteenth Monthiversary": WFF to ESF, 23 Sep 1918, ESFP 2:16.

63   "I adore, adore, adore You!": WFF to ESF, 7 Jul 1918, ESFP 2:14.

63   "Honey Mine, please," "world to you": WFF to ESF, Jun 1918, ESFP 2:13.

63   "They think the world": In late 1918, ESF heard, perhaps through WFF's brother, that WFF's parents thought she was odd. She sent WFF a combative note saying, "Good. I've been working for exactly that for a year." WFF, who was trying to get along with her family, was dismayed that she wouldn't make the same effort. "They have their faults, I know," he wrote of his parents, "but one loves in spite of faults, Dear Heart. That is what love is for. . . ." WFF to ESF, 5 Jan 1919, ESFP 2:20.

63   his room, streets so dark, seven photographs: WFF to ESF, 9 Sep 1918, ESFP 2:16; WFF to ESF, 23 Jul 1918, ESFP 2:14.

63   "I was a Hero": WFF to ESF, 7 Jul 1918, ESFP 2:14.

63   "We were together again": WFF to ESF, 18 Aug 1918, ESFP 2:15.

64   "Adored One," "to me": WFF to ESF, 31 Jul 1918, ESFP 2:14.

64   "shameless": ESF quoted in WFF to ESF, 23 Sep 1918, ESFP 2:16.

64	"I thought, last year": ESF quoted in WFF to ESF, 16 Dec 1918, ESFP 2:19.
64	"Dear Heart," "way around": WFF to ESF, 29 Oct 1918, ESFP 2:17.
64	"wishing and waiting": ESF, Diary, 45.
64	"Biwy": See, for example, WFF to ESF, 29 Sept 1918, ESFP 2:16. ESF's poems and 1922 letters sometimes lapsed into baby talk, too.
64	"Just imagine," "stand it": WFF to ESF, 7 Jul 1918, ESFP 2:14.
64	eight weeks, "infinite pain": WFF to ESF, 24 Sep 1918, ESFP 2:16; WFF to ESF, 23 Jul 1918, ESFP 2:14.
65	"'belle noir cheveux'": WFF to ESF, Jun 1918, ESFP 2:13.
65	"I may keep you": WFF to ESF, 23 Sep 1918, ESFP 2:16.
65	oil lamp and photographs: WFF to ESF, 19 Dec 1918, ESFP 2:19.
65	sixteen-hour days: WFF to ESF, 26 Aug 1918, ESFP 2:15.
65	"The work is so hard," "make good": WFF to ESF, 24 Jul 1918, ESFP 2:14.
65	"You know how much 'group work,'" "if possible": WFF to ESF, 4 Aug 1918, ESFP 2:15.
65	"I had one of those idea days," "clear blue": WFF to ESF, 26 Aug 1918, ESFP 2:15.
65	"our wizard": WFF to ESF, 10 Nov 1918, ESFP 2:18.
65–66	she discovered that Fabyan had been going through her mail: WFF to ESF, 7 Oct 1918, ESFP 2:17. ESF gave contradictory accounts about when she discovered Fabyan's trickery, but this letter proves she learned at least some of the truth in September 1918. She and WFF were still discovering details in February 1919. See WFF to J. Mauborgne, 18 Nov 1920, in WFC/NSA, ID A66329.
66	harassing her: WFF to ESF, Jun 1918 "4th installment," ESFP 2:13; 14 Jul 1918, ESFP 2:14; WFF to ESF, 18 Aug 1918, ESFP 2:15.
66	Fabyan, too: Lyle and Joyner, 94.
66	"Honey, don't be afraid": WFF to ESF, 29 Jul 1918, ESFP 2:15.
66	cabled her: WFF to ESF, 29 Sep 1918, ESFP 2:16.
66	"prison" and leaving Riverbank: ESF quoted in WFF to ESF, 11 Oct 1918. See also WFF to ESF, 29 Sep 1918, EFSP 2:16; WFF to ESF, 7 Oct 1918, ESFP 2:17; and Lyle and Joyner, 97–99.
66	"I know we shall never return," "we are free": WFF to ESF, 7 Oct 1918, ESFP 2:17.

CHAPTER TEN Escape

67   "Dearest Woman in the Universe": WFF to ESF, 10 Nov 1918, ESFP 2:18.

67   "dear, intimate things": ESF, quoted in WFF to ESF, 16 Dec 1918, ESFP 2:19.

67   "You have had a long enough vacation": Fagone, 109, citing Fabyan to WFF, 13 Nov 1918, WFFP Item 734.

67   Fabyan demanded to know: Fabyan to ESF, 2 Nov 1918 and 7 Nov 1918, Box 1:42.

67   "beginning to realize what it meant": Ed Meryl, ESF interview and Q&A, 1939, ESFP 17:14.

68   "I should be a grade higher," "better condition": Lyle and Joyner, 100, citing WFF to Fabyan, 9 Dec 1918. It was even worse than WFF thought. In February, he learned that Fabyan had cheated him of the chance to go over in October 1917 as the head of the officers he and Elizebeth had trained. That would have seen him rise higher than just one grade more. WFF to Mauborgne, 18 Nov 1920, in WFC/NSA, ID A66329.

68   Nothing they said, Elizebeth and William were outraged: ESF/ML 5:7–8; Lyle and Joyner, 104–105.

68   "Elsbeth, my Dearest": WFF to ESF, 10 Nov 1918, ESFP 2:18.

68   "Well, Honey": WFF to ESF, 20 Dec 1918, ESFP 2:19.

69   "spick and span": WFF to ESF, 10 Nov 1918, ESFP 2:18.

69   "I don't want a 'rubber stamp'": WFF to ESF, 8 Dec 1918, ESFP 2:19.

69   "Someday I may be known": WFF to ESF, 18 Aug 1918, ESFP 2:15.

69   library shut down, masks: "Fewer Books Used in 1918," *Huntington Herald*, 11 Feb 1919, 2; "Mask Order Is Issued," *Huntington Herald*, 10 Dec 1918, 1.

69   "the damfool Bolshevists": WFF to ESF, 8 Dec 1918, ESFP 2:19.

69   "all the histories": WFF to ESF, 22 Nov 1918, ESFP 2:18.

70   "Won't our reunion": WFF to ESF, 5 Feb 1919, ESFP 2:20.

70   "CAN YOU LEAVE": WFF to ESF, 6 Mar 1919, ESFP 2:19.

70   Pittsburgh, job search: Lyle and Joyner, 103; ESF, Memoir, 45; ESF/ML 2:12–13; ESF/ML 5:7–8; ESF/RWC, 12.

71   "He was having us watched": ESF/ML 5:7.

71   "Return to Riverbank": ESF, Memoir, 47; ESF/FP, 67; Lyle and Joyner, 103–104.

71   they made demands: ESF, Memoir, 47–48; Lyle and Joyner, 104–105; ESF/ML 5:7–8.

71   betrayal, William's health: WFF to Eisenhour, 8 Jun 1921, WFFP Item 734.

72   Fabyan's violent streak: ESF/FP, 70; WFF to Mauborgne, 29 Nov 1920, in WFC/NSA, ID A66329.

72   threats and false promises, "breach of loyalty": Lyle and Joyner, 106; ESF, Memoir, 49; ESF/ML 2:13.

72–73   Mauborgne recruits WFF: Mauborgne to WFF, 2 Oct 1920, and WFF to Mauborgne, 8 Oct 1920, in WFC/NSA, ID A66329.

73   heart defect: WFF to Mauborgne, 1 Nov 1920, 18 Nov 1920, and Mauborgne to WFF, 15 Nov 1920, 19 Nov 1920, 2 Dec 1920, in WFC/NSA, ID A66329, ID A66329.

73   "I expect violence": Mauborgne to WFF, 2 Dec 1920, in WFC/NSA, ID A66329.

73   secretly accepted positions: Mauborgne and WFF, 22 Nov–16 Dec 1920, in WFC/NSA, ID A66329.

73   final getaway: ESF/FP, 69–70.

73   "our secret plot": ESF/FP, 70.

74   "We've got to be": ESF/FP, 69.

RAIL FENCE LOVE LETTER

75   WFF's cipher letter: WFF to ESF, 16 Jan 1919, ESFP 2:20.

CHAPTER ELEVEN   At Home

77   arrival in Washington: ESF to Ronald Clark, n.d., ESFP 15:4; ESF, Memoir, 51–52; DeFerrari, "The Magnificent Raleigh Hotel."

78   "[E]verybody shoots": WFF to Eisenhour, 8 Jun 1921, WFFP Item 734.

78   "days very sunny," "no ice": ESF, Memoir, 52.

78   "starved for theater": ESF, Memoir, 52.

78   "We used to have crowds": ESF/RWC, 14; ESFP 12:1.

78   "new man": J. Rives Childs to V. Friedman, 28 Sep 1981, ESFP 12:14; J. Rives Childs to JRF, 16 Nov 1980, ESFP 16:26.

79   letters from Fabyan: ESF/FP, 69; WFF to GF, 10 Mar 1921, WFFP Item 734. Fabyan knew exactly how to approach WFF—by giving him technical news and promising favors. He rarely followed through.

79   "Everything is fine!": WFF to Eisenhour, 8 Jun 1921, WFFP Item 734.

79   his assistant, half the pay: J. O. Mauborgne to WFF, 19 Nov 1920; WFF to JOM, 29 Nov 1920; JOM to Hamson Black, 1 Jun 1921; all in WFC, ID A66329.

80   "By the end of the war": ESF, "Pure Accident," *The Arrow* (Feb 1930), 400, ESFP 12:9.

80   AT&T machine: WFF, "Can Cryptologic History Repeat Itself?" 21 Jul 1948, WFC/NSA, ID A516913; ESF/FP, 11–12.

80   *The Index of Coincidence:* Bellovin, 13–15; Kahn, 376.

81   "inane women's rights": ESF, Diary, 29 Jan 1916.

81   League of Women Voters work: "Feminist Outlook Divides Session," *Evening Star,* 24 Apr 1935, A4; "Vote for District One of Chief Aims of Women's Unit," *Sunday Star,* 22 Apr 1934, F2.

81   "those courageous souls": ESF to Belle Sherwin, 14 Apr 1933, ESFP 7:6.

81   WFF promoted, ESF quits: Clark, 63; ESF, Personnel Record, ESFP 7:3.

81   wanted to write, the alphabet: ESF, Memoir, 58; ESF, Diary, 38.

82   "You can write": WFF to ESF, 14 Aug 1918, ESFP 2:17.

82   "resigned in our hopes": ESF to Ronald Clark, n.d., ESFP 15:4.

82   dreaming of children: WFF to ESF, 31 Jul 1918, ESFP 2:14; WFF to ESF, 23 Sep 1918, ESFP 2:16.

82   "I want them so": WFF to ESF, 29 Sep 1918, ESFP 2:16.

82   "safe": WFF to ESF, 10 Nov 1918, ESFP 2:18.

82   It was a common belief: Molnar, 173–174.

82   William even told a friend: WFF to J. Manly, 18 Jan 1923, ESFP 13:22.

83   "went head over heels": ESF to Ronald Clark, n.d., ESFP 15:4.

83   ex-boxer: WFF, "Communications Security," Marine Corps Lectures, Second Period, WFC/NSA, ID A63403, 63.

83   "I am all alone": WFF to J. Manly, 4 Feb 1922, ESFP 13:22.

83   "Honey, the house": WFF, quoted in Lyle and Joyner, 114.

83   "Blessed Love!" "60 trillion kisses," "my five weeks": ESF to WFF, n.d., ESFP 2:2.

84   "After it got dark": ESF to WFF, n.d., ESFP 2:2.

84   manual on code breaking: ESF, Code-Breaking Manuscript, ESFP 9:12; ESF/ML 5:8.

84   "*Now, there are only two things*": Code-Breaking Manuscript, 4–5, ESFP 9:12.

84   "Eureka!": Code-Breaking Manuscript, 29, ESFP 9:12.

CHAPTER TWELVE On the Doorstep

86   "I didn't want": ESF/FP, 39.

86   Week after week: WFF to J. Manly, 18 Jan 1923, 13:22.

86   "the only way": ESF/FP, 39.

86   Agnes Meyer: ESF, Memoir, 54; Mundy, 74–77, ESF/FP, 71–72.

86   "This was a case": ESF, Memoir, 54.

86–87   "That's the story of my life": ESF/ML 5:8.

87   bargain salary: Smith, 36.

87   "could keep nothing": BF, "Family Anecdotes," ESFP 12:11.

87   she resigned from the Navy job: ESF to Secretary of the Navy, 6 Jun 1923, Personnel File, ESFP 7:3.

87   "warm barley gruel": GF to WFF, 23 Feb 1923, WFFP Item 734.

88   back treatment: BF, "Family Anecdotes," ESFP 12:11.

88   Green Mansions: ESF to Ronald Clark, n.d., ESFP 15:4; ESF, Memoir, 59.

88   Crypto, "private bodyguard," "the first": ESF, Memoir, 59–60.

88   "an extraordinarily fine person": ESF, Memoir, 59.

88   Cassie and Carlotta: ESF, Memoir, 61, 74; "Barbara" Diary, ESFP 21.

89   WFF in the news: "Photos Taken of Martian Signals," *New Britain Daily Herald,* 27 Aug 1924; "Can Get Meaning of Any Old Code," *Philadelphia Inquirer,* 7 May 1924, ESFP 18:46; Gould, 2; Undated newspaper clippings, ESFP 18:46; Martin, "Hitler's Favorite American."

89   Nordic people, "undesirable," "rendered," "We'll take our chances": Gould, 2.

89   kept records of her baby's cryptic babblings: ESF, "Barbara" Diary, ESFP Box 21.

89   expected to retire: Molnar, 170–172.

89   Edward Beale McLean: ESF, Memoir, 53–58.

90   "any demand": JRF to R. Clark, 29 Jul 1976, ESFP 14:14.

90   "We were becoming weary," "life time lesson": ESF, Memoir, 55–56.

90   3932 Military Road: WFF to GF, 10 Feb 1926, Item 734; ESF, Memoir, 59.

90   Charles Root: ESF, Memoir, 60.

CHAPTER THIRTEEN The Rum War

91   Rum War: Ensign, 2–5; Funderburg, 6, 28.

92   gangs, Al Capone: Roos, "How Prohibition Put the 'Organized' into Organized Crime"; ESF, Memoir, 70.

92   "conscientious officer": ESF, Memoir, 65.

92–93   Charles Root: Thiesen, "The Long Blue Line," 24 Sep 2015.

93   aircraft engines: Funderburg, 30–31.

93   "mother ships," "floating warehouses," "intermediates," "contact": ESF, "West Coast," ESFP 4:23, 1.

93   seventy-five vessels: Ensign, 5.

93–94   "with its coves and inlets": ESF, Memoir, 63.

94   charts and lists: Ensign, 18.

94   pigeon, bottle, radio and rumrunning: Mowry, *Listening to the Rumrunners,* 4; Ensign, 25, 48; Smith, 48.

94   Root, the Navy, and WFF: Ensign, 25; C. Root to WFF, 23 Feb 1925, ESFP 4:14.

94   "they'd get the use": ESF/RWC, 22.

95   ESF and Prohibition: ESF, Memoir, 63, 70–72.

95   "I made the condition": ESF/RWC, 15.

CHAPTER FOURTEEN The Making of Her

96   "I didn't even have an office": ESF/VV 17:16.

96   "I went to Captain Root's office": ESF, Memoir, 61.

96   "got together the present situation": ESF/VV 17:16.

97   "EBQKPI": ESFP 4:10. In the original transcription, the first letter was copied down wrong. ESF worked it out anyway.

97   "It pays to go very slowly": ESF, Code-Breaking Manuscript, ESFP 9:12; ESF/ML 5:29.

98   Pregnancy and birth of John: ESF, Service Record, 24 Feb 1931, Personnel File, ESFP 7:3; ESF to R. Clark, 12 Jul 1976, ESFP 15:1; BF, "Family Anecdotes," ESFP 12:11. John Ramsay was named partly for their friend Dr. Ramsay Spillman, who oversaw ESF's treatment during her pregnancy. See *Cornell Alumni News* 60:18 (15 Jun 1958), 639.

98   "in emergencies," April 1927: Memo, C. Root, 22 Apr 1927, ESFP 4:16.

98   "Special Investigator": ESF, Memoir, 61; "Personal History," 21 Oct 1927, Personnel File, ESFP 7:3.

98   "shrewdness," "the services of," "secret methods": Memo, C. Root, 22 Apr 1927, ESFP 4:16.

98   "Our impression": Kullback, NSA Oral History Interview, 10–11. Abe Sinkov, another one of WFF's hires, said that their team occasionally cracked rumrunner codes for the Coast Guard in the early 1930s. Perhaps this happened when ESF was on the road and her new assistants needed help, as ESF was more than capable of doing the work he describes.

98–99   "We got fun," "Inform Andrew," "Sorry": ESF/RWC, 22–23.

99   he was already snowed under at work: WFF Office Records (1919–1937), WFC/NSA, ID A66329, 296–371; WFF, Correspondence on BIA Messages, WFC/NSA, ID A4127217.

99–100   "I was . . . 'a loner'": ESF, Conexco Memo, 1928–1930, ESFP 4:23, 1. See also Ensign, 19.

100   "This traffic": ESF, "History of Work in Cryptanalysis, April 1927–June 1930," 1, ESFP 4:17.

100   working methods: ESF, "History of Work," 2, ESFP 4:17; ESF, Worksheets, ESFP 4:15.

100   "As rapidly as": ESF, "History of Work, April 1927–June 1930," 1–2, ESFP 4:17.

101   "*When I am summoned*": ESF, "Pure Accident," *The Arrow* (Feb 1930), 401, ESFP 12:9.

101   "Hittite" holiday card: ESFP 13:9.

102   sixty percent . . . 5 million: Ensign, 44.

102   a blizzard of new codes: ESF/MS, 3.

102   "nearly 50 distinct," nothing to equal it: ESF, "History of Work," 3–4, ESFP 4:17.

102   twelve thousand secret messages, twenty-five thousand messages: ESF, "History of Work," 5–6, ESFP 4:17.

103–104   ESF and intelligence work: Elizabeth Smith Friedman Dedication, ATFHQ, 17 Oct 2014, archive.org/details/youtube-20f-igw9GyA; Smith, 6, 63, 70.

104   24 different code and cipher systems: ESF, "History of Work," 4, ESFP 4:17.

104–105   *I'm Alone* case: Smith, 52–67; Helmick, 55.

BARBARA'S CIPHER

106   Trip to Spain: ESF, Memoir, 74–75.

106   Caesar cipher letter to BF: ESFP 2:12.

106–107 summer camp, "tender age": Mary Jane Brumley, "Ciphers Hold No Mysteries for Her," *Evening Star,* 5 Jun 1937, ESFP 18:23.

107 "greatest thrill": ESF, Interview by Ed Meryl, 1939, ESFP 17:14.

CHAPTER FIFTEEN Firepower

108 "Crypt Analyst": ESF, Service Record, 24 Feb 1931, Personnel File, ESFP 7:3.

108 "high-class mortician": ESF, "A Cryptanalyst," *The Arrow* (Feb 1928), 531, ESFP 12:9.

108 "Cryptanalyst in Charge": ESF, Oath of Office, 1 Jul 1931, Personnel File, 7:3. archive.org/details/ESFPersonnelFile/page/n31.

108 *"saving"*: ESF, "Memorandum Upon a Proposed Central Organization," Nov 1930, ESFP 5:6; ESF, Memoir, 69.

109 $3800—nearly three times the average U.S. salary: Smith, 48.

109 office in the Treasury Annex: Fagone, 141.

109 hours, special security pass: F. J. Gorman, Memo, 18 Jul 1931, Personnel File, ESFP 7:3.

109 recruitment, "Many times I've been asked": ESF, Memoir, 66, 69.

109 "great misgivings": ESF, Memoir, 69.

109–110 "crash course": ESF, "CONEXCO memorandum," 11, ESFP 4:23.

110 "greater experience": ESF, Federal Employee Form, 1931, ESFP 5:1.

110 Elizabeth threw herself into family life: BF to R. Clark, 26 Sep 1976, ESFP 14:14; WFF to ESF, 5 Dec 1939, ESFP 3:6; JRF to R. Clark, 29 Jul 1976, ESFP 14:14; Smith, 86.

110 "reasonable," "very loveable": ESF, "Barbara" Diary, Mar 1928, ESFP 21.

110–111 "Flimflam," "a thousand times": ESF, Diary, 284–285, 302–303.

111 "between the shower curtain": BF to Ronald Clark, 26 Sep 1976, ESFP 14:14.

111 swimmer, "ardent bicyclist," tennis: "Cryptographer," *The American Magazine,* ca. 1933, ESFP 16:29; ESF/FP, 6.

111 housekeepers: ESF to Miss Coates, 23 Jan 1930, ESFP 1:2; U.S. Census (1930), familysearch.org/ark:/61903/1:1:XM2H-R7W; BF to Ronald Clark, 26 Sep 1976, ESFP 14:14.

112 "just a little bit bothersome": WFF to GF, 26 Jun 1928, WFFP Item 734.

112 "hugging me warmly," movies, "Henry the Whale": BF to R. Clark, 26 Sep 1976, ESFP 14:14; JRF to R. Clark, 29 Jul 1976, ESFP 14:14.

112   "pack my bag": ESF, "Pure Accident" *The Arrow* (Feb 1930), 400, ESFP 12:9.

112–113   Conexco: Smith, 70–71; Conexco Decrypts, ESFP 10:21; ESF, "CONEXCO memorandum," ESFP 4:23; ESF, Memoir, 91–93.

113–114   chart, network, "blacks": Chart, May 1930, ESFP 10:21.

114   "the greatest rum-running conspiracy": Fagone, 144.

CRACKING A CONEXCO CODE

115–116   taken from Elizebeth's records: ESF, CONEXCO Memorandum 1928–30, ESFP 4:23.

116   "Golden Guess": They were quoting Tennyson, one of Elizebeth's favorite poets, who wrote, "The golden guess is morning-star to the full round of truth."

CHAPTER SIXTEEN   Fame

117   "cryptanalyst," and trial excerpts: *United States v. Albert Morrison* (E.D. La. 1933), I:141–163.

118   "made an unusual impression": ESF, Memoir, 96.

118   "Clever Mrs. Elizebeth Friedman": "How Secret Codes and a Secret Love Tracked Down the Big Dope Ring," *Spokesman-Review* [Washington, DC], 3 Dec 1933, 33. "Can Get Meaning of Any Old Code," *Philadelphia Inquirer,* 7 May 1924, ESFP 18:46.

118   She didn't mind the misspelling: In her early working life, ESF sometimes spelled her own name that way, only coming to insist on "Elizebeth" later in life. See ESF, Personnel File, ESFP 7:3.

118   "a pretty government scrypt-analyst," etc.: Fagone, 146; ESF, Memoir 83; *San Francisco Examiner,* 28 Sep 1933, 17.

118   making herself exactly one year younger: The 1910 U.S. Census gives the correct birth year, but her marriage license (familysearch.org /ark:/61903/1:1:KF2N-3SN) and marriage affidavit (familysearch .org/ark:/61903/3:1:9392-9F9K-W5?i=750&cc=1803970) do not. She repeated the 1893 date on most personnel forms, certifying it as "correct to the best of my knowledge and belief." Personnel File, ESFP 7:3. She also gave 1893 as her birth year in the 1930 and 1940 U.S. Census and in passenger records from 1928 and 1932. WFF was meticulously honest, but he gave the wrong date on sworn forms as well, suggesting that ESF kept the truth from him. The date is correct on all forms from the 1950s onward.

119   "Your Honor," "were nervously indicating": ESF, Memoir, 94–95.

119   "set the press on fire," "how experts": ESF, Memoir, 95.

119   "Complex? Code?" "While I pursued": ESF, Memoir, 93–95.

119–120   "She Breaks Up," "Millions Are Saved," "Solves Ciphers": *Sunday Star,* 22 Jul 1934; *Christian Science Monitor,* 9 May 1934; *United States News,* 18 Jun 1934; all in ESFP 18:23.

120   attention to detail mattered: ESF, Memoir, 100.

120   "No, I can't tell you how I do it": "Ezra Gang Falls in Trap of Woman Expert at Puzzles," *San Francisco Examiner,* 28 Sep 1933, 17.

121   Barbara and John at NBC: ESF, Memoir, 88.

121   NBC interview: ESF/MS, 1–16; ESFP 11:15; ESF, Memoir, 88; Fagone, 222.

122   "my own experience," "chronicle": ESF to Durward Howes, 14 Nov 1934, ESFP 1:6.

122   lack of time for writing: ESF to Miss Coates, 23 Jan 1930, ESFP 1:2; ESF to Harold M. Dudley, 15 Aug 1933, ESFP 1:5.

122–123   Andresen: W. Andresen to ESF, 12 Mar 1938, ESFP 17:1.

123   "partly on my wife," "bound": W. Andresen to ESF, 7 Sep 1938, ESFP 17:1.

123–124   "twelve year old boy," "best wishes": ESF to W. Andresen, 25 Oct 1938, ESFP 17:1.

124   "After those smugglers got out": Lunnen, "She Has a Secret Side," ESFP 11:14; ESF/BBC, ESFP 5:15; ESF/ML 3:6–7.

124   bodyguards, protection: ESF/ML 3:8–9; Chris Atchison, phone interview with the author, 19 Jan 2021.

124–125   "Daddy joked": BF, interviewed by Smith, 50.

125   a shocking ninety-seven agents died: Barbara Osteika, interviewed by Smith, 50.

125   creating new code systems: Mowry, "Cryptologic Aspects," 15.

CHAPTER SEVENTEEN   The Trip of a Lifetime

126   "very elegant gentleman": ESF/ML 3:2.

126–127   Lim case: ESF/ML 3:3–6; League of Nations, Advisory Committee on Traffic in Opium, *Summary of Illicit Transactions and Seizures,* C. 135 M. 80 (Geneva, 1938), 3 (No. 743); Dominion of Canada, *Report of the Royal Canadian Mounted Police for the Year Ended March 31, 1938* (Ottawa, 1938), 81–82; R. R. Wasche to GAO, 5 Jul 1938, Personnel File, ESFP 7:3; ESF, Memoir, 70–71; ESF, "The Gordon Lim Case," ESFP 6:29; ESF, "Memorandum for Chief Intelligence Officer," 30 Oct 1937, ESFP 6:2. ESF believed the shop was a gem shop, but the Canadian records state that it mainly sold herbs and pharmaceuticals.

127   another drug case earlier that year: ESF, Lew Kim Yuen case summary, ESFP 6:26.

127   "The shorter a message is": ESF, Code-Breaking Manuscript, ESFP 9:12.

127–128   digraphs: ESF, "The Gordon Lim Case," 3–6, ESFP 6:29.

128   "Chinese characters," Chinese code books: ESF/ML 3:2–4, 12.

129   "They considered it hopeless": ESF/ML 3:3.

129   "[T]here was something so intriguing": ESF, "The Gordon Lim Case," 7, ESFP 6:29.

129   "[O]nce in a while": ESF/ML 3:3.

129–130   "to attack *from the ends*," "had a feeling": ESF, "The Gordon Lim Case," 7, ESFP 6:29.

130   "selected three messages": ESF, "The Gordon Lim Case," 8, ESFP 6:29; ESF/ML 3:3.

130   "6010": ESF, "The Gordon Lim Case," 8, ESFP 6:29.

131   "charming and tireless": ESF, "The Gordon Lim Case," 9, ESFP 6:29; ESF/ML 3:3.

131   "I asked her to speak": ESF, "The Gordon Lim Case," 10, ESFP 6:29.

131   "I sent word to Vancouver": ESF/ML 3:4.

132   "to be without fail": ESF, "The Gordon Lim Case," 11–12, ESFP 6:29.

132   "I had one of the young men": ESF/VV 17:11. In later years, Elizebeth would remember the time as 4:00 p.m. or 4:30 p.m., but all contemporary documents show it was actually 3:40 p.m.

132   "something told me": ESF/ML 3:4.

132   "I don't know what it was.": ESF/VV 17:11.

132   "[B]less their darling hearts": ESF/ML 3:4.

132   kissed her children: ESF/VV 17:11.

132   street-corner handoff: ESF, "The Gordon Lim Case," 11–12, ESFP 6:29.

133   "not to hesitate": WFF to ESF, 18 Oct 1937, ESFP 3:5.

133–134   Flight details: all quotations from ESF to BF and JRF, 16–17 Oct 1937, ESFP 16:2.

134   plane crash: "All 19 Dead on Airliner," *Washington Daily News*, 19 Oct 1937, ESFP 9:19 and Box 6; Department of Commerce, *Report of Investigating Board;* ESF/VV 17:12.

CHAPTER EIGHTEEN Turbulence

135   "The story came," "feeling of being resurrected": ESF, quoted in Smith, 89.

135–136   "I phoned the airport": WFF to ESF, 18–19 Oct 1937, ESFP 3:5.

136   "Darling: I was awfully glad": WFF to ESF, 18–19 Oct 1937, ESFP 3:5.

136   "Well did I have a scare": Edna Smith Dinieus to ESF, 23 Oct 1937, ESFP 1:7.

136   "Well, my darling, I see": WFF to ESF, 18–19 Oct 1937, ESFP 3:5. "All 19 Dead on Airliner," *Washington Daily News,* 19 Oct 1937, 1, in ESFP 9:19 and Box 6, brown envelope.

137   "staggering number": ESF/ML 3:4.

137   "both A + B series," "Swell!": WFF to ESF, 18–19 Oct 1937, ESFP 3:5.

137   "a big idea or two," "bloomed," "very, very damning": ESF/VV 17:12; ESF/ML 3:4.

137   "good old criminal trick": ESF/VV 17:12. ESF remembered this appendicitis episode as taking place in October 1937. It actually happened in April 1938, according to RCMP records. Dominion of Canada, *Report,* 82.

137   "one of the pleasantest experiences": ESF, Memorandum to the Commandant, 14 Feb 1938, ESFP 1:9.

137–138   "good omen," "To use an old war-time expression": G. W. Fish to ESF, 3 Nov 1937, ESFP 6:27.

138   flight was "fate": Smith, 89.

138   "an extreme fatalist": BF, comment on brown envelope, ESFP Box 6.

138   "important" and "save": brown envelope in ESFP Box 6; WFF to ESF, 18 Oct 1937, ESFP 3:5; assorted newspaper clippings in ESFP 9:19.

138   "DC WOMAN ABOARD": Smith, 89.

139   She told William she wanted to quit: WFF to ESF, 18 Jan 1938, ESFP 3:6.

140   "irresistible energy": Mima Pollitt to Vanessa Friedman, 6 Oct 1981, ESFC 12:15.

140   rarely took vacation days, lunch, evenings: Pass Requests and Individual Records of Absence, ESF Personnel File, ESFP 7:3.

140   ESF and WFF work travel: ESF Personnel File, ESFP 7:3, Smith, 99; William F. Friedman, Office Records (1938–1942), WFC/NSA, ID A66325.

140 Elizabeth's health took a nose dive: Individual Record of Absence, 1938, ESF Personnel File, ESFP 7:3; WFF to T. M. Johnson, 26 Apr 1938, ESFP 13:24.

140–141 "Just never, never say anything": ESF/FP, 22.

141 "[W]e were two separate nations": Currier, NSA Oral History Interview, 53.

141 "Of course there was no truth in that": ESF/FP, 22–23.

CHAPTER NINETEEN The Black Chamber

143–144 WFF and the Black Chamber archives: Hannah, 5–8.

144 origins of the Black Chamber, Yardley, "unsavory": Kahn, 355–360; ESF/ML 2:9–10; WFF to ESF, 16 Dec 1918, ESFP 2:19.

144 he also had claimed credit: ESF/ML 2:10.

144 "*edge* on her": ESF to WFF [Summer 1922], ESFP 2:2.

145 "Gentlemen do not read": Kahn, 360.

145 Signal Intelligence Service: Kahn, 386.

146 "This is the purest bunk.": WFF's copy of *The American Black Chamber*, 149, WFC/NSA, ID A111567.

146 "undesirable publicity": H. F. Kingman, Navy Memorandum, 2 Jun 1934, WFC/NSA, ID A72637; Extract from R.I.P. No. 98, Copy 1, 5 Apr 1943, WFC/NSA, ID A66485.

146–147 "How the G-2 Woman": ESFP 18:1. ESF preferred Mary Jane Brumley's "Ciphers Hold No Mysteries for Her," ESFP 18:23— the "most intelligent, in my opinion, of all the articles ever written about me."

147 She even hoped to find a writer: ESF, Memoir, 84; Leah Stock Helmick to ESF, 3 Sep 1937, ESFP 1:8.

147–148 "Key Woman": *Reader's Digest* (Sep 1937), 51–55. After the article won the *Reader's Digest* contest, the magazine arranged to have it first published, in a different form, in an American Legion publication. The *Reader's Digest* September issue appeared in August 1937. See Leah Stock Helmick to ESF, 3 Sep 1937, ESFP 1:8; ESF, Memoir, 84.

148 "caused me no end": WFF to Mrs. N. Fabyan, 10 Nov 1937, WFFP Item 734(#2).

148 "my superiors": Clark, 95–96.

149 William believed these fears were overblown: Soon afterward, William encouraged Elizabeth to keep working on the Chinese codes in the Gordon Lim case, even though the case was likely to

attract publicity when it went to trial. He even added, "Get all the publicity you can." The latter remark, however, may not have been meant seriously, as WFF often joked with his family, and he knew that there were press restrictions on the trial. (WFF to ESF, 18–19 Oct 1937, ESFP 3:51.)

149   *"In view of the present situation,"* "I have definite reasons": ESF, "Memorandum for the Commandant," 31 Aug 1937, ESFP 6:27.

149-150   Lim trial and publicity: ESF, "Memorandum to the Commandant," 14 Feb 1938, ESFP 1:9.

CHAPTER TWENTY Ad Absurdum!

152   *"What if you had only bridge,"* "a life of mental toil": WFF to ESF, 18 Jan 1938, ESFP 3:6.

152   "It's a great life": ESF, "Pure Accident," *The Arrow* (Feb 1930), 400, ESFP 12:9.

152   Gordon Lim trial publicity: ESF, "Memorandum to the Commandant," 14 Feb 1938, ESFP 1:9.

153   "I found that my life": ESF, Memoir, 81.

153   "I have at no time": ESF, "Memorandum to the Commandant," 14 Feb 1938, ESFP 1:9. See also ESF to G. W. Fish, 13 Feb 1938, ESFP 1:9.

153   unauthorized stories and portrait: ESF, Memoir, 81, 86. For examples of the coverage, see "Deciphers Intricate Chinese Code," *Star-Phoenix* [Saskatoon], 9 Feb 1938, 8; "U.S. Woman Expert Deciphers Chinese Code, Traps Opium Ring," *Boston Globe*, 9 Feb 1938, 6; "They Make News Here and There," *Charlotte Observer*, 15 Feb 1938, 3. Many of these stories appeared in multiple papers.

154   "WHAT CIRCUMSTANCES": Theodore Adams to ESF, 25 Feb 1938, ESFP 6:4.

154   "have sickened me": ESF to Mrs. T. N. Alford, 19 Oct 1939, ESFP 1:9.

154   "no one but no one": ESF, Memoir, 83.

154-155   Her conditions?: ESF, Memos to Mr. Schwarz, 26 Feb 1938, 20 Oct 1938, ESFP 1:9; Smith, 106.

155   "the bare facts," "Greatest discouragement?" "her figure," *"she isn't exactly"*: ESF, Memoir, 83; Ed Meryl, ESF stock biography and Q&A, 1939, ESFP 17:14.

155   stopped speaking with reporters: ESF to Mrs. T. N. Alford, 19 Oct 1939, ESFP 1:9; Smith, 106.

156   "CONGRATULATIONS": WFF to ESF, 12 Jun 1938, ESFP 3:6.

156   *"Everybody"*: WFF to ESF, 16 Jun 1938, ESFP 3:6.

CAFÉ CRYPTANALYTIQUE

158   Café Cryptanalytique invitations, clues, and worksheets: ESFP 13:9.

158   "The whimsy and fun": ESF, handwritten note in ESFP 13:9.

159   "The first item was a series of dots": Virginia Corderman to Vanessa Friedman, 2 Oct 1981, ESFP 12:15.

CHAPTER TWENTY-ONE The Woman All Spies Fear

160   "The Woman All Spies in U.S. Fear.": W. K. Clark, *Miami Herald*, 1 Oct 1939, 52. The syndicated article also appeared in the *Salt Lake Tribune* and several other newspapers across the country.

160   "hodge-podge of plagiarism": Smith, 106.

161   "Forgive the sputtering": Smith, 108.

161   to speak with the White House: Smith, 108; Sweeney, 21–25; McDonnell, 59.

161   Eleanor Roosevelt had often invited her, "very thoughtful and encouraging": ESF, Memoir, 78.

161   new mission: Bennett, 21; Mowry, "Cryptologic Aspects," 15.

162   "eyes and ears": ESF, Memoir, 89.

162   "exciting, round-the-clock": ESF, "Footnote to History," 4, ESFP 9:11.

163   Coast Guard network, "10 years more advanced": Bennett, 21.

163–164 "If any text appeared": ESF, Memoir, 89.

164   secret messages: *History of Coast Guard Unit #387, 1940–1945*, 1–3; Jones, "History of OP-20-GU," 2–3, 8.

164   new code signals, spy circuits: Mowry, "Cryptologic Aspects," 16; Fagone, 188–189.

164–165 South America vulnerable to Nazis: McConahay, 11; Fagone, 180–183; "Extract from Interrogation Report on Schellenburg for June–July 1945," 12 Jul 1945, 10, NAUK, KV 2/89.

165   "complete subservience," "home country": Fagone, 180, quoting the German ambassador to Argentina.

165   Greater Germany: McConahay, xi–xii, 4; Fagone, 182.

165   Nazi and fascist sympathizers: Fagone, 182–183; ESF/RWC, 18; Weinberg, 588–593.

166   "[T]hat's what I did": ESF/RWC, 18.

167   extra funding: Mowry, "Cryptologic Aspects," 15.

167   "couldn't sleep": ESF/FP, 26.

167   sandwich, coffee, pacing: ESF/FP, 26; Clark, 107.

167   "Dad used to joke": Smith, 106.

167   "things at night": ESF/FP, 53.

168   "a certain grim look," "any expression": ESF/VV 17:16.

168   "I tried to know as little as possible," "you just hoped": ESF/VV 17:15.

168   "They aren't getting anywhere," "You drop everything": ESF/RWC, 16. See also ESF/FP, 23.

168   "Read until 1 a.m.": WFF to ESF, 10 Jun 1940, ESFP 3:7.

CHAPTER TWENTY-TWO   The War Within

170   WFF's interest in machines: "A Demolisher of Secrets," David Abarbanel, *The American Hebrew*, 2 Nov 1928, B34, ESFP 18:46; ESF, notes for Ronald Clark, ca. 1975, ESFP 15:4; Kahn, 376–377, 385.

171–172   SIGABA: Mucklow, 25–26; Clark, 152–153.

172   It was a routine that worked well: Rowlett, NSA Oral History Interview, 446, 449–450.

172   Type B, Purple: WFF, "Preliminary Historical Report on the Solution of the 'B' Machine," 14 Oct 1940, 1, WFC/NSA, ID A58137.

173   "our motion pictures": Lindbergh, Des Moines Speech, 11 Sep 1941; Calamur, "A Short History of 'America First.'"

174–175   September 20, 1940: All quotations from Rowlett, in Hannah, 5.

174   Grotjan: Gentzke, "An American Hero"; WFF, "Preliminary Historical Report," 8.

175   "almost day and night": WFF, "Important Contributions to Communications Security, 1939–1945," WFC/NSA, ID A60534.

175   alliance pact, decrypted two Purple messages: WFF, "Preliminary Historical Report," 6–7.

175   value of Magic: Kahn, 508; Hannah, 5, 19.

176   "Now wouldn't you have thought": ESF/FP, 23.

176   "cooperation and close collaboration": WFF, "Preliminary Historical Report," 8.

176 "It put a lot of psychological pressure": Rowlett, NSA Oral History Interview, 450–451.

176 The Purple machine was selected: Currier, NSA Oral History Interview, 48–50.

176–177 banks of switches: WFF, "Preliminary Historical Report," 7.

177 crates, voyage: Currier, NSA Oral History Interview, 59–62.

177 trip to Britain: "Office Orders No. 126," 23 Dec 1940, WFC/NSA, ID A66325, 257; Sinkov, NSA Oral History Interview, 1–3.

CHAPTER TWENTY-THREE Heebeegeebees

178 the "crash": ESF/FP, 28–29; Clark, 120.

178 "Fight, flight": Clark, 203.

178 "[H]eebeegeebees," "nervousness": WFF, Bletchley Park Diary, 24 May 1943. Clark, 203.

178–179 WFF, Walter Reed, William Clare Porter, and psychiatry ca. 1940: Fagone, 218–220; Sheldon, "William F. Friedman," 12–13: Standlee, 168, 235; Guise-Richardson, 23–29.

179 "There was only one psychiatrist": ESF, quoted in Clark, 120.

180 visits, rules: Smith, 111; ESF, Personnel Record, ESFP 7:3; Standlee, 334.

180 "was nothing more or less": ESF/FP, 43.

180 "dark moods": WFF to ESF, 11 Jul 1918, ESFP 2:14. In an undated note written in the early 1960s, WFF said he had suffered from "neurosis" for "50 years . . . off and on," which indicates that the problems started during his college years. Clark, 203.

180 "trying out": Zigmond M. Lebensohn, M.D., to Ronald Clark, 10 May 1976, ESFP 13:30.

180 early 1930s: Z. M. Lebensohn to R. Clark, 10 May 1976, ESFP 13:30.

180 "on the verge," "to be careful": Alexander R. George, "War Code Sleuths Find Raw Nerves Worst Foe," *Lancaster New Era,* 18 Jun 1937, 8.

181 he felt worse than ever before: Z. M. Lebensohn to R. Clark, 10 May 1976, ESFP 13:30.

181 "the military and its antisemitism": ESF to R. Clark, 8 May 1976, ESFP 13:30.

181 Army, MID, and anti-Jewish bias: Bendersky, xiii–xiv, 70–71, 132, 135, 157, 167–170, 219–220, 303–307. The Navy had problems with antisemitism, too. Smith, 123; Currier, NSA Oral History Interview, 54–55.

181–182   General George Strong: ESF/FP, 22; Bendersky, 307, 317–319; Tiltman, NSA Oral History Interview, 11; Sherman, "The National Security Agency," 201.

182   two of his brothers, "psychosis" and "severe neurosis": Z. M. Lebensohn, M.D., to R. Clark, 10 May 1976, ESFP 13:30. William's youngest brother committed suicide. Their exact diagnosis is unknown.

182   "Manic Depressive Illness," bipolar disorder: Z. M. Lebensohn, M.D., to R. W. Clark, 10 May 1976, ESFP 13:30.

182   "anxiety reaction," "prolonged overwork": Sheldon, "William F. Friedman," 12–13, 15; Clark, 120.

183   "I began to recover": Sherman, "The National Security Agency," 200.

183   recovery and discharge: Sheldon, "William F. Friedman," 12–13; Sherman, "The National Security Agency," 201–202.

183   "[E]verybody went into uniform": Davis, NSA Oral History Interview, 34.

183   "took him to work": Mima Pollitt to Vanessa Friedman, 6 Oct 1981, ESFP 12:15.

184   "indomitable spirit helped me": WFF to JRF, 13 Aug 1945, ESFP 4:8; Fagone, 152–153.

185   "my usual quadruple-decker sandwich": WFF to BF, 12 Oct 1941, ESFP 13:7.

185   several British intelligence officers: The Friedmans became especially good friends with Eddie Hastings, Kenneth Maidment, and Alistair Denniston and their wives.

CHAPTER TWENTY-FOUR   Elizebeth's War

186–187   Donovan, ESF, and the brand-new agency: ESF to Col. Donovan, 29 Dec 1941, ESFP 17:15; Smith, 114–118; Burke, 1–7. The agency was first known as the COI, after the initials of Donovan's role: Coordinator of Information.

187   code *builder:* ESF, Personnel Record, ESFP 7:3; Mowry, "Cryptologic Aspects," 15.

187   "practically sobbing," "They knew": Smith, 115–116; ESF to BF, 12 Apr 1945, ESFP 3:26; Clark, 131.

188   investigation: Sherman, "William Friedman and Pearl Harbor," 310–312, 315–319; Clark 170–171; U.S. Congress, *Pearl Harbor Attack: Hearings* (1946), Part 35: 308–309.

188   a series of mistakes: Clark, 137–138.

188   William's relapse: Clark, 141.

188 she had built several: ESF/MF 3:11; Burke, 6, mentions double transpositions and strip ciphers.

188–189 "really the only unbreakable cipher": ESF/MF 3:11.

189 one-time pad systems: ESF/ML 3:11; Kahn, 402–403, 494–495, 650, 662. See also Chambers, *OSS Training in the National Parks and Service Abroad in World War II.*

189 Donovan and "DR. E. S. FRIEDMAN": ESF to Col Donovan, 29 Dec 1941, ESFP 17:15; Smith, 117–118; Burke, 7.

189 "very rebellious": Smith, 112; Fagone, 235.

190 an officer would be put in: Smith, 123.

190 "My personal opinion," "flubdedubs": ESF/FP, 51. See also ESF/RLB, 4.

190 Agnes Meyer Driscoll, "witch": Mundy, 78–81, 146–149.

191 Treasury's response to ESF's transfer: Smith, 112–113.

191 phone call, agreement: Smith, 113; Jones, "History of OP-20-GU," 3.

191 everything stayed more or less the same: Jones, "History of OP-20-GU," 3; Smith, 134; Fagone, 253.

191–192 high-level meeting, "s" of "Mrs.": Smith, 126–127.

192 Leonard T. Jones: Smith, 123–124, 130; "Captain Leonard T. Jones, USCG," Cryptologic Hall of Honor; ESF to Col Donovan, 29 Dec 1941, ESFP 17:15.

192 frustrating setup: ESF to WFF, Aug 1945, ESFP 2:8; ESF/RLB, 2, 4; Smith, 133–134. Decades later, when writing about this time, ESF said, "a Coast Guard officer was our 'leader,'" putting "leader" in quotation marks. See ESF/RWC, 25.

193 "excessive concern": ESF/RLB, 4.

193 others looked to her: Fagone, 259.

193 "They were gone": BF, quoted in Smith, 142.

193 "grubby, ramshackle," 114: ESF, "Footnote to History," ESFP 9:11.

194 household help: ESF, Christmas letter, 1944, ESFP 4:6.

194 "It would be a cinch": ESF to BF, 12 Feb 1945, ESFP 3:26.

194 daily dinners: Smith, 114.

194 "to refrain from technical and social contacts": Sherman, "The National Security Agency," 201–202. It was General George Strong who dressed William down. See also Memo, WFF to Branch Chiefs B, C, D, E, 2 Apr 1943, WFC/NSA, ID A60573, and Memo, WFF to Colonel Corderman, 3 Apr 1943, WFC/NSA, ID A60563.

194 "tense," "hbgbs": WFF, "Bletchley Diary," 24 May 1943.

195   antisemitism, Barbara: WFF to BF, 9 Apr 1945, ESFP 3:28; Lucile
       Deen to ESF, 12 Jul 1942, ESFP 1:11; ESF to BF, [n.d.] 1944, ESFP
       3:26.

195   spy networks, Sargo: *History of Coast Guard Unit #387*, 328; Fagone,
       229–231.

CODE NAMES AND CRIBS

196   code names: Fagone, 230; Mowry, "Cryptologic Aspects," 5–7.

196   "Humberto," "Alfredo": Fagone, 231; *History of Coast Guard Unit
       #387*, 71, 76–79.

196–197 SUDAMERIAT, WEDEKIND . . . SCHOEN: *History of Coast
       Guard Unit #387*, 7.

CHAPTER TWENTY-FIVE Sargo

198   Becker: Fagone, 223–229; S. H. Noakes to R. L. Stevens, 22 Nov
       1943, NAUK: KV 2/1722; Report on Johannes Siegfried Becker, 18
       Apr 1946, 1–3, in NAUK, KV 2/89.

198–199 Becker and sabotage plans: "Extract from the . . . Report on
       Elizabeth Hedwig Weigelmayer-Sommer," 5 Oct 1945, 10–11,
       NAUK, KV 2/89.

199–200 Sargo's spy circuits: Fagone, 185, 228–229, 241–242; Smith, 120–122;
       Jones, "Memorandum to OP-20-G."

200   over a thousand Allied merchant ships: "Battle of the Atlantic
       Statistics," American Merchant Marine at War, usmm.org
       /battleatlantic.html.

200   RMS *Queen Mary:* Fagone, 242–243.

200   *counterintelligence:* Fagone, 189. *Webster's New Universal Unabridged
       Dictionary* dates the word to 1935–1940.

201   Hoover and female agents: Fagone, 202–204; Glasser, 52–53.

201   bungled the case: McDonnell, 55–61.

202   Long Island station and the FBI: *History of Coast Guard Unit #387*,
       22, 32; Mowry, "Cryptologic Aspects," 24–25, 52.

202–203 other reasons to distrust the FBI: ESF/RLB, 3; Jones, "History of
       OP-20-GU," 5–6; Jones, "Memorandum to OP-20-G," 2–3.

203   claimed in public, did their best to disguise: Sheldon, *The Friedman
       Collection*, 345–346; Fagone, 232.

203   FBI and Brazil arrests: Mowry, "Cryptologic Aspects," 25; Jones,
       "History of OP-20-GU," 6.

204   networks went dark: Smith, 130–132; Jones, "History of OP-20-GU," 6.

204   "South American stuff," "something to do": Smith, 132–133.

204   October 1942: *History of Coast Guard Unit #387*, 231.

204   Enigma: The decision to upgrade to Enigma was made before the Brazilian arrests, but the raids delayed its implementation. See "Extract from the . . . Report on Elizabeth Hedwig Weigelmayer-Sommer," 5 Oct 1945, 16–17 in NAUK, KV 2/89.

CHAPTER TWENTY-SIX Cracking Enigma

205-207 Enigma operation and history: Stripp, 83–88. See also Hinsley and Stripp, *The Codebreakers,* and Welchman's *The Hut Six Story.*

207   January 1940 Enigma case: *History of Coast Guard Unit #387*, 216–230; Fagone, 194–201.

207   a commercial Enigma machine in her office: Fagone, 187.

208   Elizebeth turned to British code breakers: Fagone, 216–217; Letter, Oliver Strachey to ESF, 16 Mar 1942, ESFP 6:7; Mowry, "Cryptologic Aspects," 88–89.

208   bombes: The first bombes were made by the Polish Enigma team, but the British had substantially improved on them.

208-209 Abwehr Enigma, "lobsters" and "crabs": Twinn, 123–131; *History of Coast Guard Unit #387*, 233.

209   48 billion possible settings: Paul Reuvers, letter to the author, 21 Apr 2020.

209   ESF and the first Abwehr Enigma messages: *History of Coast Guard Unit #387*, 231–262.

209   messages *in depth*: *History of Coast Guard Unit #387*, 231–242; Fagone, 197–199, 266–267.

210   as fast as the British: *History of Coast Guard Unit #387*, 262.

210   "outstanding problems": Smith, 132–133.

210   British alarmed: Mowry, "Cryptologic Aspects," 27.

211   Hoover left out of the loop: Jones, "Memorandum to OP-20-G," 5.

SOLVING IN DEPTH

213   December 1942 cipher messages, O and B: *History of Coast Guard Unit #387*, 232, 234–239. Their first guess was wrong, and it didn't yield anything that looked like a word. Their next guess was that O stood for E. This time they were right.

CHAPTER TWENTY-SEVEN A Spy at Sea

214   *"The new Enigma"*: *History of Coast Guard Unit #387*, 261; Mowry, "Cryptologic Aspects," 86.

214-215 GREEN and RED networks: *History of Coast Guard Unit #387*, 212, 215, 262–263; Fagone, 263–265.

215   RED messages: *History of Coast Guard Unit #387*, 262–323; Fagone, 272–274, 285–287.

215-216 a wide range of Nazi plots: Fagone, 273–274.

216-217 Hellmuth: Fagone, 279, claims ESF alone provided the vital details about Hellmuth's voyage, but other evidence suggests there were multiple sources of intelligence. ESF and her team may have been the first to discover the name of the ship. See Fagone, 276–281; Walton, 62–63; WFF, "Examples of Intelligence Obtained from Cryptanalysis," 1 Aug 1946, 8, WFC/NSA, ID A67564; NAUK KV 2/1722, especially Minutes 4, 6, 64.

217   everything he knew: H. P. Milmo to P. N. Loxley, 28 Nov 1943, NAUK KV 2/1722; Fagone, 281.

217-218 spy hunt in Argentina: Fagone, 286–291, 297, 302.

218   Sargo in 1944–1945: "Memorandum on German Activities Issued by Coordinación General on April 21st 1945," NAUK, KV 2/89/4; "Extract from the . . . Report on Elizabeth Hedwig Weigelmayer-Sommer," 5 Oct 1945, 18 in NAUK, KV 2/89.

CHAPTER TWENTY-EIGHT Overkill

219   "[T]he problem was worked," "talents of the unit": ESF/RLB, 4.

220   new kinds of traffic: Jones, "Memorandum to OP-20-G," 9–12; *History of Coast Guard Unit #387*, 12–14.

220   Barbara and John: ESF, Christmas Letter, 1944, ESFP 4:6.

220   "I will let you know": Fagone, 304.

220   "any little," "you probably need," "There now": ESF to BF, 31 Dec 1944, ESFP 3:26; ESF to BF, [n.d.] Dec 1944, ESFP 3:26.

220-221 *"Oh, my darling"*: ESF to BF, 12 Apr 1945, ESFP 3:26.

221   "a thrilling sight": ESF to BF, 20 May 1945, ESFP 3:27.

221   "glorious three days," etc.: ESF to BF & JRF, 23 May 1945, ESFP 3:27.

222   "Now I can sleep": ESF to WFF, 10 Aug 1945, ESFP 3:9.

222   William finally came home: WFF to ESF, 5 Sep 1945, ESFP 3:9; Fagone, 317–318.

222   "Reams of 'work-sheets'": ESF, "Footnote to History," ESFP 9:11.

223   FBI: Fagone, 298–300; *Army-Navy Screen Magazine* #42, "Battle of the United States," 1944.

223   awards given to Leonard Jones: Smith, 142.

223   "the pledge": ESF, "Footnote to History," ESFP 9:11.

223   "a vast dome of silence": ESF, Speech to Mary Bartelme Club, 30 Nov 1951, ESFP 7:8.

224   "usefulness of my section": ESF, handwritten note, envelope of "Reduction in force" notice, 4 Oct 1946, ESFP 6:8.

224   "It was the end": ESF, "Footnote to History," ESFP 9:11.

PROCEDURE 40

225   2008: Smith, 165.

225   Procedure 40: *History of Coast Guard Unit #387*, 203–206.

CHAPTER TWENTY-NINE Secrets

228   "A knock," "A good meal," "I am not certain": Mrs. Stuart W. Vaile to the Friedman Collection, Marshall Library, 5 Nov 1980, ESFP 17:18.

229-230 IMF: Camille Gutt to ESF, 12 Nov 1946, ESFP 7:7; Joseph G. Keyes to Vanessa Friedman, 2 Feb 1982, ESFP 12:15. She also had designed a code system for the IMF's American predecessor in the 1930s. See ESF, "Experience and Special Qualifications," ca. 1940s, Personnel Record, ESFP 7:3.

230   When France needed to devalue its currency: Smith, 166.

230   job in November 1949: "Office Memorandum, United States Government, Chief, [redacted], to Chief, Communications," 8 Nov 1949, ESFP Box 12:15; "Office Memorandum, United States Government, Commo to SED," 9 Nov 1949, ESFP Box 12:15; "Statement of Personal History" Nov 1949, ESFP 11:16. The most likely source is the Armed Forces Security Agency, but the case remains open. For expert opinions on these documents, my thanks to Betsy Rohaly Smoot, David Sherman, David Hatch, and Joseph Frechette.

231   retired from work: Smith, 167.

231   WFF's career: Sheldon, "William F. Friedman," 15–16.

231-232 "psychic giddiness," "he kissed the nurses," WFF's mental health, 1940s and 1950s: Letter, Zigmond M. Lebensohn, M.D., to Ronald

W. Clark, 10 May 1976, ESFP 13:30. WFF's struggles in 1947 may have been connected with his efforts to get rights or compensation for his cryptography patents. Clark, 159–160.

232   "I am in better health": WFF to Carter W. Clarke, 23 Apr 1952, NSA Friedman Collection, ID A70092.

232   Many of his colleagues knew: For example, Ann Caracristi (NSA Oral History Interview, 17) said, "I was simply aware that he had had problems and there were concerns." Her NSA interviewer believed WFF had only one breakdown. John Tiltman, who knew WFF well, understood that he had more than one breakdown but was wrong about the timing and causes. Tiltman, NSA Oral History Interview, 11.

232   trusted only a few close friends: Mima Pollitt to Vanessa Friedman, 6 Oct 1981, ESFP 12:15.

232   "I doubt that she ever was bored": Jackie Schukraft to Vanessa Friedman, 16 Aug 1981, ESFP 12:14. See also BJ Averitt to Vanessa Friedman, 26 Aug 1981, ESFP 12:14.

232   elaborate foreign dishes: ESF, "Statement of Personal History" form from Nov 1949, ESFP 11:16; Fagone, 330.

233   dinner parties: BJ Averitt to Vanessa Friedman, 26 Aug 1981, ESFP 12:14.

233   dangers of atomic warfare: Ruth Dean, "Action on Atom Control Urged," *Evening Star,* 14 Feb 1947, B3.

233   "your duty and my duty," "made to feel wanted": ESF, Speech to Mary Bartelme Club, 1951, ESFP 7:8, 16.

233   like the one she had started: Lyle and Joyner, 85.

233–234 "a jewel," "finding lights": BJ Averitt to Vanessa Friedman, 26 Aug 1981, ESFP 12:14.

234   "cherished home": ESF, Notes for R. Clark, ca. 1970s, ESFP 15:4.

234   their own private library: Sheldon, *The Friedman Collection,* 8–9, 21; Fagone, 155–157.

234–235 Shakespeare project, Folger: Smith, 168.

235   "I stood in the front hall": ESF, Notes for Ronald Clark, ca. 1970s, ESFP 15:4.

235   Cambridge University Press: Smith, 168.

235–236 Fabyan and Gallup had both died in the 1930s: Fagone, 158–159.

236   "cool, surgical": Smith, 168.

236   "I've always bragged": Joseph O. Mauborgne to WFF & ESF, 29 Dec 1957, ESFP 10:26.

236   Mayan glyphs: WFF to GF, 10 Mar 1924, WFFP Item 734 (#2); Smith, 109; ESF to J. O. Mauborgne, 12 Jan 1958, ESFP 10:26; WFF to Edna Smith Dinieus, 31 Jan 1958, ESFP 13:18.

236   books they might write: WFF to Edna Smith Dinieus, 31 Jan 1958, ESFP 13:18; ESF, 1959 diary, ESFP 21; Fagone, 156; Sherman, "The National Security Agency," 206, 215.

CHAPTER THIRTY The Raid

238   December 30, 1958, raid: Sherman, "The National Security Agency," 203, 209–213; S. Wesley Reynolds, Memo re: "Retrieval of Classified Agency Documents from Home of W. F. Friedman," 2 Jan 1959, WFC/NSA, ID A99780; Coffey, NSA Oral History Interview, 1–14; Carter, NSA Oral History Interview, 291–295; ESF to Marshall Carter, 8 Jan 1971, WFC/NSA, ID A2918420; S. Wesley Reynolds, Memo, WFC/NSA, ID A99780. The accounts differ in detail, but it seems that at least two men went into the house, with another possibly staying by the vehicle. At the time, S. Wesley Reynolds wrote that he, Paul Gilliam, and a "Mr. Cook" went to the house. By "Cook," he may have meant Donald Coffey. Over twenty years later, Coffey reported that he, Gilliam, and "a couple of helpers" were sent there. ESF later wrote that "two Security men from NSA" entered the library and took items from them. ESF to Marshall Carter, 8 Jan 1971, WFC/NSA, ID A2918420.

238-239 William had little common ground: Sherman, "The National Security Agency," 204–205; Carter, NSA Oral History Interview, 291–292.

239   Department of Defense tightened security: Sherman, "The National Security Agency," 209–210.

239   "All official cryptanalysis": John A. Samford, Memo, 21 Mar 1958, WFC/NSA, ID A275512.

239   "with the history": S. Wesley Reynolds, Memo, WFC/NSA, ID A99780.

239-240 materials taken from the Friedmans: Sherman, "The National Security Agency," 213; Paul E. Gilliam, Memo, 17 Apr 1959, WFC/NSA, ID A99786; "Inventory of W. F. Friedman Files / Material Taken from His House," n.d., WFC/NSA, ID A99794; Coffey, NSA Oral History Interview, 3–9.

240   six boxes: Sherman, "The National Security Agency," 212.

240   "went berserk": Coffey, NSA Oral History Interview, 11.

240   "He was obviously upset," "a gentleman": Coffey, NSA Oral History Interview, 3, 13.

240   "a very nice lady," "let it be known": Coffey, NSA Oral History Interview, 14.

240   "search-and-seizure": ESF to Marshall Carter, 8 Jan 1971, WFC/ NSA, ID A2918420.

240   "expected of Nazi Germany": Lyle and Joyner, quoted in Smith, 172.

241   "a man who flouted": Sheldon, *The Friedman Collection,* 10.

242   NSA: Bamford, *The Puzzle Palace,* 175–178, 377–379; Bamford, "The NSA Is Building."

242   "He was always," "When people": Kullback, NSA Oral History Interview, 154.

242   refusals could attract attention: Sherman, "The National Security Agency," 204–205.

243   high-stakes, high-stress encounters: Clark, 161–163; "The Gentleman's Agreement," Crypto Museum; Corera, "The Crypto Agreement."

244   "a good portion": WFF to William Bundy, quoted in Clark, 84.

244   "the collection of secret intelligence": Clark, 201.

CHAPTER THIRTY-ONE Fallout

245   NSA treatment of WFF: Paul Gilliam to WFF, 30 Jun 1959, WFC/ NSA, ID A68686; Sherman, "The National Security Agency," 206, 214; Note, ESF to R. Clark, 8 May 1976, ESFP 13:30; Z. M. Lebensohn, M.D., to R. Clark, 10 May 1976, ESFP 13:30; Clark, 198, 205.

245   "clamping down": ESF to R. Clark, 8 May 1976, ESFP 13:30.

246   *They seem to think*": Sheldon, "William F. Friedman," 20.

246   "Even at this moment": WFF to Boris Hagelin, 10 Aug 1966, WFC/ NSA, ID A2263326; Sherman, "The National Security Agency," 216.

246   fear that the NSA might raid them again: Z. Lebensohn to R. Clark, 10 May 1976, ESFP 13:30.

246   "secrecy virus": Clark, 197.

246   "the NSA considers me": Z. Lebensohn to R. Clark, 10 May 1976, ESFP 13:30.

246   "feeling of being 'has-been,'" "suicidal thoughts": Clark, 203.

246   hospitalization and slow recovery: Z. Lebensohn to R. Clark, 10 May 1976, ESFP 13:30.

246-247 moving to Europe: WFF to Boris Hagelin, 10 Aug 1966, WFC/ NSA, ID A2263326.

247   "irritable": Z. Lebensohn to R. Clark, 10 May 1976, ESFP 13:30.

247   financial worries: Mima Pollitt to Vanessa Friedman, 6 Oct 1981,
        ESFP 12:15; ESF to BF, 10 Feb 1968, ESFP 3:20.

247   "*I used to say*": ESF to JRF, 7 Feb 1967, ESFP 3:20.

247   Barbara, health issues: Z. Lebensohn to R. Clark, 10 May 1976,
        ESFP 13:30; "Nicholas" Diary, 1961, ESFP 17:19; ESF to Annie
        Hagelin, 13 Nov 1963, WFC/NSA, ID A2263295; Mima Pollitt to
        Vanessa Friedman, 6 Oct 1981, ESFP 12:15.

247–248 good days: Z. Lebensohn to R. Clark, 10 May 1976, ESFP 13:30;
        Photographs, 1966–1968, Friedman Collection, Marshall Library,
        F-111, F-112, F-113; Sheldon, "William F. Friedman," 15.

248   valued at: Smith, 173; measuringworth.com/calculators/ppowerus/
        index2.php.

248   museum: ESF/ML 1:21.

248   "scattered higgledy-piggledy": ESF/ML 1:9.

249   "No way": Carter, NSA Oral History Interview, 291–292.

249   desire to make collection accessible: ESF/ML 1:10, ESF/ML 4:8.

249   Marshall Library: ESF/ML 1:9–11; Sherman, "The National
        Security Agency," 215–217; WFF to Forrest Pogue, 1 Aug 1969,
        WFC/NSA, ID A2918414.

250   "My beloved died": ESF, Day Journal, 2 Nov 1969, ESFP Box 20.

250   "my beloved Bill": ESF to "Families and Friends," 28 Jan 1970, ESFP
        13:30.

250   "His effect": Herman Wouk to ESF, 3 Nov 1969, ESFP 14:1.

250   WFF's burial: ESF to "Families and Friends," 28 Jan 1970, ESFP
        13:30; Note, ESF to BF, Nov 1969, ESFP 13:34.

THE LAST WORD

252   WFF's tombstone: Sketch, ESFP 13:31; Dunin, "Cipher on the
        William and Elizebeth Friedman Tombstone." WFF may have had a
        hand in the overall design, since the basic sketch has capital letters in
        his style, but it was ESF's decision to add the cipher.

252   "Since WFF": ESF to R. Clark, 7 Oct 1976, ESFP 15:4.

CHAPTER THIRTY-TWO The Library

253   "It is now 2½ months": ESF to "Families and Friends," 28 Jan 1970,
        ESFP 13:30.

254   William's desk, "*Friend*": The photos and cards under WFF's desk
        are now in the Marshall Library: marshallfoundation.org/library

/photographs/photographs-glass-william-f-friedmans-desk-many
-years. ESF was quoting Gelett Burgess's "Rondel: Perfect Friendship."

254   "Washington . . . is anything but a happy place": ESF to "Families
and Friends," 28 Jan 1970, ESFP 13:30.

254   "Government," "December 17, 1970": Eugene F. Yeates, Memo,
4 Oct 1982, WFC/NSA, ID A2912470; "Present Status of the
Friedman Collection," ca. Sept 1971, WFC/NSA ID A2918440.

254–255 Elizebeth followed the movers: Melissa Davis, email to the author,
12 Nov 2020, says that this is the way Marshall Library staff
remembered it. Fagone, 336, says that ESF followed the truck, but
incorrectly states that the move happened in 1971. Sherman, "The
National Security Agency," 217, says that the collection was moved
from Fort Meade, Maryland (site of NSA headquarters) to the
Marshall Library on December 17, 1970, but this is contradicted by
declasssified NSA papers, and it is hard to square with the Marshall
Library account of ESF following the movers.

255   NSA visit to the Marshall library, removal of items: Eugene F.
Yeates, Memo, 4 Oct 1982, WFC/NSA, ID A2912470; Sheldon,
The Friedman Collection, 8–9; Fagone, 337; Sherman, "The National
Security Agency," 217–222.

255   continued to press: ESF to Marshall Carter, 8 Jan 1971, WFC/NSA,
ID A2918420.

255   declassification of Friedman materials: Sherman, "The National
Security Agency," 235–236.

255   she often made the long drive: Lyle and Joyner, 5.

255   "the epitome," "Save this": BJ Averitt to ESF, ca. 1960s, ESFP 1:11.

256   dedication on wedding date: Invitation to Dedication Ceremony for
"The William F. Friedman Memorial Auditorium," 21 May 1975,
ESFP 13:4.

256   "*afraid* of": ESF to Marshall Carter, 8 Jan 1971, WFC/NSA, ID
A2918420.

256   help of her children: JRF to Ronald Clark, 29 Jul 1976, ESFP 14:14;
BF to Ronald Clark, 8 Aug 1976, 26 Sep 1976, ESFP 14:14.

256   "the man I knew": ESF to Marshall Foundation, 14 Jul 1977, ESFP
15:4.

256   recorded interviews: Many of these interviews have been transcribed.
See ESF interviews in the bibliography.

257   "lounging," "Everything is so damn big": Lunnen, "She Has a Secret
Side," ESFP 11:14.

257   "shake and despair": ESF to "Stuart and Mabel" [prob. Hedden],
30 Apr 1974, ESFP 15:1. See also Mima Pollitt to Vanessa Friedman,
6 Oct 1981, ESFP 12:15.

257   "a voice like a lion": Smith, 177.

257   death, "love you": ESF Death Certificate, 1980, ESFP 16:26; Judith Friedman, Remarks, in ESF Funeral Material, 1980, ESFP 16:26.

257   buried in William's grave: At one point, ESF believed that as a dependent of a "*Reserve* Officer," she was not entitled to be buried with William. But Arlington records show her ashes were interred with him on November 6, 1980. ESF, Instructions on funeral, n.d., ESFP 16:23; Barbara M. Lewandrowski, Director of Public Affairs, Arlington National Cemetery, email to the author, 18 Feb 2020.

258   "A dynamo," "wispy," "Calibans": Alfred Friendly, Remarks, 1980, ESFP 16:26.

258–259 Wilma Zimmerman Davis: Davis, NSA Oral History Interview; "Wilma Davis," Women in American Cryptology, NSA.

259   about eleven thousand, "Code Girls": Mundy, 30.

259   Moody, Grabeel, Caracristi: Mundy, 339–344.

259   but still discussed: ESF/VV 18:5.

260   her notes were coded signals: Sheldon, *The Friedman Collection*, 345–346; Fagone, 339.

260   receive her due: Fagone, 339; Smith, 177.

260   resolution in her honor: S. Res. 133–116th Congress: A resolution honoring the life and legacy of Elizebeth Smith Friedman, Cryptanalyst, govtrack.us/congress/bills/116/sres133.

260   "Hero worship": ESF, Memoir, 81.

IMAGE CREDITS

Grateful thanks to those who provided images for this book:

George C. Marshall Foundation, Lexington, Virginia: ii, 5, 11, 17, 25, 26, 34, 37, 44, 48, 58, 60, 61, 70, 75, 79, 87, 99, 101, 103, 111, 112, 113 (as reconstructed by David Greenfield), 120, 123, 124, 128, 134, 136, 138, 147, 153, 156, 159, 166, 171, 184, 191, 215, 229, 234, 235, 243, 253, 261

Library of Congress: 93

Melba Edwards: 8, 9

National Archives of the United Kingdom: 199

New York Public Library, Manuscripts and Archives Division: 27

Wikimedia Commons/CIA: 205

The image on page 251 is the author's own.

INDEX

Page numbers in *italics* refer to photographs or illustrations.